KAUTILYA ON LOVE AND MORALS

KAUTILYA
ON
LOVE AND MORALS

By

Pratap Chandra Chunder

GYAN

Kautilya on Love and Morals

ISBN : 978-81-212-0096-7

First Published 1987, reprint 2013 in India by
Gyan Publishing House
23, Main Ansari Road, Daryaganj,
New Delhi - 110002
Phones : 23282060, 23261060
Fax : (011) 23285914
E-mail: books@gyanbooks.com
website: gyanbooks.com

Printed at : Sagar Color Scan, New Delhi.

CONTENTS

INTRODUCTION

Kauṭilya's *Arthaśāstra* is a work of singular importance in the field of Indology. Ever since its publication by Dr. Shama Sastry in 1909 it has made a stir among scholars throughout the world. It has caused a great deal of controversy over its date and authorship as well as the intrinsic value of its contents.

Kauṭilya's *Arthaśāstra* is essentially a work on the science of polity. He himself refers to several earlier authorities on the subject. In fact, he states in the introduction to his work: "This *Arthaśāstra* is written after compiling almost all the arthaśāstras, which have been produced by earlier masters with the object of gaining and maintaining the earth."[1]

As Dr. Mehendale observes: "The science of polity was known by various names, Arthaśāstra, Daṇḍanīti, Nītiśāstra, Rājanīti, etc. and dealt not only with the political theories and the actual organisation of administrative machinery, but also various matters connected with state and society which would now form the subject matter of law, sociology and economics. At first these subjects were treated in a section in the Dharmasūtras and later in the Dharmaśāstras. But independent treatises were also written at an early date. The *Arthaśāstras* ascribed to Kauṭilya (also called Vishṇugupta) is the earliest extant work of this class, but it contains references to a large number of treatises which were regarded as authoritative in his days. These were the products of no less than five schools and thirteen individual writers on the science of polity. Many of these are also mentioned in the *Mahābhārata* which deals with the subject under the name Rājadharma."[2] A look into the contents of Kauṭilya's *Arthaśāstra* reveals the wide variety of subjects with which he has dealt in great detail. It must, however, be stated that generally the topics are discussed by Kauṭilya from the angle of statecraft. So the matters which concern the king and his government find more emphasis in the work than the

[1] *AŚ*. I. 1.
[2] *HCIP*. VOL. II. 274.

enunciation of general rules of conduct to be followed by ordinary man.

The Dharmaśāstras often revel in generalisations on human affairs, discourses on duties, individual and collective, and polemics on merits and demerits.

Kauṭilya, on the other hand, shows a realistic attitude of mind and generally states only as much of a matter as might interest the political authority. While Kauṭilya speaks more of punishments, the Dharmaśāstras refer more to penances. Kauṭilya's work is compact, matter-of-fact and particularly useful for a practical administrator. In it there is a blending of idealism and realism. If Kauṭilya soars up in the air of ideals, he seldom loses contact with the solid rock of reality. With a clear, logical mind, he hardly betrays any confusion of thought. One might or might not agree with him on all points but he is seldom vague or inconsistent. His work bristles with technical terms. Yet, with pithy and forceful arguments he drives home his views. Kauṭilya's *Arthaśāstra*, Dr. Mehendale states, "gradually came to be regarded as the standard work on the subject and, as often happens, the previous works were cast into shade and completely lost by the pre-eminence and the well-deserved reputation of this masterly and comprehensive treatise."[3]

But the problems of its date and authorship baffle solution. Kauṭilya himself says: "This śāstra has been composed by him who from intolerance (of misrule) quickly rescued scriptures, military power and the world which had passed to the Nanda King."[4] The *Arthaśāstra* gives another name of the author, that is Viṣṇugupta.[5] Tradition identifies him with Cāṇakya whose intelligence and power of organization materially enabled Candragupta to overthrow the Nandas of Magadha and establish the Maurya empire. Old anecdotes record Cāṇakya's sagacity and exploits. The drama *Mudrārākṣasa* has a plot in which his shrewdness is the pivot. Brief adages pass off under his authorship and through the ages are looked upon as the cream of worldly prudence and sound administrative principles.

Modern scholars do not, and probably never will, agree on the

[3] *Ibid.*
[4] *AŚ.* xv. 1.
[5] *AŚ.* concluding verse.

date and authorship of the *Arthaśāstra*. Its date, according to conflicting views, fluctuates between the fourth century B.C. and the third century A.D. We must confess the impossibility of furnishing any conclusive evidence on its actual date. One should, however, remember that like all ancient works, the *Arthaśāstra* has passed through the hands of several copyists. Scholars like Hillebrandt hold that the work may have many additions and emendations by later hands. The manuscripts, so far discovered, reveal, as we shall see, many variants at important points. To base one's arguments on words like *chīnabhūmi* as some learned scholars have done in determining its date, must necessarily be an unsafe method. The work should be read as a whole.

Among the scholars who place its date in the Maurya age are Sharna Sastry, Jacobi, Smith, Jayaswal, Fleet, Ganapati Sastri, J. J. Meyer, R. K. Mookerji, N. C. Bandyopadhyaya, N.N. Law, P.V. Kane, R. G. Basak, K. A. Nilakanta Sastri and R. P. Kangle. It is out of place here to set out their arguments in support of their views.[6] On the opposite side we have Jolly, Keith, Winternitz, O. Stein, E. H. Johnston, H. C. Raychaudhuri, Atindranath Bose and others.[7] It should be noted that these scholars do not agree among themselves upon any possible date of the *Arthaśāstra*. Dr. Raychaudhuri and Dr. Bose believe that the work was composed in or about the first century A.D. Johnston places it near about 250 A.D. Keith stands for c 300 A.D. as its possible date. Jolly thinks that the work "might have been composed in the third century. This date of course is not final but may be used as a working

[6] In support of the fourth century B.C. as the date of the *Arthaśāstra*, the arguments are set out in the following among other works:
- (*a*) Shama Sastry's preface to his edition of *AŚ*.
- (*b*) Jayaswal, *Hindu Polity*, 1. Appendix C.
- (*c*) Fleet, Preface to Ganapati Sastri's edition of the *Arthaśāstra*.
- (*d*) Ganapati Sastri, Introduction to his edition of the *AŚ*.
- (*e*) R. K. Mookerji, Introduction to Dr. N. N. Law's *Studies in Ancient Hindu Polity*.
- (*f*) N. N. Law, *Calcutta Review*, September & December, 1934.
- (*g*) P. V. Kane, *HDS*. Vol. 1. 85.
- (*h*) R. G. Basak, Introduction to his Bengali translation of the *Arthaśāstra*, Vol. 1.
- (*i*) K. A. Nilakanta Sastri, *Age of the Nandas and the Mauryas*, pp. 190-211.
- (*j*) R. P. Kangle, the Kauṭilīya Arthaśāstra, Part III.

[7] Some of the arguments against the first view will be found in
- (*a*) Jolly, Introduction to Jolly & Schmidt edition of the *Arthaśāstra*.
- (*b*) Johnston, *JRAS*, 1929. 77-89.
- (*c*) H. C. Raychaudhuri, *HCIP* Vol. II. 285.
- (*d*) Atindranath Bose, 'The date of the Arthaśāstra', *IC* Vol. IV. 435.

hypothesis and does not differ much from the result arrived at by Sir R. G. Bhandarkar who considers the first or second century A.D. to be the earliest date to which we can refer K (Kauṭilya)."[8] Again, with regard to its authorship, many scholars doubt if the work was at all written by Kauṭilya. On this matter, Dr. Raychaudhuri states: "Hillebrandt ascribes the composition of the *Arthaśāstra* to a school of Kauṭilya's disciples and Keith ascribes it to some followers of Kauṭilya. But Kauṭilya is really in line with Hindu tradition in introducing his name in his own work."[9] Nilakanta Sastri holds that "the Arthaśāstra has stood the test of very vigorous criticism for so long that its genuineness must now be recognised to have been placed beyond doubt . ."[10] He also rightly mentions: "but doubts regarding the age and genuineness of the work have not been allowed to hinder the free use of the book in studies on Mauryan administration and society."[11] V. A. Smith and F. W. Thomas use the *Arthaśāstra* in connection with the Mauryas.[12] R. K. Mookerji utilises its materials in his work, *Chandragupta Maurya and His Times*. K. A. Nilakanta Sastri includes extracts from the *Arthaśāstra* in his sketch of Mauryan polity in the *Age of the Nandas and the Mauryas*.

Although it is almost impossible to assign any exact date to the *Arthaśāstra*, many ancient Indian works refer to Kauṭilya, his treatise or his technical terms. Dr. Raychaudhuri points out: "The *Arthaśāstra* certainly existed before Bāṇa (seventh century A.D.), the *Nandīsūtra* of the Jains (not later than the fifth century A.D.) and possibly *Jātakamālā* of Ārya Śūra (third or fourth century A.D. . . .). In the Junāgarh rock inscription of Skandagupta reference is made to testing officials by *upadhās*, as we find in the *Arthaśāstra*. . . . The prevalence of the study of *Arthavidyā* in still earlier days is proved by the Junāgarh rock inscription of Rudradāman I (second century A.D.) which mentions such technical terms as *praṇaya*, *vishṭi* etc." which might have been "derived from the *Kauṭilīya* itself."[13] Dr. Shama Sastry also refers to various other early Indian works

[8] Jolly & Schmidt, *Arthaśāstra*, pp. 29-30.
[9] H. C. Raychaudhuri, HCIP. VOL. II. 285.
[10] *Age of the Nandas and the Mauryas*, p. 201. Also Kangle, *op. cit.*, III, p. 106.
[11] *Ibid.* 190.
[12] V. A. Smith, *Early History of India*. F. W. Thomas, *Cambridge History of India*, VOL. I.
[13] Raychaudhuri, *ibid*. 286.

like the *Daśakumāracarita* of Daṇḍin, the *Nītisāra* of Kāmandaka, the *Nītivākyāmṛita* of Somadeva, which directly or indirectly indicate the existence of Kauṭilya's *Arthaśāstra*.[14] Hemachandra identifies Cāṇakya with Vātsyāyana, the famous author of the *Kāmasūtra*. The close similarity of language and treatment of both the works has attracted the notice of modern scholars too. Even at a modest estimate the *Arthaśāstra* has not been placed later than 300 A.D. Dr. A. L. Basham suggests a compromise: "Yet it is certainly pre-Guptan, and is, we believe, the elaboration of a Mauryan original which was perhaps the work of Kauṭilya himself."[15]

Another controversy relates to the intrinsic value of its contents. The work itself became highly controversial even from early days. Kāmandaka is full of praise for Viṣṇugupta and his work. He states: ". . . to the wise and Brahma-like Viṣṇugupta we make salutation. From the scientific work of that learned man who had reached the limits of knowledge, the favourite learning of the kings, brief yet intelligible and useful in the acquisition and maintenance of earth, we are going to extract and teach kings in the manner acceptable to those learned in the science of polity."[16] Daṇḍin in a spirit of fun says: "Learn then the science of polity. Now this has been by the revered teacher Viṣṇugupta abridged into six thousand ślokas in the interest of the Maurya (king) that, when learnt and well observed, it can produce the results expected from it."[17] On the other hand, the Jain *Nandīsūtra* includes the work of Kauṭilya among the pseudo-sciences. Bāṇa denounces Kauṭilya's Śāstra. "Is there anything," asks he, "righteous for those to whom the science of Kauṭilya, detestable for its extremely merciless precepts, is an authority ?"[18]

Modern scholars too hold divergent views on the merits of this work. Dr. Winternitz remarks that it is improper for an author to profess himself to be a follower of Dharma and at the same time adopt unfair methods.[19] Johnston comments that Kauṭilya "pays lip service" to the ideal of Dharma "but the essential doctrine underlying the

---

[14] Shama Sastry's Introduction to the *Arthaśāstra*.
[15] A. L. Basham, *The Wonder that was India*, p. 77.
[16] *Kāmandakīya Nītisāra*. I. 6-8.
[17] *Dāśakumāracarita*, II. 8.
[18] Quoted in Shama Sastry's Introduction to the *Arthaśāstra*.
[19] Winternitz, *Calcutta Review*, April, 1924 (Kauṭilya *Arthaśāstra*).

entire work is that a king's sole preoccupation is with his own self-aggrandisement and that in its pursuit he should be restrained by no consideration except those of enlightened self-interest."[20] Dr. B. K. Ghosh holds: "What Kauṭilya teaches with so much pedantry is the art of violating law and justice with impunity in the ceaseless struggle for political power and economic aggrandisement . . . . Kauṭilya was not a Real-politiker in any sense, but simply a political Pandit revelling in subjective speculations which with disconcerting frequency develop in the fashion of Occam's Razor"[21].

He adds: "Kauṭilya need not have been any more dangerous a person than an innocent theoretician devoid of any direct experience of state-craft."

On the other hand, Dr. Radhakumud Mookerji writes: "As an exposition of an ancient polity it takes its place by the side of the other ancient compilations such as the Babylonish code of Hammurabi and the works on Greek politics such as those of Aristotle and Plato . . . . . In the *Arthaśāstra* we find a combination of theory and practice, principles of government as well as administrative details and regulations, treated with a touch of refreshing realism which is born only of a living experience of actual problems and contact with facts."[22] Dr. N. C. Bandyopadhyaya refers to the veneration with which Cāṇakya or Kauṭilya is held throughout South Asia for the wise sayings or nītis attributed to him.[23]

In this work we do not try to solve the problem of the date of the *Arthaśāstra*. We take its authorship for granted. But we venture to take part in the controversy over its intrinsic worth, specially with regard to the problems of morality. We also seek to comprehend Kauṭilya's view of life. We propose to study his attitude towards social institutions and family relationship, towards morals in general and sexual morality in particular. We do not intend merely to catalogue facts concerning marriage and other social institutions found in the *Arthaśāstra*. We seek to assess, as far as practicable, Kauṭilya's mental reactions to those facts. Fustel De Coulanges observes: "History does not study material facts and institutions alone; its true object of study is the human

---

[20] Johnston, *op.cit.* 77.
[21] Batakrishna Ghosh, *Hindu Ideal of Life*, p. 70-1.
[22] Introduction to Dr. N. N. Law's *Studies in Ancient Hindu Polity.*
[23] *Kauṭilya*, p. 1.

mind; it should aspire to know what this mind has believed, thought and felt in the different ages of the life of the human race."[24] In this work we make efforts to probe into Kauṭilya's mind in so far as it reveals itself in his writings. We also try to evaluate his views by comparison or contrast on the one hand with the epics and the principal Smṛiti literature (collectively referred to as the orthodox school) and on the other hand with Vātsyāyana's *Kāmasūtra*, Bharata's *Nāṭyaśāstra* and some other non-canonical works. We know well that there are large gaps in the dates and situations of these different works. But comparison and contrast alone might help us to see moral ideals in their proper perspective. For this reason we shall also refer to the ancient and the medieval writers of Europe as well as modern scholars and scientists. The bibliography lists some of the works which have been consulted or quoted.

With this end in view, we have studied the *Arthaśāstra* in its three different Sanskrit versions, that of Dr. Shama Sastry, of Ganapati Sastri (with his admirable commentary) and of Jolly and Schmidt. Its English translation by Dr. Shama Sastry and Bengali translation by Dr. R. G. Basak have been useful. We have tried to elicit from the *Arthaśāstra* many new facts, specially relating to sexual matters, which have hitherto received little or no attention. Even some well-known materials have been studied from the ethical point of view.

A cogent question might arise in this context. How far was the Kauṭilyan code of conduct actually put into practice ? It is difficult to answer this question categorically. If the *Arthaśāstra* could have been dated with absolute certainty, matters stated in it might have been compared with contemporary practices. But its date, as we have seen, is still highly controversial. Frankly speaking, we have not been able to throw any fresh light on the vexed question. Or perhaps no answer to the problem posed above is strictly necessary. As L. T. Hobhouse states: "There is no social measuring rod by which we could compare degrees of obedience to law. Civilized societies, with their records of criminal statistics, might, indeed, repay investigation from this point of view, though there is no department in which statistics are more apt to mislead, and that is saying a good deal. But if we were to

[24] *The Ancient City* (English translation), p. 123.

take ruder societies into account, the means of investigation would wholly fail. All that we can hope to do in comparing different stages of growth is to deal with recognized customs, accepted maxims, and ideas expressed in mythology, in literature, or in art. In other words, we could only hope to give the history of those ethical conceptions which are recognized as rules of conduct, and we must give up as wholly beyond our power the investigation of the degree in which conduct itself conforms to those rules. In Ethics there are principles and principles, and the distinction between them is often clear enough. A rule of conduct may be a genuine expression of what people actually feel and think, or it may be an ideal bearing as little relation to common practice as the Sermon on the Mount to the code of the Stock Exchange. In other words, there is a difference between the rule to which society expects you to conform and the rule which it keeps for Sunday use only. Both are rules and both may be broken. Hence to record either of them is to record not what conduct always is, but what it is thought it ought to be."[25] Sir P. S. Sivaswamy Aiyar also remarks: "The ethical progress of a community has to be judged more by the ideals of conduct which it sets before itself than by the extent of the conformity of its members to the ideals. Shortcomings and deviations from the rules are bound to occur in every society."[26] We have tried to show possible deviations from the internal evidence of the *Artha-śāstra*.

It is, of course, true that many learned scholars have compared Kauṭilya with Megasthenes and other classical writers to find out the 'real' state of affairs.[27] We have also at some places made such comparisons. Others have compared the *Arthaśāstra* with the Aśokan Edicts.[28] This too we have done at places. But our purpose has been not so much to ascertain how far the conduct of men conformed to the Kauṭilyan code as to make an effort to understand his ideals and their moral content. Dr. Basham, perhaps, rightly remarks: "Many errors have been made by historians through their uncritical accep-

---

[25] L. T. Hobhouse, *Morals in Evolution*, p. 23.

[26] *EHMI.* 4.

[27] Monahan, *Early History of Bengal.* F. W. Thomas in *Cambridge History of India*, Vol. 1. etc.

[28] R. K. Mookerji, *Chandragupta Maurya & His Times*, Appendix II. p. 236.

tance of these political texts as giving an exact picture of things as they were."[29]

In fine, our modest effort seeks to give a broad idea of Kauṭilya's conception of social morality in general and sexual morality in particular. We hope to be excused if in course of our investigation some emphasis is laid on the question of sex. That is perhaps somewhat normal in any discourse on morals. Westermarck states: "Sexual behaviour has always been a subject of moral judgment; indeed, so much so that when people speak of 'morality' they think chiefly of sex. To call a man 'moral' and a woman 'virtuous' means that they are continent outside of wedlock, although these words have other meanings in dictionaries and treatises on ethics."[30]

There is one special danger connected with the study of sexual morality. It is the subjective element which interferes with the dispassionate appraisal of the matter. Rattray Taylor rightly holds: "To summarise sexual history is the more difficult for the fact that it is almost impossible to view it objectively. From earliest youth we are taught to approve and condemn, and these judgments derive from buried emotions, so that they are held with great force and passion. All judgment tends to be egocentric, but in this field unusually so: the very word moral is derived from mores, customs. The moral is what is customary. And what is customary constantly changes. The range of possible variation is wide—just how wide the anthropologists have taught us."[31] One should, therefore, always approach the subject with a great deal of caution.

Kauṭilya's *Arthaśāstra* has been studied by learned scholars from the angles of politics, economics and sociology. In this work we propose to study the *Arthaśāstra* from the point of view of morals in general and sexual ethics in particular.

---

[29] A. L. Basham, *The Wonder that was India*, p. 81.
[30] Westermarck, *Future of Marriage in Western Europe*, p. 228.
[31] Rattray Taylor, *Sex in History*, p. 14.

Chapter I

LOVE AND LIFE

The *Arthaśāstra* of Kauṭilya reveals a spirit of happy moderation. Extremism in any form is generally avoided. Whether in the exercise of governmental power or in the enjoyment of sensual pleasures, Kauṭilya seeks to strike a middle course. Discoursing on the use of state power, Kauṭilya observes[1]: "Whoever imposes severe punishment becomes repulsive to the people; while he who awards mild punishment becomes contemptible. But whoever imposes punishment as deserved becomes respectable." Applying this idea to the field of social morality, Kauṭilya proposes to penalise extreme addiction to sensual pleasures on the one hand and untimely abstinence or asceticism on the other. A person excessively addicted (*prasakta*) to hunting or gambling or drinking is a suspicious character in the eye of law.[2] Vices (*vyasana*) include extreme attachment (*prasaṅga*) for women and other pleasures.[3,4] On the contrary, marriage and copulation are sacred duties of a householder. A husband refusing to cohabit with his wife after her monthly ablution (*ṛitu*) commits a punishable offence.[5] Unregulated asceticism is contrary to Kauṭilya's policy. The law punishes escape from the burdens of the family by recourse to asceticism. One has to make an adequate provision for one's wife and children before one can take to asceticism. Even the senescent can wear the monk's robe only upon notice to the civil authorities, otherwise he is punishable.[6]

---

[1] *AŚ*. I. 4. Cf. *Mbh*, Śānti. 58. 21-22; 14. 65-66.

[2] *AŚ*. IV. 6.

[3] *AŚ*. VIII. 1.

[4] The *Mbh*. (Śānti. 140. 26) recites the views of Bharadvāja, who holds a similar opinion: Drinking, gambling, women, hunting, songs and music are to be enjoyed reasonably (*yuktyā seveta*), extreme attachment for them is blameworthy (*prasaṅga hyatra doṣavān*). *Manu*. VII. 46 states: "If the king is extremely addicted to sensual pleasures (*kāmajeṣu prasakta*), he will be deprived of Dharma and Artha."

[5] *AŚ*. I. 3; III. 2: The epics also mention similar views. Meyer, *SLAI*. 216-18.

[6] *AŚ*. II. 1.

Between the two extremes of addiction and abstinence lies the middle course of Kauṭilya.[7]

"Be not without happiness" (*na nissukhassyāt*) is his bold assertion.[8] Happiness, as contemplated by Kauṭilya, is not an elusive, shadowy pleasure felt by escapists from raw life. On the contrary, it comprises manifold pleasures of the senses. Kauṭilya enjoins one to light up the flames of desire (*kāmaṁ seveta*).[9] Like the traditional Brāhmaṇical philosophers he believes in the well-known threefold objective of life, namely, spiritual (*dharma*), economic (*artha*) and sensual (*kāma*).[10] But the pursuit of sensual pleasures should, according to Kauṭilya, be tempered with spiritual and economic considerations. "*Kāma* is to be enjoyed without detriment to *Dharma* and *Artha*." Rather, all the different objectives should be pursued equally (*sama*) or in connection with one another (*samaṁ vā trivargamanyonyānubandham*).[11] The concept of co-ordination of the threefold objective of life is well-known to the schools of Indian social philosophers. The term *anubandha* occurs prominently in the *Mahābhārata*, Kauṭilya's *Arthaśāstra* and Vātsyāyana's *Kāmasūtra* in connection with Trivarga. Vātsyāyana mentions[12] *anubandha* to mean "the attainment of one (end) while pursuing the others" (*teṣvācaryamāneṣvanyasyāpi niṣpattiranubandhaḥ*). Kauṭilya elaborates the concept of *anubandha*.[13] His

[7] According to Aristotle, "Excess and deficiency are alike fatal in conduct. Excess or deficiency of gymnastic exercise is fatal to strength, excess or deficiency of meat and drink to health. Similarly in respect of courage, temperance and the other virtues, excess or deficiency is destructive, the mean or intermediate state is preservative of the virtue" (Ethics, II. 2, summary in Carlton House Edition, p. 253). Elsewhere, "Moral virtue then is a mean state as lying between two vices, and as aiming at the mean in the emotions and actions. Hence the difficulty of virtuous living, as it is always difficult to find the mean" (*ibid.* II. 9, p. 257).

[8] *AŚ*. I. 7.

[9] Bharadvāja, quoted in the *Mbh.* (Śānti. 140. 26), also enjoins reasonable enjoyment of pleasures (*yuktyā seveta*). In Śānti. 167 Bhīma appears as the protagonist for sensual pleasures (*kāma*).

[10] Aristotle (*Ethics*, I. 3) too holds a somewhat parallel view. He describes lives of men as sensual, political and speculative. According to him the sensual life is chosen by slavish or brutish men.

[11] *AŚ*. I. 7: The *Mbh.* (Śānti. 167. 40) recites the well-known passage: "*Dharma*, *Artha* and *Kāma* are to be pursued equally; he who is attached to one only is a contemptible person (*Dharmārthakāmāḥ samameva sevyā yo hyekabhaktaḥ sa naro jaghanyaḥ*)." In several passages of the great epic a similar view is expressed. (Śānti. 69. 70; 123. 2-11; 140. 57; etc.).

[12] *KS*. VI. 6. 6.

[13] *AŚ* IX. 7.

discourse bears a close similarity with that in the *Kāmasūtra*. While Kauṭilya discusses the topic from the angle of statecraft, Vātsyāyana does so from a courtesan's point of view.[14] According to both, *Artha*, *Dharma* and *Kāma* are Artha-trivarga and the reverse of these, *Anartha*, *Adharma* and *Śoka* (*Dveṣa*) are Anartha-trivarga.[15] In Kauṭilya's opinion, of *Artha*, *Dharma* and *Kāma*, the objectives to be attained are in the order mentioned.[16] In both the works as well as in Bharata's *Nāṭyaśāstra*,[17] there is a schematic treatment of the permutations and combinations of the three objectives of life. Kauṭilya, however, holds that all-round material success (*sarvārthasiddhi*) means that material success (*arthasya siddhi*) which promotes *dharma*, *artha* and *kāma* (*dharmārthakāmānubandhā*) inasmuch as *artha* is the root of *dharma* and leads to *kāma* (*dharmamūlatvāt kāmaphalatvāt*).[18] The *Mahābhārata* quotes Bharadvāja's view thus: "There are three objectives, three abuses and three interconnections (among them). Knowing the interconnection (*anubandham*) one should avoid the abuse (*pīḍā*)" (*trivargastrividhā pīḍā anubandhastathaiva ca anubandham tathā jñātvā pīḍāṁ ca parivarjjayet*).[19] Bhīṣma too elaborately discusses the inter-dependence of these objectives of life.[20] Vātsyāyana conveys a similar idea.[21]

---

[14] *KS*. VI. 6.

[15] *AŚ*. IX. 7=*KS*. VI. 6. 5.

[16] *AŚ*. ibid.

[17] *NŚ*. XX. 72-75: "In this connection three kinds of love to be presented through different actions are: That in relation to duty (*dharma*), that actuated by material gain (*artha*) and that actuated by passion (*kāma*). When in (discharging) the duty one attains one's (much) desired well-being accomplished in many ways and in this connection means like observing vows, austerities and penance are adopted, it is to be known as love in relation to duty (*dharma-śṛiṅgāra*). Love in which attainment of material gain occurs in various ways is called in relation to material gain (*artha-śṛiṅgāra*) or it may be that love in which the enjoyment of pleasure with women is for the purpose of some material gain. Love actuated by passion (*kāmaśṛiṅgāra*) includes the seduction of a maiden and it causes secret or excited intercourse of a man with a woman." (Translation by M. Ghose)

[18] *AŚ*. ibid.

[19] *Mbh*. Śānti. 140. 57. [20] *ibid*. 123. 3-14.

[21] *KS*. I. 2. "Man whose span of life is hundred years should divide his (life) time and pursue threefold objectives in such manner as they may be attained in harmonious combination with one another and without detriment to one another. Thus in his boyhood, reception of education and other economic pursuits; in youth, erotic pursuits and in old age, religion and mokṣa. Or considering the uncertainty of life, one may pursue these objectives as desirable". "One should strive to do such acts as are conducive to the attainment of all the Trivargas or any one or two of them. None of these Trivargas should be pursued if it is likely to be injurious to the interest of the other two." (I. 2. 51).

According to Manu, the king should be well-versed in *dharma*, *artha* and *kāma* and, exercising his royal power, properly progress in the threefold objective (*dharmakāmārthakovidam; trivargenābhivarddhate*).[22]

The implication seems to be that these three objectives should be followed in such a way that the pursuit of one will automatically lead to that of the other two. For example, a lawful wedlock primarily satisfies sexual cravings but incidentally leads to spiritual merits through the birth of sons and economic gains through family life and social connections. So lawful wedlock is highly approved. On the contrary, the husband's abstinence from intercourse with his wife after her menses is discouraged as it leads to the loss of spiritual merits (*dharmabadha*)[23] probably due to the consequential failure of progeny.

Kauṭilya is opposed to an exclusive attachment for *dharma*, *artha* or *kāma*. Too much devotion to *dharma* or *artha* is as bad as excessive addiction to sensual pleasure (*kāma*). For, Kauṭilya cryptically observes: "If, among *dharma*, *artha* and *kāma*, any one is pursued excessively (*atyāsevita*), it harms not only itself but also the other two objectives."[24] In short, for Kauṭilya, extremism of any sort in spiritual, temporal or sensual matters is a taboo. This idea, based on the harmonious blending of the threefold objective, is reflected in many of the measures advocated in the *Arthaśāstra*.

In spite of this idea of inter-dependence of three objectives of life, the ancient Indian thinkers cannot agree upon their importance inter se. Kauṭilya believes in the economic basis of all human endeavours. To Kauṭilya, both spiritualism and sensuality are rooted in economics (*artha-mūlau hi dharmakāmau*) and so economics is of primary importance (*artha eva pradhāna*).[25] The Dharmaśāstras no doubt give dharma the principal place.[26] The *Kāmasūtra* places *Dharma* first for ordinary people, but *Artha* first for kings and *Kāma* first for public women.[27] The *Mahābhārata* records all the divergent views. In the great epic there is an interesting debate on the relative importance of the three objectives. Vidura champions *dharma*, Arjuna

[22] *Manu*. VII. 26 & 27.
[23] *AŚ*. III. 4.
[24] *AŚ*. I. 7.
[25] *Ibid.*
[26] *Rāmāyaṇa*, I. 21. 57-58.
[27] *KS*. I. 2. 14-17.

asserts the claim of *artha* and Bhīma advocates the importance of *kāma*, but Yudhiṣṭhira supports the ideal of *Mokṣa* (Salvation).[28] Elsewhere Arjuna avers: "From *artha* (come) *dharma* and *kāma* and, indeed, the heaven; O King, without *artha* people's living would certainly not succeed."[29] If we do not forget that Kauṭilya's work is meant primarily for the rulers of the land, his special emphasis on the importance of *artha* is quite intelligible.

For his emphasis on economic considerations, Kauṭilya is attacked by a modern writer. "As for Kauṭilya, he would simply not be bothered about questions of right or wrong in affairs of state, for he boldly declares that even virtue (*dharma*) depends upon politico-economic power (*artha*)."[30] Elsewhere he characterises this view of Kauṭilya as 'the sinister principle'.[31] The learned critic does not appear to be impartial in his judgment. Kauṭilya definitely has a great concern for ethics and even in the sphere of statecraft he tries to set a high moral tone, as we shall see later. His emphasis on the material considerations of life seems to be supported by the well-known modern social philosopher Benedetto Croce, who remarks: "There is no moral life unless economic and political life is first established; as the ancient used to say, first the 'living' and then 'good living'. On the other hand, there can be no moral life that is not both economic and political life, just as there can be no soul without a body."[32] However, we have observed from other Indian sources, that a powerful section of opinion believes *artha* to be of primary importance.

It appears that efforts were made to give effect to the theory of a regulated balanced living in the life and manners of the people. In the eyes of the Greek envoy, Megasthenes, the Indian manners and customs, however, reveals a distinct 'contrast'. It is reported that on the one hand "the Indians all live frugally, especially in camp. They dislike a great undisciplined multitude and consequently they observe good order. . . . They live, nevertheless, happily enough, being simple in their manners and frugal", and on the other hand, "In contrast to the general simplicity of their style, they love finery and

[28] *Mbh.* Śānti. 167.
[29] *Ibid.* 8. 17.
[30] B. K. Ghosh, *Hindu Ideal of Life*, p. 75.
[31] *Ibid.* p. 87.
[32] B. Croce, *Politics and Morals*, p. 22.

ornament. . . . for they have a high regard for beauty and avail themselves of every device to improve their looks".[33] It seems strange to the Greek envoy that such a 'contrast' in manners should exist—simplicity and frugality set against finery and ornaments (and every psychologist knows that the love of physical beauty has its roots in sensuality). But this apparent 'contrast' in the manner of the Indian people can possibly be explained by a reference to the ideal of a well-balanced life.

Even Aśoka the Great, who accepted the Buddhist faith, did not discard this useful social ideal. For the laity he did not preach the asceticism of the orthodox Buddhists, but emphasised those social and ethical virtues, which were more or less the common heritage of the people. It is sufficient to quote here some views of well-known authorities on the subject. "Aśoka was attracted more by the ethical than the philosophical aspect of Buddhism and laid stress upon the practical benevolent activities and pious thoughts inculcated by it",[34] or elsewhere "Aśoka's edicts reveal that he wanted good citizens and not recluses. He laid emphasis on a heavenly life hereafter and not on Nirvāṇa."[35] Hopkins has ably summarised the orthodox Buddhist view on sensual pleasures: "Gratification of desire therefore only bound one the more and the way of escape was to eliminate desire of everything except of the highest good, which was to be reached eventually by absolute indifference but the way to it was found in a preliminary elimination of everything tending to postpone the desired state".[36] But Aśoka was not influenced by this pessimistic outlook on the life on earth. He honoured ascetics and householders alike. Thus, in *RE.* XII we read: "King Priyadarśin, Beloved of the Gods, honours (men of) all sects, ascetics and householders and honours (them) with gift and manifold honour." Like his predecessors, Aśoka strove after "comforts (*sukhāyanāya*) of the people". "For with various comforts have the people been blessed both by former kings and by myself."[37] And these 'comforts' mean happiness both in this world and the other (*hitasukhena hidalokika pālalokikena*).[38] Elsewhere, we

[33] *Meg.* 68-69.
[34] *HCIP.* Vol. II. 75.
[35] *Ibid.* p. 385.
[36] Hopkins, *Ethics of the Hindus,* p. 141.
[37] *RE.* VII.
[38] *ṢRE.* I,

also note Aśoka's measures for the material welfare of all people, which more or less tally with the provisions laid down in the *Arthaśāstra*. Unlike the orthodox Buddhist's contempt for family, Aśoka stressed devotion to parents, friends and relations, as well as slaves and servants.[39] This, according to Kauṭilya, is an important duty of a householder (*gṛihastha*) viz. 'gifts to Gods, ancestors, guests and servants' (*deva-pitratithibhṛtyeṣu tyāga*).[40] Well-versed in the ways of human life, Aśoka was fully conversant with the various desires (*chanda*) and passions (*rāga*) of the common people. "But men possess various desires (and) various passions. Either they fulfil the whole or they fulfil (only) a portion (of their duty)."[41] Aśoka sought to sublimate these passions by ethical precepts. But the fact remains that the royal idealist was realist enough not to ban sensual pleasures, the basis of a virtuous family life, and glorify 'the mortification of the flesh'.

The ideal of a balanced life, Kauṭilya believes, can be realised through discipline (*vinaya*), self-control (*saṁyama*) and certain other virtues.

According to the *Arthaśāstra*, discipline may be natural or acquired through efforts, mainly education.[42] But education and discipline can be had only through a "victory over the organs of senses" (*indriya-jaya*).[43] Control over the senses is an ethical ideal preached by various sects in India throughout the ages.[44] Kauṭilya also lays much emphasis on it. To him, this victory can be achieved through 'abandoning (*tyāga*) sensual pleasures, anger, greed, vanity, haughtiness and joy'.[45] These are collectively designated as 'the group of six enemies' (*ariṣaḍvarga*) (an expression popular with many Indian moral philosophers).[46] A doubtful fragment of Megasthenes seems to confirm this traditional view: "There is war, the Brachmanes hold, in the body wherewith they are clothed, and they regard the body as being the fruitful source of wars, and as we have already shown, fight against it

[39] *RE*. VII.
[40] *AŚ*. I. 3.
[41] *RE*. VII.
[42] *AŚ*. I. 5.
[43] *AŚ*. I. 6.
[44] *Manu*. VII; *Mbh*. Śānti. 275.
[45] *AŚ*. I. 6.
[46] *AŚ*. I. 6 & 7.

like soldiers in battle contending against the enemy. They maintain, moreover, that all men are held in bondage, like prisoners of war, to their own innate enemies, the sensual appetites, gluttony, anger, joy, grief, longing desire and such like, while it is only the man who has triumphed over these enemies goes to God".[47] The informants of Megasthenes claim that the philosopher Dandamis is a god on earth as 'he conquered in the warfare against the body'. Later we shall discuss more details of the life and preachings of this philosopher but the truth remains that, according to the Greek testimony, there was at least one person who had attained the high ideal indicated above. Kauṭilya repeatedly exhorts the king to control the organs of senses. In his several edicts, Aśoka, too, inculcates self-control (*saṁyama*).[48] In *RE.* III he observes: "These (passions) viz., fierceness, cruelty, anger, pride, envy are called sinful. Let me not ruin (myself) by (these) very (passions)." The great king claims to practise what he preaches and gloats over the fact that "everywhere (people) are conforming to Devānāmpriya's instructions in morality."[49]

The general precept in favour of 'abandoning' sensual appetites and joy is obviously hedged round by exceptions. Life is certainly not meant to be joyless and dull. Happiness (*sukha*) is a necessity and, as we have seen, pursuit of sensual pleasures tempered with spiritual and economic considerations is enjoined by the *Artha-śāstra.* Moreover, it is a prescribed duty of the state to exercise its power in such a way that the subjects can follow spiritual, economic and sensual pursuits—that is to say—proper, approved pursuits.[50] So Kauṭilya hastens to give us an alternative connotation of *indriyajaya* viz., "directing for the purposes laid down in the Śāstras (approved texts) the natural inclination of sensory organs towards their respective functions", in other words, proper attachment of the ears, nose, eyes, skin and tongue for sound, smell, sight, touch and taste respectively.[51] Unlike Vātsyāyana Kauṭilya does not define *kāma* but his ideas concerning it may be derived from stray references. In general, it connotes the natural cravings of the various organs of senses, for

[47] *Meg.* 122-23.
[48] *RE.* VII; XIII.
[49] *RE.* XIII.
[50] *AŚ.* I. 4.
[51] *AŚ.* I. 6.

example, cravings of the ears, nose, eyes, skin and tongue for sound, smell, sight, touch and taste respectively.[51] In other words, *kāma* means sensual pleasures.[52] Vātsyāyana states: "There are five organs of perception, viz., ears, touch, eyes, tongue and nose. To experience any kind of pleasure one or other of these organs should come into contact with the objects, themselves being acted upon by mind in combination with soul. The desire for securing these objects as causes man's happiness as also its fulfilment is termed *kāma*. But the thing chiefly and commonly known by the word *kāma* is the pleasure felt at the time of sexual intercourse between man and woman attended with other kinds of amorous sports—kissing, embracing and similar acts."[53] It is, however, the regulation and not repression, of the pleasures of the senses that is actually enjoined by Kauṭilya. The cravings of the flesh are to be curbed and guided by the injunctions of the approved texts, that is, proper education.

Incidentally, Kauṭilya is liberal in framing his syllabus for education. It includes not only the traditional, orthodox and dogmatic education, viz., the study of *Trayī*—the three Vedas with their subsidiary works, but also *Ānvīkṣikī* (science of reason), *Vārttā* (economics) and *Daṇḍanīti* (politics).[54] By his emphasis on *Ānvīkṣikī*, Kauṭilya seems to have intended to cool down the dogmatism of the Vedas with the help of reason. According to him, *Anvīkṣikī* consists of Sāṁkhya, Yoga and Lokāyata. These texts challenged the Vedas on many points. Some are known to have disowned the Vedas and rebelled against their sanction. Lokāyata, for instance, includes

[52] *Mbh.* Vana. 33. 30 defines *kāma* as the pleasure caused in connection with touch, wealth or properties. Also verses 37-38. Sir Sivaswamy Aiyar observes: "The term *kāma* is used to denote *viṣayānubhavajanyasukha*, i.e., pleasures or happiness derived from contact with the external objects of sense or the sources of intellectual or emotional satisfaction. The word *kāma* would include not merely the pleasures of the senses, but also all pleasures derived from the exercise of the mental faculties . . . Similarly the word *kāma* is often popularly used to signify the coarser pleasures of the senses and the word has attracted the same prejudice as the English word 'pleasures'." *EHMI.* p. 152. Dr. Basham explains: "In its broadest sense the word *Kāma* means desire of every kind and its fulfilment, but, like such English words as 'desire' and 'passion', it usually had a sexual connotation. Of all legitimate pleasures sexual pleasure was thought to be the best." *The Wonder that was India*, p. 170.

[53] *KS.* I. 2. 11-12 (Iyenger's translation).

[54] *AŚ.* I. 2; *Manu.* (VII. 43) and *Yāj.* I. 311 prescribe the same course of study for a king. The practical importance of the subjects was so great that even the orthodox school had to adopt them for the ruler's education.

extreme hedonistic philosophy. Yet these subjects are not excluded from Kauṭilya's catholic course of study. "Light to all knowledge, way to all actions and shelter of all virtues is the Science of Reason ever deemed to be."[55] Kauṭilya's emphasis on the study of economics and politics is also significant. It seems to suggest that he is not bound by the dogmatic prescriptions of religious scriptures, although he has a high regard for them. He is practical enough to conclude that the preachings of the orthodox texts might have to be modified in the light of reason, political and economic considerations.

This discussion was necessary to show Kauṭilya's attitude towards life. With all his devotion to Brāhmaṇical faith, he is not prompted by blind orthodoxy. For material and political considerations, he does not disdain to advocate measures which the orthodox moralists will forthwith frown upon, just as they do in the case of many modern societies which place the state before the individual. At other times, like a true rationalist, he draws certain facts of life to their logical conclusions and frames rules in consonance with them. For instance, if a husband deserts his wife, Kauṭilya requires the latter to wait for certain periods and thereafter to take a second husband, whereas Manu stops short with 'waiting', without any provision in that context for the remarriage of the unfortunate wife.[56] However, in most of his measures relating to social, sexual or other matters, Kauṭilya is, in the happy company of one or the other of the well-known exponents of the orthodox Brāhmaṇical school. Kauṭilya does not share the views of the extreme hedonists who discard the belief in Heaven and after-life. At several places he refers to *Svarga*. He believes in the orthodox view that the performance of one's duties in this life will lead one to Heaven.[57] Nor does he disown the importance of the three Vedas as Bṛihaspati and Uśanas, two earlier writers on *arthaśāstra,*

---

[55] *AŚ.* I. 2. The great importance of *Ānvīkṣikī* is admitted even in the *Mbh.* (Śānti. 318. 46-48), which states that the Vedas are to be interpreted in the light of Reason. Also *Manu.* XII. 105. But the *Rām.* denounces this science (II. 100. 39) and in particular the 'Loukāyatika' (II. 100. 38).

[56] *AŚ.* III. 4; *Manu.* IX. 76. The commentators of Manu are puzzled over the question of the wife's duty after the period of waiting. Medhātithi refers to the remarriage on the strength of other Smṛitis. Kullūka following Vasiṣṭha suggests that she should rejoin her husband. The topic has been discussed in Chapter IV infra.

[57] *AŚ.* I. 3. *Svadharmas svargāyānatyāya ca;* also *AŚ.* III. 1; III. 7. The *Mahābhārata* (Śānti. 291. 13-15) refers to some views of the hedonists with disapproval. Bandyopadhyaya: *Kauṭilya,* p. 30, f.n. The *Rāmāyana,* II. 100. 38. deprecates the *Loukāyatika.*

quoted in Kauṭilya's work, do.[58] "The spirit of Kauṭilya was, however, quite different. He was a believer in material joys and aspirations, yet he did not go to extremes. His ideal was a compromise or a moderate synthesis of the two extreme views of life and its aims."[59]

Kauṭilya's practical bias towards life is indicated by his comparative silence over the topic of salvation. While he emphasises the threefold objective of life (*Trivarga*) he hardly speaks of *Mokṣa* as the fourth objective which is so much liked by the Dharmaśāstras. Kauṭilya only incidentally mentions that the performance of one's own duties (*svadharma*) will lead one to Heaven and Eternity (*ānantyāya*).[60] Manu also preaches a similar ideal. He condemns the pursuit of *Mokṣa* without previously discharging one's duties to the world.[61]

The positive aspect of Kauṭilya's ethics comprises the practice of certain duties. In general, Kauṭilya calls them *Svadharma*. In the first instance, Kauṭilya believes in the traditional *Varṇāśrama* dharma, which had already taken concrete shape in the Vedic age. It means the well-known division of the Aryan society into four *varṇas* (castes) and of the Aryan life into four *āśramas* (stages). In this connection, it is better to quote Kauṭilya *in extenso:* "The rule of the three Vedas is beneficial because it lays down the respective duties of four *varṇas* and four *āśramas*. The special duty of a Brāhmaṇa is study, teaching, performing and acting in the performance of sacrifices, making and receiving gifts. That of a Kṣatriya is study, performing sacrifice, making gifts, military profession and protection of life. That of the Vaiśya is study, performing sacrifice, making gifts, agriculture, cattle-breeding and trade. That of the Śūdra is serving the twice-born, economic activities, and the profession of craftsmen and artistes."[60] Theoretically, the Aryan society is split up into four major groups on the basis of duties, but actually there are many divisions and subdivisions.

The *Arthaśāstra* makes a broad division of mankind between the Ārya and the rest, a division comparable with 'the Greek and the Barbarians', 'the Jew and the Gentile', 'the faithful and the kafir'

[58] *AŚ.* I. 2.
[59] Bandyopadhyaya, *op.cit.* 31.
[60] *AŚ.* I. 3.
[61] *Manu.* VI. 35.

The rest includes various groups like *Caṇḍālas*, *Śvapākas*, *Patitas* (outcasts), *Mlecchas* and the like. Aryan society is ideally divided into four *Varṇas* noted above. In practice, however, division exists between the twice-born castes, viz., Brāhmaṇas, Kṣatriyas and Vaiśyas on the one hand and Śūdras on the other. It is noteworthy that despite their degraded position, the Śūdras according to Kauṭilya, stand within the bounds of 'Aryandom'.[62] Again, there are various 'mixed castes' (*saṅkara*) supposed, according to the traditional theory followed by Kauṭilya, to have originated from marriages between different castes and mixed castes. Apart from the adherents to the Brāhmaṇical faith, there are so many heretical, often influential sects like the Buddhists, Ājīvikas, Nirgranthas and the like. Megasthenes mentions[63] seven 'castes' viz., (*i*) philosophers, (*ii*) husbandmen, (*iii*) hunters and shepherds, (*iv*) artisans, (*v*) military, (*vi*) overseers and (*vii*) councillors and assessors. Aśokan edicts mention Brāhmanas and Gahapatis (Vaiśyas), Śramaṇas, Ājīvikas and various sects *(pāsaṁda)*. In any event, Aśoka accepts the caste system. The strict rules of endogamy, commensality or profession might not hold good in all cases, but all the ancient sources indicate that the concept of caste was, in the main, a strong reality.

Caste and other divisions of society have significant bearing on morals. These divisions often led to different standards of morality. For example, a higher standard of morality is prescribed for the Āryas who claim greater privileges than the rest. The State is called upon to uphold the status of the Ārya (*āryamaryādā*).[64] Untouchability makes its mark. A Caṇḍāla is to be fined for touching an Ārya woman.[65] For violating her chastity, capital and other deterrent punishments are prescribed.[66] A Caṇḍāla is made to reside near the cremation ground.[67] His well cannot be used by any other person.[68] Except under special circumstances, an Ārya cannot be enslaved, nor can his children be sold or mortgaged into slavery, whereas it was proper for a Mleccha

[62] *AŚ*. III. 13. Also Kangle, *op. cit.*, Part III, 144-50.
[63] *Meg*. 38-41.
[64] *AŚ*. I. 3.
[65] *AŚ*. III. 20: For the orthodox views in the Smṛiti, *HDS*. II. Chap. IV.
[66] *AŚ*. IV. 9.
[67] *AŚ*. II. 4.
[68] *AŚ*. I. 14.

to do so.[69] Half the fine is prescribed for stealing or destroying certain goods of a *caṇḍāla* or a wild tribesman, whereas full fine or mutilation in the case of the rest.[69a]

Discrimination is also prompted by the caste system. Thus, drinking spirituous liquor is an offence for a Brāhmaṇa leading to his banishment, but not for the rest.[70] Although endogamy within a caste is the approved conduct, mixed marriages between a male of a higher caste with a female of a lower caste is allowed, but not *vice versa*.[71] Thus, a Brāhmin has a much wider choice of brides who may be from any of the four castes, whereas a Kṣatriya has a choice from the three castes, a Vaiśya from two and a Śūdra from his own caste only. But love is traditionally blind. A deviation from the approved conduct is not rare, but the law seeks to stamp out such gallantry. Again, adultery with a woman of higher caste is sought to be ruthlessly suppressed. For adultery with an unguarded Brāhmana woman, a Kṣatriya is to suffer the highest amercement, a Vaiśya is to forfeit all his properties but a Śūdra is required to be 'burnt alive wound round in mats'.[72] For adultery with a Śvapāka woman, a man of the higher caste was either banished or degraded to the lower caste.[71] Similar discriminations exist in connection with food,[72] assault,[73] defamation,[74] battery,[75] etc. A Śūdra trying to pass himself off as a Brāhmaṇa commits a grave offence like treason and is liable either to be blinded or heavily fined.[76]

The degradation to a lower caste or complete ostracism has, as we shall see later, a grave effect on morals. It spells serious dangers, the curtailment of civil rights and social privileges, and even break up of the family tie.[77]

With regard to discrimination based on differences in races, castes and creeds Kauṭilya largely follows the orthodox school.[78]

One might relevantly ask how far the discriminations prescribed

[69] *AŚ*. III. 13.
[69a] *AŚ*. IV. 10.
[70] *AŚ*. IV. 8; Chapter XV, *infra*.
[71] Chapter IV. *infra*.
[72] *AŚ*. IV. 13.
[73] *AŚ*. IV. 10.
[74] *AŚ*. III. 14.
[75] *AŚ*. III. 19.
[76] *AŚ*. IV. 10.
[77] Chapter XIII. *infra*.
[78] Kane, *HDS*. II. Part I, Chapter III.

in the Brāhmaṇical law books were actually put into practice. There must have been many exceptions, but the law books set a norm and a society dominated by the Brāhmaṇa intellectuals would generally enforce such discriminations. At any rate, scholars have shown from non-Brāhmaṇical sources that the discriminatory rules of castes were often a real force.[79]

No less important from the point of view of morals is the Brāhmaṇical division of the human life into four stages (*āśramas*). According to Kauṭilya, the respective duties of different stages are as follows:—

"The duty of a householder is earning livelihood by his own profession, marriage among his equals, of different ancestral *Riṣis*, intercourse with his wedded wife after her monthly ablution; gift to gods, ancestors, guests and servants and the eating of the remainder.

"That of a student (*Brahmacārin*) is learning the Vedas, fire-worship, ablution, living by begging and devotion to his teacher even at the cost of his own life, or in the absence of his teacher, to the teacher's son, or to an elder classmate.

"That of a *Vānaprastha* (forest-recluse) is observance of chastity, sleeping on the bare ground, keeping twisted locks, wearing deer skin, fire-worship, ablution, worship of gods, ancestors and guests and living upon foodstuffs procurable in forests.

"That of an ascetic retired from the world (*Parivrājaka*) is complete control of the organs of sense, abstaining from all kinds of work, disowning money, keeping from society, begging in many places, dwelling in forests and purity both internal and external."[80]

---

[79] *HCIP*. Vol. II. 544; Fick, *Social organization* etc. p. 50.

[80] *AŚ*. I. 3. (Shama Sastry's translation). Kauṭilya's description of the *āśramas* largely tally with those in the *Mbh.* (e. g. Śānti 61; 191; 192; 242-45 and the principal Dharmaśāstra. Jolly, *Hindu Law and Custom* (Eng. translation), Chap. VI; Kane, *HDS.* II(I). Ch. 8. The great epic gives us conflicting views regarding the relative importance of the *āśramas* inter se. Śānti. 11, 242-45. According to some, the stage of the householder is the best, for, on it depend the other *āśramas*. The householders carry on productive activities and maintain persons in the other stages of life. In his description of *āśramas*, Kauṭilya mentions householders first, implying, perhaps, their special importance in society. Kauṭilya takes special care to keep ascetics and wanderers within proper bounds. "On the whole the tendency of most of the dharamśāstra works is to glorify the status of a householder and push into the background the two *āśramas* of *vānaparastha* and *sannyāsa*, so much so that certain works say that these are forbidden in the Kali age." Kane, *HDS*, ibid. 424. Thus in his special concern for the stage of a householder, Kauṭilya does not deviate from the predominant orthodox view.

Kauṭilya does not tell us if this plan of life applied to all, but we may infer that it did not, at least in the cases of women, *Śūdras* and outcasts, for the Vedic study is not open to them and the stage of *brahmacarya* is apparently inapplicable to their cases. In spite of some confusion in his assessment of the *āśramas*, Megasthenes seems to suggest that these stages of life are possibly meant for the philosophers only.[81] He alludes to these different stages, although mixing them up to some extent. At any rate, two *aśramas*, viz., *Gṛihastha* and *Pravrajita*, are well known to Aśoka.[82] Megasthenes mentions women celibates engaged in the pursuit of learning.

According to Kauṭilya, the faithful performance of the duties assigned to different castes and stages of life will lead one to Heaven and salvation (*Svadharmas Svargāyānantyāya*).[83] Indian philosophers generally hanker after salvation. This can be attained through the well-defined stages of life. Thus Mm. Kane remarks: "Therefore the ancient Indian writers devised according to their lights a scheme which is embodied in the theory and practice of the *āśramas*. In *brahmacarya* the individual goes through the discipline of the will and the emotions, makes himself acquainted with the literary treasures of the past and learns obedience, respect, plain living and high thinking. Then he marries, becomes a householder, tastes the pleasures of the world, enjoys life, has sons, discharges his duties to his children, to his friends, relatives and neighbours and becomes a useful, industrious and worthy citizen, the founder of a family. It is supposed that by the time he is fifty years or so he has become convinced of the futility of human appetites and the pleasures of the world and is therefore called upon to resort to a forest life for pondering over the great problem of the life hereafter and to accustom himself to self-abnegation, austerities and a harmless life. This would lead on to the last stage, viz., *sannyāsa*. He may succeed in this very life in realising the supreme goal of *mokṣa* or he may have to continue to rise in spiritual height until after several births and deaths the goal is in view. The theory of *varṇa* dealt with man as a member of the Aryan Society and laid down what his rights, functions, privileges, responsibilities

[81] *Meg*. 99-102.
[82] *RE*. xii; *PE*. vii.
[83] *AS*. i. 3

and duties were as a member of that society. It was addressed to the mass. The theory of *āśramas* addressed itself to the individual. It tells him what his spiritual goal is, how he is to order his life and what preparations are required to attain that goal."[84]

In any event, the scheme of *āśramas* arranges personal ethics on a chronological basis. According to this arrangement, certain conduct is moral at some point of time in life and immoral at other points. For instance, sexual intercourse within the ambit of marriage is an essential duty for a householder, whereas sexual abstinence is compulsory for a student, a recluse and a wanderer. Likewise, the pursuit of vocations. Consequently, untimely celibacy or untimely abstention from fruitful work is irreligious, illegal and immoral. The *Arthaśāstra* repeatedly calls upon the king to uphold this chronological plan. According to this scheme, *Kāma* and all that it stands for seem to be confined to the stage of householders, and that also generally within the ambit of marriage, although connection out of wedlock is suffered by law in some special cases.[85]

Apart from special duties relating to castes and stages of life, *svadharma*, according to Kauṭilya, includes some common virtues of universal observance. These are non-violence, truthfulness, purity, freedom from hatred and cruelty, and forgiveness.[86] The Greek envoy also speaks of the Indian people's love of simplicity, frugality and truthfulness. He testifies to their 'good, sober sense'. "Truth and virtue they hold alike in esteem".[87] Aśoka also inculcates similar virtues. "But what does morality include ?" he asks in *PE.* II: "(It includes) few sins, many virtuous deeds, compassion, liberality, truthfulness (and) purity." Again in *PE.* VII he records: "For noble deeds of morality and practice of morality (consist in) this, that (morality) viz., compassion, liberality, truthfulness, purity, gentleness and goodness will thus be promoted among men." Elsewhere he extols

---

[84] *HDS.* II. Part I, 423.

"The oldest Upanishads speak of these *Aśramas* only as three types or branches of life, but not as successive stages. It is only in the late Upanishads, the Great Epic, and the Dharmaśāstras that the theory of successive stages of life is formulated and is developed further by the addition of the fourth stage, that of the *sannyāsin*"...*HCIP.* Vol. I. 493.

[85] Chapter IX, *infra.*

[86] *AŚ.* I. 3.

[87] *Meg.* 69.

non-violence. One is struck by the close similarity between the moral teachings of Kauṭilya and Aśoka. The virtues inculcated by them are in a large measure the common characteristics of the Indian people, as the Greek testimony leads us to believe.

Thus, a critical study of Kauṭilya's *Arthaśāstra* shows how he inculcates a broad principle of synthesis in life. In his philosophy of good living he tempers orthodoxy with rationalism, combines moderate enjoyment of pleasure with the pursuit of spiritualism and economic gains and supports self-control and not self-repression. Dr. N. C. Bandyopadhyaya rightly remarks: "It is difficult to designate this ethical system under any specific name, following the western thinkers on ethics and social morality. There is in it a predominance of elements of hedonism and a belief in pleasure. Next to it, there is not only an element of rationalism in it, but an altruistic tendency is also present there. Hence in Kauṭilya we find a fine synthesis of all these."[88]

In fine, Kauṭilya's view of life is not revolutionary. It is rooted deeply in the Indian traditions. The pattern of life as drawn in his *Arthaśāstra* resembles that of the orthodox school given in the Mahābhārata and the Dharmaśāstras. No doubt he lays emphasis on economic considerations. This view, too, may be in line with traditional experts in the science of polity as other sources suggest.[89] His comparative lack of enthusiasm for the concept of salvation as the goal of life reveals his practical bias. In this view too he may have followed that branch of the orthodox school which lays stress upon the stage of householders and the performance of the prescribed duties in this life.

---

[88] Bandyopadhyaya, *Kauṭilya*, p. 39.
[89] *Mbh.* Śānti. 167, Arjuna's view; *KS.* I. 2. 14-17.

CHAPTER II

RELATIVITY OF MORALS

"Ethical relativity," writes Westermarck, "implies that there is no objective standard of morality, for objectivity presupposes universality. As truth is one it has to be the same for any one who knows it and if morality is a matter of truth and falsity, in the normative sense of the terms, the same must be the case with moral truth. If a certain course of conduct is good or bad, right or wrong, it is so universally, and cannot be both good and bad, right and wrong."[1]

Relativity of morals has been a pet subject for debate among philosophers. Is there any objective standard of moral judgment ? Is there anything intrinsically good ? Or is the same thing good or bad according to the circumstances of each case ? As a modern poet has exclaimed,

> "The wildest dreams of Kew are the facts of Khatmandu,
> And the crimes of Clapham chaste in Martaban."[2]

Kauṭilya gives us an interesting discourse on the merits and demerits of certain 'vices' (*vyasana*).[3] On the basis of human conduct (*puruṣa-vyasana*), the *Arthaśāstra* classifies 'vices' under two heads: (*a*) those arising from anger (*kopaja*) and (*b*) those originating from desire (*kāmaja*). These, again, have their sub-heads. Kauṭilya's classification of human vices can be set out in a diagram (*see* page 19).

Kauṭilya records an illuminating comparison between anger and lust.

According to Bhāradvāja, quoted in the *Arthaśāstra*, both anger and desire are good because "anger is customary with an honest man; it prompts revenge upon foes, stops insults and keeps people in fear. The recourse to anger is always necessary for the prevention

---

[1] Westermarck, *Ethical Relativity*, p. 183.

[2] Chesterton quoted in Preface to Philosophy; Hocking and others, p. 119.

[3] *AŚ*. VIII. 3.

Puruṣa-vyasana (human vices)

- *Kopaja* (due to anger)
  - *Vākpāruṣya* (harsh words)
  - *Arthadūṣaṇa* (financial offences)
  - *Daṇḍapāruṣya* (harsh punishment)
- *Kāmaja* (due to desire)
  - *Mṛgayā* (hunting)
  - *Dyūta* (gambling)
  - *Striyaḥ* (addiction to women)
  - *Pāna* (drinking)

of sin. Desire leads to success, sweet speech, liberality and suavity. The recourse to desire is always necessary for the enjoyment of the fruits of work done."

For Kauṭilya, both anger and desire are bad but anger is worse. Thus Kauṭilya observes: "Of these two, anger is worse, for anger goes against all. Often kings, slave to anger, are heard to have been killed through popular fury, (whereas) those, slave to desire, were, through wastage and expenditure, destroyed by enemies and disease."

Again, contradicting Bhāradvāja's view, Kauṭilya states: "No, anger causes hatred, troubles from enemies and unhappiness (whereas) desire leads to contempt, loss of property, and close association with thieves, gamblers, hunters, singers, players on musical instruments and other undesirable persons. Of these, hatred is more serious than contempt, for a contemptible person is oppressed by his own people as well as his enemies, whereas a hated person is totally destroyed. Troubles from enemies are more serious than loss of properties, for the latter injures the purse, the former injures life. Unhappiness is more serious than close association with undesirable persons, for the latter is pleasant for the moment, but the former causes long pain. So anger is worse."

Vātsyāyana's discussion on the merits and demerits of *Kāma* bears a close similarity with the arguments set out above. He writes: "Some argue against *Kāma*—One should not have recourse to *Kāma*. For it is detrimental to the cause of the other two objects, viz., *Dharma* and *Artha*, as a person addicted to *Kāma*, being always in the pursuit of sensual pleasures, is liable to neglect *Dharma* and *Artha*. For these reasons he will be shunned by good people. *Kāma* will lead to an association with wicked and dangerous people and will lead to many unworthy undertakings and impure habits and loss of future prospects. It will likewise be the source of many other evils and the man will be looked upon with contempt. He will neither be trusted nor associated with by people at large. It is traditionally stated that many persons through falling victims to *Kāma* (sensuality), perished with all their family and followers. To cite the example of King Daṇḍakya, a descendant of Bhoja, who through sensuality having had sexual intercourse with a Brāhmiṇ girl perished with all his relations and kingdom......But there are the following arguments in favour of *Kāma*. *Kāma* (sexual intercourse) is as indispensable to the bodily existence as food is (as, through unsatisfied passion, madness and other evil consequences will follow). Moreover, *Kāma* is the aid of *Dharma* and *Artha*, as they are pursued with the object of securing worldly pleasures including sexual enjoyment (the proper *Kāma*) and happiness in the next world."[4]

It is highly interesting to note that Aristotle makes a similar comparison between anger and lust. His *Ethics*[5] states that anger is less disgraceful than sensual desire. The grounds may be summarised as follows: "Anger follows reason in a sense but desire does not; anger is more natural than desire for excessive pleasure; anger is less cunning than desire; anger causes pain but wantonness is associated with pleasure."

The Indian arguments, though seemingly naïve, contain some fundamental psychological truths. The very juxtaposition of anger and desire finds prominent place in works on modern psychology. "In the language of Freud, man has two inborn capacities, and each may manifest in a nobler or a baser form. There is Eros, which is love and creativity, but also lust; and there is Thanatos, which is hate and destruction, but may also become the power to control and manipulate for useful purposes. Often these two drives become fused. Love can make a divine marriage with mastery, just as lust can make a diabolic marriage with pain. Sadomasochism is the reverse side of a coin whose obverse is creative achievement."[6] The

---

[4] *KS.* I. 2. 40-47, Iyenger's translation.
[5] *Ethics*, VII. 7.
[6] G. Rattray Taylor, *Sex in History*, 13-14.

opinion of the modern writer seems to reconcile the divergent views of the ancient lawgivers.

Kauṭilya elaborately discusses the conflicting views of the ancient social philosophers on 'vices' originating from desire and then gives his own opinion on the topics.[7] His discourse on the relativity of sensual licence attracts notice. The arguments might better be expressed in the form of a debate in which the participants were Kauṇapadanta (identified with Bhīṣma), Vātavyādhi (identified with Uddhava) and Kauṭilya himself.

Kauṇapadanta: "Of the vices of gambling and womanizing, gambling is more heinous; for the gambler always plays, even at night by lamplight and even when his mother dies; the gambler gets angry when accosted (even) in danger. But in the company of women it is possible to discourse on spiritual and financial matters even at the places of bath, toilet and feasts. Moreover, it is possible to engage the woman in the king's welfare or (otherwise) to do away with her by secret means or remove her by causing her disease."

Kauṭilya: "No, it is possible to recover lost wealth in gambling but not so from women. (The evils of sensuality are) lack of vision, breach of duty, troubles due to procrastination, loss of virtue, weakness of policy and addiction to drinks."

Vātavyādhi: "Of the vices of womanizing and drinking, the former is more reprehensible. There are various intrigues among womankind whereas from drinking result the enjoyment of sound and other objects of the organs of senses, affectionate gifts, honouring followers and the removal of fatigue from work."

Kauṭilya: "No, in the case of attachment for women, there is birth of children and self-preservation through wedded wives (although) there is trouble through public women and total destruction through (erotic connection with) prohibited women; both these dangers (may result from) drinking. (Further) evils of drinking are loss of sense, madness of a sensible person, death in life, nudity, loss of sacred knowledge, life, wealth and friends, separation from the good and association with the undesirable, indulgence in playing on stringed instruments and songs and close contact with money-grabbers."

---

[7] *AŚ.* VIII. 3.

The elaborate discussion on the pros and cons of certain common human habits and propensities clearly indicates that the idea of the relativity of morals makes an impression on Kauṭilya's mind. He appears to have noticed the good and the bad sides of human conducts. Let us take a concrete example, the attachment for women. Kauṭilya himself sets out its bright as well as dark sides. Wives bear children and preserve life, although illicit connections bring about one's downfall. The inference seems to be that association with women cannot be intrinsically good or bad.

Similar inferences may be drawn in the cases of hunting, drinking and gambling. Aristotle also agrees: "There are some desires and pleasures which are noble and virtuous of their kind."[8] Even then excessive devotion to them is thought to be foolish.

Moreover, a close study of the *Arthaśāstra* shows that Kauṭilya and his forerunners encourage lies, treachery, violence and lust for certain ulterior ends; principally of the State.[9] Politics rule over ethics. In theory nothing is inequitable for the benefit of the State. Seduction, adultery, rape, torture, chicanery, murder—nothing is bad, if the ends of the State require it. For this view, many ancient and modern writers condemn Kauṭilya.[10] But in assessing his attitude towards ethics, one should not forget the age-old controversy over the end justifying the means.

The Kauṭilyan State is a welfare state par excellence in which the king, a model of personal purity and sobriety, is called upon to work for the happiness of the people. The law requires him to control his evil propensities and avoid greed for the wives and wealth of others.[11] Yet the glorification of the state at the occasional expense of personal morality finds numerous parallels in the ancient and the modern worlds.[12]

From a study of old texts as well as from the internal evidence of the *Arthaśāstra* it appears that Kauṭilya attempts to bring in a higher moral tone to politics than that of some of his predecessors.

---

[8] *Ethics*, VII. 6.
[9] *AŚ.* V. 1 & 2.
[10] *Vide* Introduction, *supra.*
[11] *AŚ.* I. 7. (*evaṁ vaśyendriyaḥ parastri-dravyahiṁsāśca varjayet*).
[12] *Vide* Chapter XVII, *infra.*

For example, to keep restive princes under control, *Vātavyādhi* quoted in the *Arthaśāstra*, is said to have prescribed gross immorality: "Princes may be suffered to dissipate their lives by sensual excess, inasmuch as rebelling sons do not dislike their indulgent father." "This," contradicts Kauṭilya: "is death in life, for as soon as a royal family with dissipated princes is attacked, it collapses like a moth-eaten wood." Other politicians, Āmbhīyāḥ, are reported to have advised that princes should be allured into dissipation. Kauṭilya stoutly protests: "There can be no greater crime or sin than making wicked impressions on an innocent mind."[13] Similar instances have been cited elsewhere in this work.[14]

Moreover, Kauṭilya prescribes devious means only in exceptional circumstances. For example, a righteous (*dharmaruchi*) king is advised to cause the secret murder of powerful enemies who cannot be controlled openly.[15] To fill the state's coffer, the king is allowed to engineer any crime, but this is directed against evil characters only. Kauṭilya categorically states: "These devices are applicable against blameworthy (*duṣya*) and irreligious (*adhārmika*) persons but not against others."[16] In other words, he seems to think that there is nothing wrong in fleecing ill-gotten wealth for the state purposes.

Right conduct seems to allow exceptions, and in this view of the matter Kauṭilya is in good company. The *Mahābhārata* gives us an excellent discourse on the relativity of moral conducts. In certain circumstances, the great epic justifies manifestly sinful acts. To cite a few instances, the Śāntiparvan[17] tells us that it is not sinful to drink for the purpose of curing diseases, to cohabit with the preceptor's wife at the command of the preceptor for raising an issue; to steal for the maintenance of the preceptor's family in emergency; to rob wealth of persons other than Brāhmaṇas for the preservation of others; to tell lies before women or in connection with marriage; to commit adultery with another's wife if she, oppressed by desire, makes

---

13 *AŚ*. I. 4.

14 Chapter XVI, *infra*.

15 *AŚ*. v. 1; also Chapter XVII, *infra*.

16 *AŚ*. v. 2; also Chapter XVII, *infra*.

17 *Mbh*. Śānti, 34. 16-32; 109. 13-15; 141. 39; 142. 9. For relativity in following different courses of conduct, Sivaswamy Aiyer, *EHMI*. 164-65.

entreaties; to tell lies before robbers and to steal for self-preservation in danger.

Manu, the greatest exponent of orthodox morality, allows theft or robbery in certain cases.[18] Thus, a poor Brāhmaṇa may with impunity rob another's property for the completion of an unfinished sacrifice. A hungry man is allowed to steal food from another's field in special circumstances. Manu even forbids the king to punish the man in such cases. Hunger and religiosity are thus no respecters of private property. So, even according to Manu, theft or robbery, it seems, is not inherently bad.

In Europe too, as Lecky shows: "The Fathers laid down as a distinct proposition that pious frauds were justifiable and even laudable" and he adds: "immediately, all ecclesiastical literature became tainted with a spirit of the most unblushing mendacity."[19]

Moreover, the stern ends of politics do not brook ordinary morality. Bhīṣma in the *Mahābhārata* calls upon a king to kill oppressive persons, be they friends or elders, to distrust even near relations, to rob the wicked and pay the good and to bribe opponents into submission.[20] In times of emergency the king is allowed to overstep the limits of common morality. Bhīṣma allows him in such cases to collect money by force or fraud (*tasmādāpadya-dharmo'pi śrūyate dharmalakṣaṇaḥ/adharmo jāyate tasminniti vai kabayo viduḥ*).[21] The *Mahābhārata* gives us an elaborate discourse on the duties of a king in emergent circumstances. It bears a close resemblance to the views of Kauṭilya.

Speaking on the *Maṇḍala* theory of Kauṭilya, Professor K. A. Nilakanta Sastri observes: "Modern writers have often remarked on the unscrupulous and 'Machiavellian' nature of these precepts; but one may well doubt whether the work of modern foreign and war offices described with a due regard, not to their professions, but to what they actually perform, will be seen to evince a better respect for morality. On the other hand the Indian text-books often developed

---

[18] *Manu*, XI. 11-21.
[19] Rattray Taylor, *Sex in History*, p. 56.
[20] *Mbh.* Śānti. 57.
[21] *Mbh.* Śānti. 130. 16; also 131ff.

extravagant theories having little relation to practice for the sake of the completeness of the śāstra."[22]

In any event, if the champions of orthodox morality make clear exceptions to right conduct, why should one find so much fault with Kauṭilya for advocating oppressive devices to attain the ends of a welfare state ?

It will not be out of place to quote the view of a modern philosopher on politics and morals: "In political action, in attempts to reach a definite goal, everything becomes a political means —everything, including in certain respects morality and religion, that is, moral and religious ideas, sentiments and institutions. The initial situation is given in each case: the men with whom we have to deal are always what they are; their ideas, their prejudices, their good or bad dispositions, their virtues and their defects furnish the material on which and with which we must work and there is no way of substituting for them more pleasing material. If, in order to agree with men in a common action or to induce them to come to an agreement, it is necessary to soothe their illusions, flatter their vanity, appeal to their most superstitious and childish beliefs (as, for example, the miracle of St. Gennaro), or to their most superficial or most superficially understood ideas (for example, equality, liberty and fraternity and the other so-called "principles of '89", which are big emotional realities, whatever may be their theoretical value), then it will be well to adopt these means. We must not be shocked by them. Every form of human activity, as it unfolds, takes strength from all other activities and it subjects and makes its own the products of all the other activities. It would be the same as being scandalized by the poet who uses thoughts and affections, joys and griefs, good and evil, all as materials for his poetry and turns all to winged images.

"But there is still another reason for not being shocked. Pure poetry does not dispel reflection, criticism and science from the spirit and from the world, but, rather, prepares for and almost summons them. Just so, politics, which is pure politics, does not destroy, but produces morality, in which it finds its completion and highest expression."[23]

---

[22] *Age of the Nandas and the Mauryas*, p. 188.
[23] B. Croce, *Politics & Morals*, pp. 20-21.

One might, however, explain away the supposed encouragement of ordinary immorality in extraordinary cases by citing an illuminating passage from Vātsyāyana.[24] The sage describes some debased sex practices but promptly justifies himself by stating, "There is no reason why anything should be done merely because there is the *Śāstram* (ordinance) sanctioning the act. The śāstras ordain things in general. But their application is to be confined to a few approved acts only. In the *Vaidya Śāstra* (Medical Science), even the flesh of a dog is said to be contributing to taste, virility and strength of the body. Is it therefore to be eaten by wise men ? But nevertheless, there are certainly some men who are addicted to such acts. There are some countries where such acts prevail generally. There may also be times when such acts would not be useless, as sometimes they may tend towards attaining some desired objects. Therefore, one should consider the place, time and the means of accomplishment, sanction of the śāstra and his own position before deciding whether or not one should adopt one or the other of these acts."

In other words, as modern writers state, "Moral rules are not absolute, but relative: relative to the time and place, perhaps even to the individual person."[25]

The *Mahābhārata* expresses the same attitude: dharma turns into adharma and *vice versa* on account of place and time. (*Bhavatyadharmo dharmo hi dharmādharmāvubhāvapi/karaṇāddeśakālasya deśakālaḥ sa tādṛiśaḥ*).[26]

Megasthenes perhaps records a similar ideal of relativity when he speaks of Brachmanes as follows: "They consider nothing that befalls men to be either good or bad, to suppose otherwise being a dreamlike illusion, else how could some be affected with sorrow and others with pleasure by the very same thing and how could the same thing affect the same individuals at different times with these opposite emotions ?"[27]

What, then, is the test of the right conduct ? The answer seems to lie in Kauṭilya's cryptic definition of *vyasana* or vice.[28] "That which

---

[24] *KS.* II. 9. 37-40 and also *KS.* VIII. 2. 55 (Iyenger's translation).
[25] Hocking & others, *Preface to Philosophy*, p. 120.
[26] *Mbh.* Śānti. 78. 32.
[27] *Meg.* 100.
[28] *AŚ.* VIII. 1.

diverts one from the good is a vice (*vyasyatyenaṁ śreyasa iti*)." He, however, omits to define "*śreyas*" or the good but gives us some characteristics of vice, viz., "absence of or opposition to virtues, excessive faults, excessive attachment (for sensual matters) and oppression (from others) (*guṇa-prātilomyamabhāvaḥ pradoṣa prasaṅga pīḍā vā vyasanam*)". Moreover, vices are, according to Kauṭilya, due to lack of education and discipline.[29]

Thus, in deciding what is right and what is wrong conduct, one, as Kauṭilya seems to think, is left, in the last analysis, with education and discipline. Personal feeling or individual emotion cannot be the proper guide in this matter as the Hedonists seem to believe. Education and discipline connote a social consideration. "What counts above all in conduct is neither the motive that it springs from nor the pattern of behavior itself but the results to which the conduct leads. With this we turn from act-theories to end-theories."[30] "For the right was a means to the good."[31]

Kauṭilya's moral attitude bears a remarkable similarity with the Greek view on morals. As modern writers have ably summarised it, "Yet of course the Greek, like rest of us, had his view as to what made life good or bad. What was this view ? Put generally, it was as follows: everyone had his part to play in the life of the community, a complex part in which he must try, for example, to be an effective provider for his family, an expert carpenter, and a useful citizen at the same time; the good life for him consisted simply in filling his station and its duties as best as he could.

" 'As best as he could'; but how is one to know what is best ? The Greek's reply was characteristic. That activity of any kind is best, he said, which achieves most completely and with the greatest economy of means the end it is meant to serve. What do we mean by a good knife ? One that is good *for* its special end, which is cutting. What do we mean by a good general ? A man who is effective in his responsibilities such as supplying and ordering troops, which are necessary to victory. What is a good man ? That is an immensely harder question. But when Aristotle came to discuss it in the classic

[29] *AŚ*. VIII. 3.
[30] Hocking & others, *Preface to Philosophy*, 159.
[31] *Ibid.* 160.

work of Greek ethics, he held that it must be answered by the same method. If we are to know what is meant by a good or bad man, by right or wrong conduct, we must know the *end* that man should pursue."[32]

Thus, reversing Kauṭilya's definition of 'vice' we may arrive at his definition of 'right'. He seems to think that right is what leads to the good (*śreyas*).

How is one to discern the good ? Kauṭilya's answer seems to be, through education and discipline, for, according to him 'vices' are due to lack of education and discipline.

Aśoka too lays an emphasis on education and discipline. To do good is difficult. "Good (*kalyāna*) is difficult to perform. He who initiates good does something difficult to perform . . . verily.sin is easy to commit (*sukaraṁ hi pāpam*)."[33] *Kalyāna* of Aśoka may be equated with *śreyas* of Kauṭilya.

Ultimately, Kauṭilya rounds off his discussion on the relativity of morals by observing: "*Kāma* is excessive contact (*pragraha*) with the bad and *Kopa* is oppression (*avagraha*) of the good. Due to excess of evils both are deemed to be grave vices. So a person, self-possessed, victor of the organs of senses and associate of the aged, should abandon both anger and desire, which sap the root (of life)."[34]

Kāma in this context becomes a vice as it exceeds all limits of propriety. So it is to be abandoned. But *Kāma* (Desire), not opposed to spiritual and economic considerations, ought to be pursued (*Dharmārthāvirodhena kāmaṁ seveta*).

In this context, Vātsyāyana observes: "As to the possible evil consequences of *Kāma*, we should know how to avoid them and seek remedial measures as in cases such as the following: 'Are not vessels placed over stoves for cooking food in spite of the existence of beggars ? . . . Are not the seeds of *yava* sown in spite of the existence of deer and other grazing animals ?' As in these cases, so, precautionary measures should be taken against the evil results of *Kāma*."[35]

---

[32] Hocking & others, *Preface to Philosophy*, 160.
[33] *RE*. v.
[34] *AS*. VIII. 3.
[35] *KS*. I. 2. 48 (Iyenger's translation).

Thus, the regulation of sensuality was, and still is, the chief concern of law-givers, ancient or modern.

In conclusion, we might observe with some amount of confidence that Kauṭilya does not in fact swerve from the path of morality.[36] His advocacy for devious means in some cases is prompted by the special circumstances of each case. Even many orthodox moralists do not hesitate to prescribe similar methods in such unusual cases. Moreover, Kauṭilya bases his political ideal on the welfare of the people. His king is the model of perfection. Even if he is asked to adopt doubtful steps in emergencies, he aims only at the good of his subject.

[36] Ganapati Sastri, Preface to *AŚ.* Vol. 3, pp. 3-5.

Chapter III

EROTIC BELIEFS AND PRACTICES

Kauṭilya stands for a practical approach to erotic matters. He considers happiness to be necessary. Yet he holds that sensual pleasures should be enjoyed without conflict with moral principles and economic considerations (*na nissukhas syāt dharmārthāvirodhena kāmaṁ seveta*).[1] His stray references to erotic beliefs and practices further reveal his attitude towards sensuality.

He knows the tremendous force of sexual urge in human beings, particularly women. He is fairly conversant with the ordinary physiology of sex. As in the *Mahābhārata* and the Dharmaśāstras,[2] he recognizes the importance of the *ṛitu* or the period in the life of a woman. He requires the householder to copulate with his wife during her *ṛitu* (*ṛitugāmitvam*). According to Kauṭilya, to allow the period of a woman to go in vain is immoral as well as illegal. Kauṭilya enunciates a broad view: "*Tīrthoparodho hi dharmavadha iti.*"[3] Modern psychologists too stress the importance of copulation during this period when the sexual craving in a woman is heightened and the chances of procreation enlarged.[4]

Humanism, rather than religiosity, it seems, prompts him to take up this liberal attitude. He allows, as we later on note, sexual connec-

---

[1] *AŚ.* I. 7.

[2] J. J. Meyer writes: "..... with the *ṛitu* love begins, with it ends, in it it has always its central point. *Ṛitu* denotes the monthly cleansing, and then in particular those days after the period, from the fourth day onwards, which in the Indian view, are proper for conception." *SLAI.* 216-17.

[3] *AŚ.* III. 4. Jolly summarises the orthodox view as follows: '..... the loss of a *ṛitu*, i.e. the day regarded as appropriate for the raising of progeny involves the sin of killing an embryo (*bhrūṇahatyā*). This is no doubt the reason why marriageable daughters who are not yet married may after three *ṛitus* herself to go out to seek a husband.' *HLC.* 121. Manu also directs the husband to approach the wife during her *ṛitukāla* but he should avoid the holy days. The *ṛitu*, according to Manu, is usually the first sixteen days (after the menstruation begins) of which the first four, the eleventh and the thirteenth nights are to be excluded. *Manu.* III. 45-47.

[4] *ESP.* 660-61.

tions in some cases even out of lawful marriage, perhaps for the satisfaction of a woman's sex-hunger.[5] If a father fails to get a grown-up daughter married, Kauṭilya like other orthodox moralists allows the girl to find a mate on her own.[6] According to Kauṭilya, the father forfeits his dominion over the daughter, if he allows her monthly period to go in vain (*ṛitupratirodhibhiḥ svāmyādapakrāmati*).[7] From the point of view of the girl, the provisions ensure the chance of a normal sexual relationship. A modern authority on sex observes: "With the appearance of menstruation and even before, the normal girl begins to take an interest in everything concerning love. But restraint, arbitrarily exercised over the sexual instinct, can induce pathological indifference."[8] Thus, Kauṭilya's view is based on the foundation of psychological truth recognised also by modern scientific writers.

Kauṭilya quotes Bhāradvāja who mentions a popular saying that a woman making love of her own accord will, in the case of a refusal, curse the man.[9] In other words, ancient common sense does not encourage the refusal of a woman who voluntarily offers herself to a man. The *Mahābhārata* even curiously observes that it is not sinful to cohabit with another's wife, if she asks for such a pleasure.[10] Yājñavalkya allows the elopement with a woman who asks for it, provided she is below one's caste.[11] Kauṭilya prescribes a lighter punishment for one who violates a willing maiden.[12] The girl, too, is let off with a light fine.[12] The sex-urge in a woman at the time of copulation should receive due respect. Kauṭilya repeats like a refrain that no one should have sexual connection with a woman against her inclination (*na ca prākāmyamakāmāyāṁ labheta*).[13] In the matter of carnal connections, the cravings of a prostitute, too, call for consideration. A man violating even a prostitute against her wish is punishable according to the *Arthaśāstra*.

Even on the marital bed a spouse is supposed to consider the sexual

---

[5] Chap. IX, *infra*.
[6] Chaps. IV & IX, *infra*.
[7] *AŚ*. IV. 12.
[8] Stekel quoted in *ESK*. 138-39.
[9] *AŚ*. V. 6. (*svayamārūḍha hi strī tyājyamānā' bhiśapatīti lokapravādaḥ*).
[10] *Mbh*. Śānti. 34. 27 (*bhikṣite pāradāryaṁca tadādharmasya na dūṣakam*).
[11] *Yāj*. II. 291 (*sakāmāsvanulomāsu na doṣaḥ*.)
[12] *AŚ*. IV. 12.
[13] *AŚ*. IV. 12.

craving of the other. As we shall observe, a spouse is allowed to refuse sexual intercourse with the other, if the sexual desire is absent, provided, of course, certain conditions pre-exist. Thus, a wife who is barren or has a son or has reached menopause or gives birth to still-born babies or is inclined towards religion (*dharmakāmā*) can avoid the sexual act with the husband, if she lacks the urge for it (*akāmā*). One condition at least obviously depends on the wife herself. That is her inclination for religion. So, where religion and sex clash with each other, Kauṭilya allows the wife to choose the former, if she likes. And in this matter her choice is final. The husband is not allowed to impose his will on her.[14]

A mature woman is compared to a tree in fruits (*phala*).[15] Elsewhere a woman is compared to a field and the man, a sower of the seed (*paraparigrahe vījamutsriṣṭaṁ kṣetrinaḥ*).[16] This analogy is very popular with the orthodox school.[17]

Copulation (*maithuna*) is known to be the ultimate end in erotic bouts, and is often preceded by love-play. The *Arthaśāstra* cursorily mentions special efforts for Cupid's art (*anaṅgaviceṣṭita*) with a view to the final union.[18] Kauṭilya is well-aware of the usual methods of love-making, so much elaborated in the ancient works on sexology. He refers to the lovers' mumblings, secret rendezvous and escapade at night. The significance of the hair, the girdle, teeth and nails in love-play is also well-known to him. He does not allow the holding out the hair or girdle or teeth or nails with a view to heightening the sexual ardour, obviously outside the lawful union (*keśa-nīvidantanakhā-valambaneṣu pūrvaḥ sāhasadaṇḍaḥ puṁso dviguṇaḥ*).[19]

---

[14] *AŚ.* III. 2: Chap. V. *infra.*

[15] *AŚ.* IV. 12.

[16] *AŚ.* III. 7.

[17] *Manu.* IX. 25-55.

[18] *AŚ.* III. 3.

[19] *AŚ.* III. 3. The *Nāṭyaśāstra* describes a courtezan's lovemaking as follows: "A courtezan is to be considered overpowered with love when she expresses her passion by casting sidelong glances, touching the ornaments, itching the ears, touching the toes, showing the breast and the navel, cleansing the nails and gathering her hairs" (XXIV. 163 ff. Ghose's translation). Mm. Ganapati Sastri and Dr. Basak find in the relevant passage of the *Arthaśāstra* a reference to the application of the teeth and the nail-marks in course of love play (*dantakṣatakaraṇa nakhakṣatakaraṇe ca*). Yājñavalkya too does not allow such love-plays outside the lawful union. *Yāj.* II. 286-87. For courtship of a girl in the *Kāmasūtra vide* Chakladar, *Social Life in Ancient India*, pp. 134-35.

According to Kauṭilya, adultery may be inferred from play with each other's hair (*keśākeśikam*), or the signs of enjoyment with one's body (*upaliṅganādva śarīropabhogānām*).[20]

In the game of love, go-betweens play a dominant rôle. They carry love-letters and costly presents, communicate messages of love and stimulate the desire for the lover.[21] The *Arthaśāstra* makes several references to them. As in the *Kāmasūtra* and the *Nāṭyaśāstra*, female ascetics, mendicant women and nuns very often act as go-betweens.[22] Kauṭilya seeks to protect a good wife from contact with such persons. On the other hand, he requires them to be employed for the purpose of espionage. He mentions several cases of possible betrayal by messengers.[23] He refers to the fringe of the forest and the play-house (*vanānte krīḍāgṛihe*) as the places for a tryst.[23] He restricts the free movement of married women as a precaution against temptation. He does not allow a woman in many cases to travel with unwanted persons on the highway (*pathyānusaraṇa*).[24]

Commenting on the ancient Hindu attitude towards sexuality, Dr. Basham observes: "Sexuality was not looked on as a mere vent for the animal passions of the male, but as a refined mutual relationship for the satisfaction of both parties."[25]

The *Arthaśāstra* frequently refers to sexual intrigues and tries to exploit them for the furtherance of political ends. Wily politicians are asked to take the full advantage of moral weakness of others. Of various intrigues in the matters of sex, we hear of spies rousing the jealousy of rival lovers, instigating one lover to kill another, and so on. An offence against women might lead to sudden murder.[26] Suspected persons in a house include a woman who has placed her heart elsewhere.[27] A heart-broken lover commits suicide.[28] Cupid's arrow is no respector of castes or relations or status, although the *Arthaśāstra* seeks to prevent it. Kauṭilya is keen to punish the cases of rape and

---

[20] *AŚ*. IV. 12.
[21] *AŚ*. XI. 1.
[22] *KS*. V. 4. 44-65, *NS*. XXIV. 198-200.
[23] *AŚ*. XI. 1.
[24] *AŚ*. III. 4.
[25] A. L. Basham, *The Wonder that was India*, p. 171.
[26] *AŚ*. IV. 7.
[27] *AŚ*. IV. 6.
[28] *AŚ*. V. 7.

abduction.[29] We also hear of robbers carrying off women at night.[30] But Dr. Basham rightly remarks that the *Arthaśāstra* is "comparatively lenient towards sexual crime."[31]

Kauṭilya is not unmindful of magic and witchcraft with reference to erotic matters. He mentions aphrodisiacs[32] and witchcraft[33] to which one spouse might take recourse for rousing the flagging love of the other. It is no offence to practise witchcraft (*abhicāra, saṁvanana*) to gain love of an indifferent husband or wife, unless it leads to some injury.[33] Mendicant women are found in the *Arthaśāstra* to administer to wives medicines to arouse affection in the husband. Sometimes the drugs prove fatal.[34] Medicinal ointments are believed to be capable of attracting the beloved.[35]

A belief in magic and witchcraft often influences sexual adventures. An interesting device to trap adulterers is mentioned in the *Arthaśāstra*.[36] "On availing themselves of the opening made by ordinary spies sent in advance, spies pretending to be endowed with supernatural powers may, under the pretence of knowing such incantations as cause rapid speed in running away or render persons invisible or cause hard-fastened doors to open, induce highway robbers to robbery; and may, under the pretence of knowing such incantations as secure the love of women, entice adulterers to take part in criminal actions planned for the purpose of proving their criminal intentions.

"On taking these enthusiasts thus induced to a village where persons under the guise of women and men are previously stationed, and which is different from the one intended to be reached, the youths may be told that it is difficult to reach in time the village aimed at, and that the power of incantation may be seen then and there alone.

"Having opened the doors seemingly with the power of incantation, the youths may be asked to get in. Having in the midst of wakeful watchmen under concert, rendered the youths invisible with incantation, they may be asked to go into the interior. Having caused the

---

[29] *AŚ*. IV. 12.
[30] *AŚ*. VIII. 4.
[31] A.L. Basham, *op.cit.* p. 119.
[32] *AŚ*. V. 1.
[33] *AŚ*. IV. 13.
[34] *AŚ*. V. 1.
[35] *AŚ*. XII. 2.
[36] *AŚ*. IV. 5 (Shama Sastry's translation).

watchmen seemingly sleepy, the youths may, as ordered, move the beds of watchmen with no hesitation. Persons under the guise of others' wives may seemingly under the influence of incantation, please the youths." This proposed adventure in love is likely to end in a charge of theft and other crimes on the part of the young gallant and, ultimately, punishment.

The Kauṭilyan state attempts to detect witch-doctors and banish them from the realm. Thus, the *Arthaśāstra* provides:[37] "Whoever is believed to secure for others the love of women, by magical charms, drugs or ceremonials performed on cremation grounds may be approached by a spy with a request that the wife, daughter or daughter-in-law of someone, whom the spy pretends to love may be made to return the love and that a certain amount of money may be accepted. If he consents to it, he shall be proclaimed as one engaged in witchcraft (*saṁvanana-kāraka*) and banished." Similar steps may be taken against persons engaged in witchcraft which is hurtful to others. The *abhicāra* rites are meant to injure others. The law inflicts the intended injury upon the very person who plans it.[38] Elsewhere[39], Kauṭilya gives us some details of *Jambhakavidyā*: "Or a spy under the garb of an ascetic, may offer inducements to seditious persons to acquire more wealth by taking in aid the art of witchcraft and say: 'I am proficient in such witchcraft as brings inexhaustible wealth or entitles a man to get admission into the king's palace or can win the love of any woman or to put an end to the life of one's enemy or can lengthen the duration of one's life or can give a son to any one, if desired.' If the seditious person shows his desire to carry on the process of witchcraft, securing wealth, the spy may make rich offerings, consisting of flesh, wine, and scent, to the deity near an altar in a burial ground wherein a dead body of a man or a child with a little quantity of money has been previously hidden. . ." In fact, Kauṭilya devotes a whole book (Book XIV) to recipes and magical rites for various purposes including the increase of sexual potency (*vīrya*) and making one impotent. In some of these rites even human excreta, female menstrual blood, foetus after abortion and genitals of dead women play important rôles.

---

[37] *AŚ.* IV. 4 (Shama Sastry's translation).
[38] *AŚ.* IV. 13.
[39] *AŚ.* V. 2. (Shama Sastry's translation).

The magical processes which find mention in the *Atharvaveda* continue unabated in the *Arthaśāstra* and ultimately culminate in the later Tāntric cults.[40]

The various magical formulas for opening doors, sending watchmen, watchdogs and inmates to sleep, acquiring invisibility and seeing in darkness are described by the *Arthaśāstra* (Book XIV). Eroticism is clearly reflected in some of these rites. Certain deities are supposed to possess the genital (*bhaga*) of a woman. "O, *Chaṇḍālī*, *Kumbī*, *Tumbha*, *Kaṭuka* and *Sāragha*, thou art possessed with the *bhaga* of a woman (*sanārībhago' si*), oblation to thee ! When this mantra is repeated, the door will open, the inmates fall to sleep."[41] There are recipes for causing various diseases including gonorrhoea (*prameha*).[42]

Modern scientific writers have noted the prevalence of aphrodisiacs, magic and witchcraft in sexual matters throughout the world in all ages. In the chapter entitled "The Alchemy of Love", the learned authors of the Encyclopaedia of Sexual Knowledge have analysed the various reasons behind the popularity of the use of aphrodisiacs. They observe: "As we have seen the use of them was widespread during antiquity and the Middle Ages, and in our times, in the guise of chemical preparations, they play an enormous part in the life of civilised society. It would, however, be a mistake to regard this as a sign of the decadence of the times" Concerning superstition, they state: "According to the most widely accepted definition, that of Albert Hellwig, it is 'those elements in popular beliefs which modern scientific concepts qualify as erroneous'. That is to say that certain beliefs which are today classified as superstitions, may a century hence be reinstated by new scientific discoveries."[43]

---

[40] *HCIP*. Vol. I. Chap. XXII. "It is a remarkable fact, however, that in spite of this aversion to the Veda of magic, the ritual texts which describe the great sacrifices do incorporate exorcism—formulas and magic rites whereby the priest can destroy 'the enemy whom he hates and who hates him,' and the law book of Manu (XI. 33) sanctions the use of exorcism against enemies" *ibid.* p. 438-39 (*śrutiratharvāṅgirasīḥ kuryāditya vicārayan vākśastraṁ vai Brāhmaṇasya tena hanyādarīn dvijaḥ*).

[41] *AŚ*. XIV. 3: The *Ṛig Veda* (VII. 55. 5.8) contains a similar charm. (*Ṛig Veda* quoted in *HCIP* Vol. I. 389).

[42] *AŚ*. XIV. 1. Megasthenes (102) also mentions diviners and sorcerers. He speaks of persons who know drugs which are said to make marriages fruitful. The *Kāmasūtra* also devotes a chapter on aphrodisiacs and love potions.

[43] *ESK*. 369.

In conclusion, Kauṭilya is, obviously, conversant with the basic psychology of sex. He makes suitable provisions for the normal outlet of the sexual urge preferably through the institution of marriage, but failing that, in exceptional cases, even outside wedlock. He does not accept Manu's proposition that a girl should die as an old maid, if a suitable match is not found.[44] Jolly[45] refers to some commentators according to whom Manu's utterances in this behalf are not to be taken literally. Jolly further cites Baudhāyana who holds that marriage with even an unworthy suitor is to be preferred to remaining in the parents' house (*avidyamāna sadṛiśe guṇahīnamapi śrayet*). As a matter of fact, like Kauṭilya, Manu also allows a mature girl to choose her husband in some cases.[46] Thus, there is no inherent contradiction between Kauṭilya and the champion of the orthodox school in this matter. Moreover, modern scientific knowledge also justifies Kauṭilya's emphasis on the necessity for sexual inclination of a woman during copulation.[47]

With regard to aphrodisiacs, magic and witchcraft Kauṭilya continues the Vedic traditions. On the one hand, he seems to suppress the practitioners of these nefarious arts; on the other hand, he attempts to exploit the superstitions of the common people for the furtherance of the ends of the state. Perhaps he himself succumbs to such superstitions of the age when he prescribes magical rites and formulas for various purposes (Book XIV). But it is difficult to judge whether he does so through a genuine belief in them or as a matter of expediency. It is quite possible that Kauṭilya seriously pins his faith on these methods. In any event, as modern writers have observed, belief in such inexplicable practices does not necessarily imply moral decadence of the age.

---

[44] *Manu.* IX. 89.

[45] Jolly, *Hindu Law & Custom*, p. 122.

[46] *Manu.* IX. 90-93; also *Baudh.* IV. 1. 15-16.

[47] Commenting on the Indian works on erotics, the authors of *ESK* state: "They did not look upon the pleasure derived from 'love-play' and healthy sensuality as 'animal' but on the contrary regarded intercourse that was joyless, gloomy, and lacking in subtlety as a sordid act." They further observe: "Once the satisfaction of the sexual instinct has been accepted not only as a means but also as an end it becomes obvious that the lack of satisfaction deprives a woman of her natural right and may besides induce serious organic troubles." p. 347. Thus sexual desire in a woman becomes a condition precedent to copulation. That Kauṭilya harps on this fact several times shows the great concern he felt for the existence of sex-cravings in a woman during intercourse.

Even with regard to the exploitation of moral weakness of the people, specially concerning sexual matters, one should not find too much fault with the Kauṭilyan state. We know how Croce justifies "appeal to their most superstitious and childish beliefs" for political ends.[48]

[48] Croce, *Politics & Morals*, p. 21; also Chap. XVII *infra*.

Chapter IV

WEDLOCK

Unlike the *Mahābhārata*,[1] Kauṭilya does not speculate on the origin of marriage. He takes it for granted. The *Mahābhārata* postulates a state of promiscuity in ancient times and also in the country of Uttarakuru. It also states how Śvetaketu introduced the institution of marriage and Dīrghatamas enforced the rules of monogamy for woman.[2] No doubt Kauṭilya refers to a state of anarchy (*Mātsyanyāya*) in which the absence of a controlling political power causes the strong to oppress the weak (*apraṇīto hi mātsyanyāyamudbhāvayati/balīyānabalaṁ hi grasate daṇḍadharābhāve*).[3] The *Mahābhārata* elaborates this concept of *Mātsyanyāya*. It presupposes an invasion of private property and family life (*na dhanārtho na dārārthasteṣām yeṣāmarājakam . . . hriyante ca valāt striyaḥ . . . na dārā na ca putrāḥ syānna dhanaṁ na parigrahaḥ*).[4] To Kauṭilya, however, marriage is an established institution. He calls upon the king himself to control his senses and avoid other people's property and wives (*parastrīdravyahiṁsāśca varjayet*).[5] Thus, even the powerful head of the state is asked to uphold the sanctity of marriage. Kauṭilya, further, calls upon the king to induce the people to follow their *svadharma*.[6] This conception of duties as we have seen includes the duty to marry (*vaivāhyam*).

Thus, as a champion of the *āśramas* or four stages comprised in the plan of life, Kauṭilya enjoins marriage (*vaivāhya*) and cohabitation (*ṛitugāmitvam*) as the duties (*svadharma*) of a householder (*gṛihastha*).[7] Abstinence from carnal connection is meant only for those in the other

---

1 *Mbh.* Ādi. 122. 148.
2 *Ibid.* 10-20; 104. 23-37.
3 *AŚ.* I. 3; I. 13.
4 *Mbh.* Śānti. 67. 12-17; 68.
5 *AŚ.* I. 7.
6 *AŚ.* I. 2.
7 *AŚ.* I. 3.

three stages of life, viz., the *Brahmacārin*, the *Vānaprastha* and the *Parivrājaka*.[8]

Westermarck cites many instances which show "the curious notion that there is something impure and sinful in marriage as in sexual relations generally."[9] Kauṭilya along with the orthodox Indian school of thought is against this notion. As in the *Dharmaśāstras*, Kauṭilya stresses the duty to marry. There might be exceptional cases of perpetual bachelorhood, for example, *Naiṣṭhika Brahmacārin*, who might pass his single life in the family of his teacher in pursuit of knowledge.[10] But such cases are definitely rare in the *Arthaśāstra*.

According to Kauṭilya, marriage is the foundation of the family and of civil rights (*vivāhapūrvo vyavahāra*).[11] No doubt, a family can, by legal fiction, consist of persons not linked up by marriage. Thus, even persons born out of wedlock or raised by levirate or adopted, are sometimes recognised as members of the family.[12] Concubinage, prostitution and other connections outside marriage receive limited recognition in the *Arthaśāstra*.[13] But these cases are obvious exceptions to the general rule providing for marriage.

Such is the importance of marriage that it can cure even the initial taint in the method of obtaining a bride. This brings us to a discussion of the so-called 'forms' of marriage. The *Arthaśāstra*[14] describes eight forms as follows:

"The gift of a bride, decked with ornaments, is *Brāhma* marriage; for the joint performance of sacred duties (by the couple), *Prājāpatya;* upon receipt of a pair of cows, *Ārṣa;* made to an officiating priest at a sacrificial altar, *Daiva;* upon voluntary union (of the couple), *Gāndharva;* upon receipt of *śulka* or bride price, *Āsura;* upon forcible capture, *Rākṣasa;* and upon getting a sleeping or drunken girl, *Paiśāca*." These different 'forms' of marriage have with some variations been described in other ancient texts and thoroughly discussed by modern

---

[8] *AŚ.* ibid.

[9] Westermarck, *History of Human Marriage*, pp. 151ff. He also refers to the Buddhist attitude in favour of monastic life.

[10] *AŚ.* I. 3.

[11] *AŚ.* III. 2.

[12] *Vide* Chapter VIII, *infra.*

[13] *Vide* Chapters IX and X, *infra.*

[14] *AŚ.* III. 2.

writers.[15] They have shown that these 'forms' do not mean different kinds of marriage but rather different ways in which wives may be secured. Thus, in the *Brāhma, Prājāpatya* and *Daiva* forms we find gift of the bride. In the *Ārsa* form, there is a nominal exchange. Mm. Kane, however, states[16] that in this form "the pair is not given as a price (i.e., there is no purchase)", as "the gift is made to show one's regard for the girl". The *Āsura* form, however, contemplates marriage by purchase. According to Kauṭilya, the parents take the daughter's bride price (*tau hi śulkaharau duhituḥ*).[17] The *Gāndharva* form is based upon mutual agreement between the bride and the bridegroom. The *Rākṣasa* form connotes nothing but marriage by capture. *Paiśāca* is the most reprehensible form, involving, as it does, fraud or rape of the girl. We must hasten to state that mere fornication, abduction or rape is not tantamount to marriage. The Kauṭilyan law as well as the *Smṛitis* in general seek to penalise such offences severely.[18] To create the marital bond, something else is required. According to Kauṭilya, the last four forms, *viz. Gāndharva, Āsura, Rākṣasa* and *Paiśāca* require the approval of both the parents of the girl (*mātāpitṛipramāṇāḥ*),[19] whereas in the first four forms the consent of the father (*pitṛipramāṇā*) of the bride is considered sufficient.[19] Some Smṛitis insist upon the rites of marriage in all cases.[20] Even Vātsyāyana describes simple marriage ceremonies before a sacrificial fire in the cases of the *Gāndharva* and the *Paiśāca* forms. He states that the affair is disclosed to the bride's father and mother who are then compelled to ratify the marriage for avoiding scandal.[21] Vātsyāyana, however, at one place considers the *Gāndharva* marriage to be the best.

Like the orthodox writers, Kauṭilya makes a distinction between the sacramental (*dharmya*) and non-sacramental marriages. According to him the first four are sacramental and the rest non-sacramental marriages.[22] Jayaswal holds: "The Dharma school, it should be re-

[15] Kane, *HDS.* Vol. II. 516-26. Jolly, *HLC.* 107ff. Mayne, ***Hindu Law & Usage.*** Meyer, *SLAI.* Chapter II. N. C. Sengupta, ***Evolution of Ancient Indian Law,*** Chapter IV and many other authorities.

[16] Kane, *HDS.* Vol. II. 518.

[17] *AŚ.* III. 2.

[18] Chapter IX, ***infra.***

[19] *AŚ.* ibid.

[20] Kane, *ibid.* 520-21.

[21] *KS.* III. v.

[22] *AŚ.* ibid.

membered, regarded marriage as a sacrament. But the Artha regarded it as a contract, whether entered into by parties themselves or vicariously through guardians (mostly, guardians for the brides)."[23] With great respect to the learned scholar we are unable to accept this view. Kauṭilya clearly recognises four forms of marriage as sacramental (*dharmya* or *dharmiṣṭha*), while the rest according to him are non-sacramental.

The husband has much greater right of enjoyment of the wife's property in the case of a sacramental marriage than in the rest;[24] divorce is not allowed or is probably very much restricted in the former but not so in the latter (*amokṣo dharmavivāhānām*);[25] the remarriage of a virgin wife is postponed for a longer time in the case of the former than in the latter;[26] for the purposes of succession and inheritance children born of sacramental marriages are preferable to those born of the rest.[27] Thus, sacramental marriages mean greater honour, better rights for the male and probably comparative permanence of the union. But in the rest, the union prompted by free love or force or fraud or money is less durable and praiseworthy, but confers greater rights on the wife. It might very well be that these non-sacramental marriages receive left-handed approval only as a matter of compromise, for customs reflected in these marriages were —and still are—prevalent among many tribes and communities throughout the world.[28] Dr. N. C. Sengupta compares the inferior forms of marriage in ancient India with those in ancient Rome and suggests: "In India too it seems probable that these inferior forms of marriage entered into the Vedic Society by a similar adoption or adaptation of rites which prevailed amongst persons who did not belong to the Aryan culture."[29] Indeed, the Greek writers too noted various marriage customs in India. Megasthenes says of the Indians: "They marry many wives whom they buy from their parents, giving in exchange a yoke of oxen."[30] This surprisingly confirms the prevalence

---

[23] Jayaswal, *Manu & Yājñavalkya*, p. 221.
[24] *AŚ*. III. 2; *Infra*. Chap. VI.
[25] *AŚ*. III. 3, read with III. 4.
[26] *AŚ*. III. 4.
[27] *AŚ*. III. 5 & 6.
[28] Westermarck, *op. cit.* Chapter XX.
[29] N. C. Sengupta, *op. cit.* p. 89.
[30] *Meg*. 69.

of the *Ārṣa* marriage. Arrian states: "They marry without either giving or taking dowries, but the women, as soon as they are marriageable, are brought forward by their fathers and exposed to the public, to be selected by their victor in wrestling or boxing or running or by some one who excels in any other manly exercise."[31] We wish we could have more details of these marriage bouts. The exposure of a marriageable girl to the gaze of a prospective suitor is a practice well-known to Vātsyāyana. "Daily in the afternoons the girl of the marrying age should be properly decked and allowed to play freely with her friends. She should invariably be taken to places where people congregate, such as a *yajña* or a marriage and also to other festivals, so that people may see her, she being like a merchandise which should be exposed to the public view."[32] The absence of bride price or dowries in the kingdom of Sophytes in the Punjab drew the attention of the Greek writers.[33] The *Arthaśāstra* indicates different customs also. Thus, in some cases, the bride receives ornaments and other gifts from her parents, husband, kinsmen on both sides and strangers; in other cases, *śulka* or bride price goes to her parents or any survivor of them or to the bride.[34]

Marriage is usually arranged.[35] For details of match-making we can profitably study the *Kāmasūtra* which contains much of popular psychology and common sense.[36] Like Vātsyāyana,[37] Kauṭilya enjoins marriage between equals (*tulyaiḥ*)[38]. Matchmaking is often done by mendicant women. High praise is often lavished on the bride and the bridegroom. Before the choice, the bride-to-be is sometimes shown for approval.[39] Sometimes there is fraud in the course of negotiations for marriage. A person might pretend to secure a particular bride for one and get her for another. A bride is engaged to a particular man, but another gallant impersonates him in marriage.[39] A girl shown for marriage might be changed for another.[39] Suppression of faults and

[31] *Meg.* 227.
[32] *KS.* III. 1. 16.
[33] *MC. I.* p. 280.
[34] *AŚ.* III. 2.
[35] *AŚ.* IV. 12.
[36] *KS.* III. 1.
[37] *KS.* III. 1. 23-25.
[38] *AŚ.* I. 3.
[39] *AŚ.* III. 15; IV. 12.

exaggeration of virtues of the parties to the marriage are also mentioned. The state is required to stop such frauds by punishments, viz., imposition of fines, award of damages, forfeiture of property and even mutilation of limbs.[39]

If the girl is approved, betrothal (*varaṇa*) takes place. Occasionally, a long waiting period might elapse. The impatient young man might with law's approval cohabit with the betrothed, 'if she has passed seven menses.'[40]

It is the duty of the father to give his daughter in marriage. If he fails to do so within three years from her puberty, he loses dominion over her and the girl is allowed to unite with any one she likes.[41]

This view of Kauṭilya, which, as we shall see later, is supported by some orthodox lawmakers, is a significant step in the evolution of the institution of marriage. Westermarck believes that "the paternal authority of the archaic type . . . formed only a transitional stage in the history of human institutions. It declined gradually, according as the religious basis on which it rested became more unstable. The introduction of a new religion with higher conceptions of human rights particularly contributed to its fall."[42] Kauṭilya's rule seems to be midway between absolute paternal dominion and full liberty of choice in respect of marriage. The *Gāndharva* form of marriage, based upon mutual love between the parties to matrimony, requires, according to Kauṭilya, the approval of both the parents. But Vātsyāyana suggests that to avoid scandal the parents are sometimes forced to grant their consent. He says: "He (the lover) should so contrive that her relatives, in order to free their family from sin and out of fear of punishment from their community, may be compelled to give the girl in marriage to him alone."[43] But, as S. Bhattacharyya points out, the *Gāndharva* marriages in the epic seldom call for the approval of the parents.[44] Yet, according to J. J. Meyer, the *Gāndharva* wedding "is not altogether free love affairs as has been thought . . . for however lightheartedly such a union is often entered upon there, it is mostly held to be binding."[45] Yet, as we have already seen, love-marriages in

[40] *AŚ.* IV. 12.
[41] *Ibid.* also *infra* Chapter IX.
[42] *History of Human Marriage,* p. 235.
[43] *KS.* III. 5. 15.
[44] S. Bhattacharyya, *Māhābhārater Samāja,* p. 8.
[45] Meyer, *SLAI.* 95.

Kauṭilya's view rank lower than the sacramental marriages. Even free love of a maiden seems to be an exception rather than the rule in the *Arthaśāstra.*

The *Arthaśāstra* does not tell us much about marriage ceremonies. These are perhaps governed by the *Gṛihya Sūtras.* Of these, the *Arthaśāstra* mentions giving of the bride (*kanyādāna*)[46] and clasping of her hands (*pāṇigrahaṇa*).[47] The bride is probably carried by several persons (*kanyāvāhika*) along the public thoroughfare, perhaps in a procession.[48] Aśoka's *RE.* IX records: 'People perform various rites (*maṅgalas*) . . . at marriages . . . In this matter, however, womankind performs much manifold, trivial, useless rite'. The great king, however, allows these rites to be performed. Kauṭilya requires the state to encourage marriage. For example, the commodities intended for marriage or taken by the bride from her parent's house to her husband's are exempt from tolls.[49] In marriage receptions, wine is sometimes used lavishly.[50]

According to the *Arthaśāstra,* among the three upper castes, marriage becomes final with the ceremony of *pāṇigrahaṇa* or hand-clasping; but with the Śūdras, on *prakarma* or consummation.[51] Until then marriage can be disowned (*upāvartana*).[51] Even after *pāṇigrahaṇa,* a spouse can be rejected, if he or she is found to have lain with another person prior to marriage. The rejection is not allowed if a child is born of the union (*vṛittapāṇigrahaṇayorapi doṣamaupaśāyikaṁ dṛiṣṭvā siddhamupāvartanaṁ/na tvevābhiprajātayoḥ*).[51]

In the choice of a spouse, tastes obviously differ. Sometimes the good omen in a girl might induce one to marry her. For instance, Kauṭilya suggests that spies in the garb of an astrologer might tempt a leader of a corporation to marry a girl already engaged to another and say, "This man's daughter deserves to be the wife of a king, and will bring forth a son destined to be a king, purchase her with your wealth or seize her by force."[52] But men are, as Kauṭilya suggests attracted also by youth and beauty in a woman (*strībhiḥ paramarūpa-*

[46] *AŚ.* III. 2.
[47] *AŚ.* III. 15.
[48] *AŚ.* X. III. 3.
[49] *AŚ.* II. 21.
[50] *AŚ.* XI. 1.
[51] *AŚ.* III. 15.

yauvanābhiḥ).[52] Indeed, speaking of the kingdom of 'Sopithes' in the Punjab, Curtius Rufus writes: "In contracting marriages they do not seek an alliance with high birth, but make their choice by the looks, for beauty in the children is highly appreciated."[53] Diodoros Siculus confirms this: ". . . in selecting a bride they care nothing whether she has a dowry and a handsome fortune besides, but look only to her beauty and other advantages of the outward person."[54]

Vātsyāyana too quotes a view which lays stress upon beauty in selecting a match. "A man will find happiness and prosperity in such a woman who creates love in his mind and brings pleasure to his eyes at first sight. He should marry such a woman only not any other, provided she is satisfactory in other respects. This is the opinion of some."[55]

It seems probable that according to the *Arthaśāstra* the usual age for marriage is sixteen for boys and twelve for girls.[56] To protect girls from premarital intercourse and also to avoid loss of nuptial fees, the father of a girl must have been anxious to give her away in marriage not long after she reaches the age of puberty.[57] Kauṭilya prescribes a sixteen-year long student-life for the prince and then marriage.[58] According to Megasthenes, Brāchmanes marry after thirty-seven years of student life.[59] The virginity in a bride is usually preferred in the *Arthaśāstra*. In the case of succession, a son born of a mother who was virgin at the time of marriage has precedence over a son whose mother was not so.[60] The lack of virginity may be a ground for rejecting the bride (*upāvartana*).[61]

Yet, according to the *Arthaśāstra*, the marriage with a deflowered girl is not always voidable.[61] As we have seen, if a child is born of the marriage, the rejection is not allowed. In some cases, the remarriage of a widow and of a wife whose husband has deserted her receives legal sanction, though limited in extent. Ordinarily, a spouse should

---

[52] *AŚ*. XI. Ancient *sūtras* refer to some mystical methods for the selection of a bride. Kane, *op. cit.* 433-34.

[53] *MC. I.* 219.

[54] *Ibid.* 280.

[55] *KS*. III. 1. 14.

[56] *AŚ*. III. 3, as interpreted by Jayaswal, Manu & Yājñavalkya, p. 225.

[57] *AŚ*. IV. 12.

[58] *AŚ*. I. 5.

[59] *Meg.* 99.

[60] *AŚ*. III. 6.

[61] *AŚ*. III. 15.

be free from secret blemishes (*kanyādoṣa, varadoṣa*)[62]. Yājñavalkya even asks for a test of the virility of a bridegroom.[63] Many Smṛitis and the *Kāmasūtra* give us details of the qualities to be expected of the parties to the marriage.[64] Still it appears from the *Arthaśāstra* that the marriages of outcasts, eunuchs, idiots, lunatics, blindmen and lepers are not void.[65]

According to Kauṭilya, a householder's duty is to marry a girl who is his 'equal' (*tulyaiḥ*) and is born in the clan of a different ancestral *Ṛiṣi* (*asamānaṛiṣibhiḥ*)[66]. The last requirement perhaps hints at the ban on the *sagotra* marriage. But we do not get any details of prohibited degrees in marriage. As we shall observe later, incest with certain near relations is declared to be a capital offence.

Ordinarily, caste is an important consideration in marriage. It is well known that in early days in India, the rule as to marrying within one's own caste was not compulsory. Mm. Kane cites the Vedic references to show that inter-caste marriage was allowed.[67] A similar view appears from the Sūtras and the Smṛitis, although a marriage between a man of one of the three upper castes and a Sūdra woman was falling into disrepute and later on prohibited.[67] As in the orthodox works, Kauṭilya does not make marriage within one's caste compulsory but advocates certain limitations upon inter-caste marriages.[68] Thus a man of an upper caste is allowed to take a wife from a lower (*anuloma*). Even a son born of a marriage between a Brāhmaṇa or a Kṣatriya with a woman of the next lower caste is considered to be *savarṇa* or as belonging to the same caste as the father, but not so in the case of a marriage with a woman belonging to a caste after the next. Again, the marriage between a woman of a higher caste with a man of a lower is disapproved (*pratiloma*).[68] Kauṭilya gives us a list of such *pratiloma* marriages and sons born of such unions are placed in special categories. He holds that *pratiloma* marriages occur when the king deviates from the rules of conduct (*svadharma*) (*ta ete pratilomāḥ svadharmātikramādrājñassambhavanti*).[68]

[62] *AŚ.* III. 15.
[63] *Yāj.* I. 54-55.
[64] Kane, *op. cit.* pp. 431-32.
[65] *AŚ.* III. 5.
[66] *AŚ.* I. 3. The Jātakas commonly refer to *Sadisī bhāriyā*. Mehta, *PBI.* 279.
[67] Kane, *ibid.* pp. 447-52; also Aiyar, *EHMI.* pp. 36-37.
[68] *AŚ.* III. 7.

Moreover, among sons born of mothers belonging to different castes, the shares in patrimony are reduced in the cases of those born of a mother belonging to a lower caste. Thus, of the sons of a Brāhmaṇa, one born of a Brāhmaṇa wife gets four shares, of a Kṣatriya wife three shares, of a Vaiśya wife two shares and of a Sūdra wife one share. Likewise in the cases of other castes.[69] Kauṭilya does not ban the marriage between an upper caste male with a Sūdra female, but appears indirectly to discourage it by placing the sons born of such a union in some mixed castes, like Niṣāda or Ugra in the cases of the Brāhmaṇa and the Kṣatriya fathers respectively, and in the Sūdra caste itself in the case of a Vaiśya father.[68] Megasthenes also states: "The custom of the country prohibits intermarriage between the castes:—for instance the husbandman cannot take a wife from the artizan caste, nor the artizan a wife from the husbandman caste."[70] Similar customs are also recorded by him elsewhere.[71] "No one is allowed to marry out of his own caste." But, as we have seen, mixed marriage is allowed subject to some restrictions.

According to the *Arthaśāstra*, monogamy appears to be the ideal but pologyny is not rare. A man is allowed to marry any number of wives subject to certain restrictions.[72] The usual grounds for a man's remarriage in the life time of the first wife are: (*i*) that she cannot conceive after her first child-birth (*aprajāyamānā*) or (*ii*) that she does not give birth to a son (*aputrā*) or (*iii*) that she is barren (*vandhyā*) or (*iv*) that she brings forth a still-born child only (*nindu*) or (*v*) she gives birth to daughters only (*kanyāprasavinīm*). In all such cases the husband is required to wait for (*ākāṅkṣeta*) a few years before remarriage. For example, he has to wait in the first three cases for eight years, in the fourth case for ten years and in the last case for twelve years. Then if he wants a son, he may remarry (*tataḥ putrārthī dvitīyāṁ vindeta*).[72] But if he violates (*atikrame*) these rules, he is required to pay

[69] *AŚ.* III. 6.
[70] *Meg.* 218.
[71] *Ibid.* 41, 85.
[72] *AŚ.* III. 2. There are different readings and interpretations of the text. According to Dr. R. G. Basak, *aprajāyamānā* may also mean 'one who does not give birth to a child' and *vandhyā*, 'one who cannot conceive'. Mm. Ganapati Sastri reads *vindum* for *nindum*; *vindum* means, according to him, 'one who bears only still-born child'.

her *śulka* (bride-price), her property (*strīdhana*) and monetary compensation for supersession (*arthaṁ*[73] *cādhivedanikam*) in addition to a fine of 24 paṇas to the state. Kauṭilya does not tell us if the second marriage by the husband in contravention of the above regulation will be void. It does not seem so. Thus, the husband gets exemption from waiting for long periods before remarriage, provided he is willing to spend. Money, it seems, enables the husband to purchase the right of remarriage without any restriction whatsoever. Thus, by paying the first wife *śulka* and *strīdhana* where she has got them or monetary compensation equivalent to *śulka* and *strīdhana* where she has not got them as well as suitable maintenance (*anurūpāṁ vṛittim*), a husband is allowed to marry any number of wives (*bahvīrapi vindeta*). For the wives, asserts Kauṭilya, are for giving birth to sons (*putrārthā hi striyaḥ*). It must, however, be noted that upon the remarriage by the male, the earlier marriage is not dissolved. The Greek envoy also points out the main reason for polygyny. It is for getting sons. Thus Megasthenes speaks for Brāhmaṇas: "They marry as many wives as they please with a view to have numerous children, for by having many wives greater advantages are enjoyed and since they have no slaves, they have more need to have children around them to attend to their wants."[74]

Vātsyāyana, however, repeats two of the grounds mentioned by Kauṭilya, viz., the wife's barrenness or bearing daughters only. He adds other grounds, viz., wife's incurable disease or bad character or the husband's love of pleasure or the absence of mutual love between the spouses.[75] He asks the wife to take precautions against such contingencies. He paints a clear picture of a polygynous household.

In the *Arthaśāstra*, the economic bar to polygyny seems to be important. A man with a lean purse would think twice before remarriage while the first wife is alive. Many Smṛitis speak against polygyny practised in contravention of the approved texts but, as

---

According to Dr. Shama Sastry, *aprajāyamānā* means the woman who brings no (live) children.

[73] Mm. Ganapati Sastri and Dr. Jolly read *ardham* for *artham*. Dr. Basak seems to read *argha*.

[74] *Meg.* 100.

[75] *KS.* IV. 2. 1.

Mm. Kane points out, "it is extremely doubtful whether a man was ever punished by the king for so doing."[76]

On the ethics of polygyny opinions always differ. Westermarck admits: "Even in the Christian world monogamy has not always been the only form of marriage in the past. And there are writers who maintain that it should not be so in the future."[77] He cites[78] the cases of Merovingian kings, Charlemagne and Prussian rulers who practised polygyny. He also quotes the views of modern authorities like Norman Haire and others who support it on medical and social grounds. But Westermarck concludes: "Numerous facts show that advancement in civilization has been adverse to polygyny."[79]

Though polygyny is allowed by Kauṭilya, we do not get in the *Arthaśāstra* any direct evidence of polyandry. In some cases, however, a wife is allowed to take a second husband, even though the first is alive. This usually happens when the husband stays away from his wife for a period, long or short. In view of the importance of the topic it is better to quote Kauṭilya *in extenso:* "Wives who belong to Sūdra, Vaiśya, Kṣatriya or Brāhmaṇa caste, and who have not given birth to children, should wait as long as a year, two, three and four years respectively, for their husbands who have gone abroad for a short time; but if they are such as have given birth to children, they should wait for their absent husbands for more than a year. If they are provided with maintenance, they should wait for twice the period of time just mentioned. If they are not so provided with, their well-do-do *jñātis* should maintain them either for four or eight years. Then the *jñātis* should leave them to marry, after taking what had been presented to them on the occasion of their marriages. If the husband is a Brāhmaṇ, studying abroad, his wife who has no issue should wait for him for ten years; but if she has given birth to children, she should wait for twelve years. If the husband is a servant of the king, his wife should wait for him till her death; but even if she bears children to a *savarṇa* husband, (i.e., a second husband belonging to the same *gotra* as that of the former husband) with a view to avoid

---

[76] Kane, *ibid.* p. 552.

[77] Westermarck, *op. cit.*, p. 172.

[78] *Ibid.* Chapter IX.

[79] *Ibid.* p. 193. *The Hindu Marriage Act, 1955*, provides for the compulsory monogamy for both the sexes.

the extinction of her race, she shall not be liable to contempt therefor (*savarṇataśca prajātā nāpavādaṁ labheta*). If the wife of an absent husband lacks maintenance and is deserted by well-to-do *jñātis*, she may re-marry one whom she likes and who is in a position to maintain her and relieve her misery.

"A young wife (*kumārī*) who is wedded in accordance with the customs of the first four kinds of marriage (*dharmavivāhāt*), and whose husband has gone abroad and is heard of shall wait for him for the period of seven menses (*saptatīrthanyākāṅkṣeta*), provided he has not announced his departure; but she shall wait for him for a year in case of his having announced the same. In the case of a husband who has gone abroad but who is not heard of, his wife shall wait for the period of five menses, but if the absent husband is heard of, his wife shall wait for him for the period of ten menses. In the case of a husband who has gone abroad and is not heard of, his wife shall if she has received only a part of *śulka* from him, wait for him for the period of seven menses. A young wife who has received the whole amount of *śulka* shall wait for the period of five menses for her absent husband who is not heard of; but if he is heard of, she shall wait for him for the period of ten menses. Then with the permission of judges (*dharmasthairvisṛiṣṭā*), she may marry one whom she likes; for neglect of intercourse with wife after her monthly ablution is, in the opinion of Kauṭilya, a violation of one's duty (*tīrthoparodhohi dharmavadha iti Kauṭilyaḥ*).

"In the case of husbands who have long gone abroad (*dīrghapravāsinaḥ*), who have become ascetics, or who have been dead, their wives, having no issue, shall wait for them for the period of seven menses; but if they have given birth to children, they shall wait for a year. Then (each of these women) may marry the brother of her husband. If there are a number of brothers to her lost husband, she shall marry such one of them as is next in age to her former husband, or as is virtuous and is capable of protecting her, or one who is the youngest and unmarried. If there are no brothers to her lost husband, she may marry one who belongs to the same *gotra* as her husband's or a relative, i. e., of the same family. But if there are many such persons as can be selected in marriage, she shall choose one who is a nearer relation of her lost husband."[80]

[80] *AŚ.* III. 4 (Shama Sastry's translation). The expression *savarṇataśca prajātā* may

The separation need not amount to actual desertion. Periods ranging from one to ten years are prescribed, before a separated wife is permitted to take a second husband. The length of the period depends on various factors, viz., caste, children and provisions for maintenance. Deserted by kinsmen, such a wife may remarry anyone she chooses for maintaining herself or for tiding over difficulties. Shorter periods are prescribed for wives whose marriages have not been consummated. These might be as short as three menstrual periods only. On the expiry of the prescribed period, a virgin wife can with the permission of civil judges marry any one she likes. The period of waiting is usually short, if the separation is actually or likely to be long or, more or less, permanent. But in the case of long or permanent separation, the choice of the second husband is usually restricted to the nearer relatives of the first husband, in the following order of preference, viz., (*a*) husband's sole brother, (*b*) in case of many brothers, the next in age or one who is virtuous or capable of maintaining her or one who is the youngest or unmarried, (*c*) if there is no brother, a near kinsman of the husband (*sapiṇḍaṁ kulyaṁ vā*) and (*d*) in case of many such relations, the one nearest to the husband. If she marries any man outside this circle, she is liable to punishment along with the man and all those who consent to such a marriage. It is not stated if such a marriage is declared to be null and void.

What will happen to her first marriage? It is not clear if the tie is completely broken. Presumably, that is the case.[81] Otherwise the text cited above will indicate the existence of polyandry which militates against Kauṭilya's general view on marriage.

If our conclusion is correct that the first marriage is automatically dissolved on the remarriage by the wife in the life time of the first husband, one important result follows. That is, indirect divorce. Mm. Kane is right in holding that remarriage by the husband whose

---

not connote a marriage with the father of the child. Dr. Basak's interpretation is "if the wife gets a son by another man of the same caste" (Vol. I. p. 201). Mm. Ganapati Sastri takes the word *ca* to connote "or man of a higher caste than one's own" (*cakārāt svoṭkṛiṣṭavarṇādapi*), Vol. II. p. 28.

[81] Sir Sivaswamy Aiyar holds a similar view: "The text of Parāśara which permits the remarriage of women clearly contemplates the dissolution of marriage otherwise than by death." *Evolution of Hindu Moral Ideals*, p. 33. Dr. Basham also states: "The *Arthaśāstra* would allow divorce even after religious marriage to a wife who has been deserted by her husband." *The Wonder that was India*, p. 173.

first wife is alive does not dissolve the first marriage. In the case of the wife remarrying, however, in the life time of the first husband, the first marriage probably comes to an end. In other words, on the husband's default, the aggrieved wife is allowed to terminate the first marriage and to take another husband. Even in the case of a sacramental marriage (*dharmavivāha*) a deserted wife may thus divorce her husband indirectly. But the corresponding right does not appear to have been granted to the husband.

Kauṭilya mentions many reasons for allowing the remarriage of a wife. The principal reason is that it is a sin to allow a wife's periods to go in vain (*tīrthoparodho hi dharmavadha iti Kauṭilyaḥ*). Elsewhere, we have discussed this view in detail. Other reasons include making provisions for her existence (*jīvitārtham*) and overcoming privations (*āpadgatā*).

Like Kauṭilya, several Smṛitis point out that the wife is to wait for certain periods when her husband has left her.[82] For instance, Manu states: "The wife should wait for her husband for eight years, if he has gone to a foreign country; six years, if he has left for gaining knowledge for fame; three years, if he has gone for love."[83] But Manu does not say what the wife is to do on the expiry of the periods of waiting. His commentators are puzzled. Kullūka follows Vasiṣṭha's view: "A wife whose husband has gone abroad should wait for eight years and thereafter go to her husband." Mm. Kane puts a cogent question: "This may be all right as far as it will go. But if the husband is unheard of, how is she to reach him ? Vasiṣṭha says nothing on the point."[83] Medhātithi, however, refers to the conflicting views on the question, viz., that some allow her remarriage, that others ask her to earn her living by decent means and so on. In fact, Nārada says: "Hence there is no sin if a woman resorts to another man (in such cases)."[84] He and some other Smṛitikāras clearly allow the remarriage of the wife in five cases of dangers (*pañcasvāpatsu*). We have elaborately dealt with this question in the chapter on the position of widows.[85] It must, however, be observed that Kauṭilya speaks of *proṣitavidhavā* also,

[82] Kane, *op. cit.* p. 613.
[83] *Manu.* IX. 76.
[84] *Nārada* (*strīpuṁsa*, 101).
[85] *Infra.* Chapter VII.

that is to say, the wife whose husband is away. She is allowed to earn her livelihood by working at home for the state textile factory.[86] This seems to indicate that there might be a wife who leads the life of a widow when the husband is away. In fact, the Smṛitis and the *Kāma-sūtra* elaborately lay down the duties of a devoted wife during her husband's absence.[87] In substance these duties may be compared with those of a chaste widow as laid down in many Dharmaśāstras. Perhaps Kauṭilya has such a devoted wife in view.

Kauṭilya does not stop with indirect dissolution of marriage. He goes a step ahead and provides for divorce or *mokṣa*. But here his religious scruples perhaps get the better of his logic. For he does not allow divorce or *mokṣa* in the cases of sacramental marriages (*amokṣo dharmavivāhānāmiti*).[88] Or perhaps, he is not at all illogical. In the cases of '*dharma-badha*' mentioned above, he does not hesitate to permit the wife to dissolve even the *dharmavivāha* or sacramental marriage. But the 'direct' divorce, which is prompted by mutual hatred or perhaps misconduct (*viprakāra*), is not allowed in the case of a sacramental bond.

On this point Kauṭilya states: "A woman, hating her husband, cannot dissolve her marriage with him against his will. Nor can a man dissolve his marriage with his wife against her will. But from mutual enmity, divorce may be obtained (*parasparaṁ dveṣānmokṣaḥ*). If a man, apprehending danger from his wife, desires divorce (*mokṣamic-chet*), he shall return to her whatever she was given on the occasion of her marriage. If a woman, under the apprehension of danger from her husband, desires divorce, she shall forfeit her claim to her property; marriages contracted in accordance with the customs of the first four kinds of marriages cannot be dissolved."[89]

Kauṭilya is practical enough to provide for divorce in case of mutual hatred. It is considered better to part than fight. So, according to him, marriage can be dissolved by mutual enmity. Unilateral

---

86 *AŚ*. II. 23 (*yāścāniṣkāsinyaḥ proṣitavidhavā nyaṅgā kanyakā vā'tmānaṁ vibhṛiyustāḥ svadāsībhi-ranusaryasopāgrahaṁ karma kārayitavyāḥ*). *Cf.* Manu. IX. 75.

87 *KS*. IV. 1. 43-52. Kane, *op. cit.* p 565-66.

88 *AŚ*. III. 3.

89 *Ibid.* (Shama Sastry's translation). *Viprakāra=aparādha* (offence) according to Mm. Ganapati Sastri; danger according to Dr. Shama Sastry; *asadvyavahāra* (misconduct) according to Dr. R. G. Basak.

aversion is of no avail. Either spouse can, however, get a divorce for misconduct (*viprakāra*) on the part of the other. In such cases, the husband claiming divorce is required to return her property to her but the wife demanding divorce forfeits her claim to her property.[90]

Mm. Kane thoroughly discusses the attitude of the orthodox school towards divorce. In general, divorce is not acceptable to this school of lawmakers. Although Nārada and some other Smṛitis allow remarriage of a wife in her husband's lifetime, Mm. Kane points out that "according to the digests and commentaries these rules apply to a former yuga (age)."[91] He further observes: "The position of the writers on *dharmaśāstra* is that marriage is a *saṁskāra*, that the status of wifehood arises from that *saṁskāra*, that even if the husband or wife became *patita*, the *saṁskāra* already performed is not annulled by that fact, that even if a wife committed adultery she still remains a wife and that when she performs a penance for her lapse, it is not necessary to have a fresh *saṁskāra* of marriage performed on her." Dr. N. C. Sen Gupta also confirms this view: "There is no text anywhere laying down a law of divorce, a procedure by which the husband or wife could sever the marriage."[92] Yet it may be suggested that divorce is indirectly allowed wherever the remarriage of a wife is permitted. In spite of the ideals set up by the Smṛitis, we find that custom allows divorce for the Hindus in many groups and localities. Kauṭilya, however, does not differ from the orthodox school in the question of prohibiting 'direct' divorce or *mokṣa* in the cases of sacramental marriages. Only in the cases of non-sacramental marriages, he allows 'direct' divorce. It is well-known that modern Hindu law allows divorce, on certain conditions, in all marriages.[93] Yet, as Westermarck points out: "But the woman's subordinate position and her inability to support herself makes separation more difficult for her than for the man. Moreover if the woman claims a divorce the purchase-sum paid for her has to be returned, and she may even, in certain cases forfeit her dowry and whatever property

[90] Dr. Basak suggests another reading which seems to be more appropriate. According to this, the wife need not return the property she has received from the husband.

[91] Kane, *ibid.* p. 620.

[92] N. C. Sen Gupta, *Evolution of Ancient Indian Law.*

[93] *Hindu Marriage Act, 1955.*

she brought with her marriage."[94] Comparing this observation with the Kauṭilyan law which probably provides for the forfeiture of the wife's property if she claims divorce on the ground of her husband's cruelty (*pativiprakārāt*) we have to admit that she will generally shrink from the idea of divorce.

[94] *History of Human Marriage*, p. 534.

Chapter V

ETHICS OF THE MARRIED LIFE

"There are three essential elements in every normal marriage," states Westermarck: "the gratification of the sexual impulse, the relationship between husband and wife apart from it, and procreation."[1] Kauṭilya seems to have grasped the full implications of these essential elements in marriage. In his characteristically cryptic way, he mentions the main factors behind a successful marriage and frames his laws accordingly. The *Arthaśāstra* defines the conjugal rights and duties carefully and directs the state to enforce them properly.

Moreover, Kauṭilya is also aware of the religious aspect of marriage. Since the Vedic times the wife married in some approved form associates with her husband in religious rites.[2] In the *Prājāpatya* form of marriage the spouse, says Kautilya, perform their religious acts together (*sahadharmacaryā*).[3] The wife's *strīdhana* may be utilized for the husband's religious performances (*dharmakārye ca patyuḥ*).[4] Again, in some cases of elopement, the wife forfeits her right to her association with the husband in all religious works (*gamyena vā puṁsā sahaprasthāne caturviṁśatipaṇaḥ; sarva dharmalopaśca*).[5] It must however be admitted that this religious aspect of marriage has not received much prominence in the *Arthaśāstra*. Kauṭilya, as it were, takes this aspect for granted. Manu, however, states the various aspects of marriage in a short verse: "Indeed on the wife depend progeny, religious performances, service (*śuśruṣā*), the highest sexual pleasure (*ratiruttamā*) and Heaven for oneself and one's ancestors."[6]

---

[1] *Future of Marriage in Western Civilization*, p. 21.

[2] Kane, *op.cit.* pp. 556-57.

[3] *AŚ.* III. 2.

[4] *Ibid.*

[5] *AŚ.* III. 4. This interpretation is suggested by Mm. Ganapati Sastri and Dr. Basak. According to Dr. Shama Sastry, the expression means 'lose all kinds of social privileges'.

[6] *Manu.* IX. 28.

Kauṭilya is not blind to the sexual side of marriage. The sexual cravings of both husband and wife receive due attention in the *Arthaśāstra.* Marriage is not simply for procreation but for pleasure as well. In the *Arthaśāstra* rules are laid down for approaching wives in a polygynous household. "If many or all of the (wives) are at the same time in menses, he (the husband) shall lie first with that woman among them whom he married earlier or who has a living son. In the case of his concealing the fact of her being in menses or neglecting to lie with any of them after her menses he shall pay a fine of 96 *paṇas*" (*tīrthasamavāye cāsāṁ yathāvivāhaṁ pūrvoḍhām jīvatputrām vā pūrvaṁ gacchet. Tīrthagūhanāgamane ṣaṇṇavatirdaṇḍaḥ*).[7]

Mutual company is thus ensured by the law but for certain sound reasons a spouse is allowed to refuse cohabitation. "If a wife has a son or is inclined towards religion or is barren or brings forth only a dead child or is beyond the age of menstruation, she shall not have intercourse against her desire. If a man has no inclination, he may not lie with his wife who is either afflicted with leprosy or is a lunatic. But if a woman is desirous of having sons, she may lie with men suffering from such disease" (*putravatīṁ dharmakāmāṁ vandhyāṁ ninduṁ nīrajaṣkāṁ vā nākāmāmupeyāt / na cākāmaḥ puruṣaḥ kuṣṭhinīmunmattāṁ vā gacchet strī tu putrārthamevaṁbhūtaṁ vopagacchet*).[8] According to Mm. Ganapati Sastri's reading, the husband who does not feel any inclination should not have sexual union with his wife.

Although intercourse at the time of *ṛitu* (*ṛitugāmitvam*) is a pious and legal duty for a husband it seems that a man without sexual urge may with impunity stay away from his wife. Likewise, the sexual urge of the wife is in certain cases taken into account. It is to be noted that a wife devoted to religion (*dharmakāmā*) is allowed to refuse sexual connection, if she has no craving from within (*akāmā*). Further, it is known that a woman who has attained menopause might not lose her sex-hunger. However, when she has lost it, sex acts cannot be forced upon her.

The desire for sons is, therefore, not the only purpose of cohabita-

---

[7] *AŚ.* III. 2.

[8] *Ibid.* The readings of this passage are different. Dr. Shama Sastry and Dr. Jolly have the above reading. But Mm. Ganapati Sastri has a varient reading: "*na cākāmaḥ puruṣaḥ/kuṣṭhinī-munmattāṁ vā na gacchet.*" This really means that the husband should not cohabit with his wife if he has no inclination.

tion between the spouse. The pleasure of the sexual act is an important consideration. In many cases, the feeling of the wife is respected.

What will happen in the case of continuous frigidity? The husband, as we have seen, might pass over the frigid wife and take to another wife. If the husband is discovered to be impotent (*klība*) the wife is allowed to desert him. Again, she might take recourse to magical rites to win over her husband's love. If, however, positive hatred instead of passive aversion mars the relation between the spouse, Kauṭilya allows them certain periods to make amends. In default, he advocates some special rules of the bed. "A woman who hates her husband, who has passed the period of seven turns of her menses and who loves another (*anyaṁ kāmayamānā*), shall immediately return to her husband both the endowment and jewellery she has received from him and allow him to lie down with another woman. A man, hating his wife, shall allow her to take shelter in the house of a mendicant woman or of her lawful guardians or of her kinsmen."[9]

Kauṭilya allows for some sort of judicial separation upon unilateral hatred of one spouse for another. But a hateful wife is liable to lose some right to property and the husband is permitted to take another woman to bed. On the other hand, the innocent wife receives only the right to a separate residence only. One-sided hatred, as we have seen, does not dissolve the marriage. Mutual hatred does so provided the marriage is in an inferior form.

Again, a wife is permitted to desert her husband and live separate from him if he "is of bad character or is long gone abroad or has become a traitor to the state or is likely to endanger the life of his wife or has fallen from his caste or has lost virility" (*nīcatvaṁ paradeśaṁ vā prasthito rāja-kilbiṣī/prāṇābhihantā patitastyājyaḥ klibo'pivā patiḥ*).[10]

Thus, the *Arthaśāstra* allows *kāma* or desire for sexual pleasure to play an important rôle in conjugal life. In some cases a spouse who does not want sexual connections is permitted to avoid it. In the case of the wife's hatred the husband may take to another woman. And if the husband deserts the wife, she is permitted to remarry. A husband, who refuses to cohabit with his wife without a proper cause, is even

---

[9] *AŚ.* III. 3. Mm. Ganapati Sastri and Dr. Jolly read *amaṇḍayamānā* for *anyaṁ kāmayamānā*. This will mean the wife "who does not put on her ornaments" possibly to displease her husband.

[10] *AŚ.* III. 2.

punishable with a fine of 96 paṇas. He also incurs sin for allowing his wife's menses to go in vain.

In this emphasis upon the sexual aspect of marriage Kauṭilya is in company with the exponent of the orthodox school. Thus, according to Manu, the highest sexual pleasure (*ratiruttamā*) of a man depends on his wife (*dārādhīnā*).[11] He permits a husband to cohabit with his wife even outside her *ṛitu* with the desire for sensual pleasures (*ratikāmyayā*).[12] The *Mahābhārata* too holds that women are for sexual enjoyment and progeny (*ratiputraphalā nārī*).[13] Baudhāyana and other orthodox writers make it a sin for the husband to avoid cohabitation with the wife after her monthly ablutions (*ṛitusnātām*).[14]

In this respect Kauṭilya and the Smṛitikāras differ from the ancient Greek view which allows marriage only for procreation and household chores. "The ordinary Greek feeling on the object of marriage is no doubt expressed in the oration against Neaera, ascribed to Demosthenes, where it is said: "We keep mistresses for our pleasures, concubines for constant attendance, and wives to bear us legitimate children and to be our faithful house-keepers."[15] Kauṭilya and the Smṛitikāras, as we shall see, permit concubinage and prostitution but do not neglect the importance of sexual pleasure within matrimony. In this view they cannot possibly agree with the orthodox Christian opinion[16] that the continuance of the human species is "the only legitimate object of sexual intercourse even between husband and wife."

Fear of punishment, as Kauṭilya seems to suggest, cannot induce love. A spouse might take recourse to aphrodisiacs[17] and witchcraft (*abhicāra, saṁvanana*)[18] to arouse love in the other. It is no offence to practise witchcraft to gain the love of an indifferent husband or wife, unless it leads to injury to the other.[18] Mendicant women are found to supply a wife with medicines to arouse love in the indifferent

[11] *Manu.* IX. 28.
[12] *Manu.* III. 45.
[13] *Mbh.* Sabhā. 5. 112.
[14] Kane, *op.cit.* p. 571, note 1327.
[15] Westermarck, *op.cit.*, p. 23.
[16] *Ibid.*, p. 24.
[17] *AŚ.* v. 1.
[18] *AŚ.* IV. 13.

husband. It is quite possible for designing persons to supply poisonous drugs to the credulous spouse which might prove fatal in the end.[19]

In the *Arthaśāstra* the husband generally dominates home. To discipline the wife (*vinaya-grāhaṇam*), he may reasonably abuse and chastise her. Kauṭilya says: "Women of refractive nature shall be taught manners by using not even such expressions as 'Thou, half-naked; thou, full-naked; thou, cripple; thou, fatherless; thou, motherless.' "[20] He may even inflict on her some degree of physical punishments. "Or three beats, either with a bamboo bark or with a rope or with the palm of the hand may be given on her hips."[20] But if he exceeds the limits prescribed by law, he is punishable by the state.[20]

The wife has an equal right to abuse and beat her husband if she is herself faultless but jealous on account of the husband's gallantry outside home (*bāhyavihāreṣu*).[20] The law, however, authorises the husband as well as the state to control the conduct and movements of the wife. Her participation in sports (*darpa*) and drinking bouts (*madyakrīḍā*) depends upon the permission of the husband. Penal misconducts of the wife include visiting amusement halls for men or women, leaving home while the husband is asleep or drunk, refusal to let him in the house and indulging in various love plays with others.[21]

Is there any purdāh mentioned in the *Arthaśāstra*? Kauṭilya refers to a class of women who do not come out of their house (*Aniṣkāsinī*).[22] When the state provides these women with work in the public textile industry, they do not attend the factory personally but send their materials through maid servants. To enter into any legal transactions relating to partition or deposit of *strīdhana* these women are not required to come out of their houses. The transactions are valid even if completed at home (*antarāgāra*). Ordinarily, a wife is not allowed to leave her husband's home without his consent. Otherwise, she is liable to fine or other punishments. Generally, she is not permitted to call at others' houses. The privacy of the matrimonial home is well-guarded by the law. Without the husband's consent the wife cannot give

---

[19] *AŚ.* v. 1.
[20] *AŚ.* III. 3.
[21] For details Chapter III, *supra.*
[22] *AŚ.* II. 23; III. 1.

shelter to neighbours, alms to mendicants or goods to traders. She cannot allow any forbidden person access to the house. A man is also forbidden to give shelter to another's wife. Otherwise he is liable to a fine of 100 paṇas. This precaution is necessary in view of the fact that spies or other designing persons are found to take advantage of human frailty and bring about a rupture in the matrimonial home or cause other injuries to the family.[23]

The wife, however, is granted limited freedom of movements in special cases. "My teacher says: With a view to avoiding danger, it is no offence for women to go to any male person who is a kinsman of her husband, or is a rich and prosperous gentleman (*sukhāvastha*), or is the headman of the village, or is one of her guardians (*anvādhi-kula*), or who belongs to the family of a mendicant woman, or to any one of her own kinsmen."

But Kauṭilya questions: "How is it possible for good women (*sādhvījana*) to know at least this fact, that the family of her own kinsmen consisting of a number of males is good ? It is no offence for women to go to the houses of kinsmen under the circumstances of death, disease, calamities and confinement of women. Whoever prevents her going under such circumstances shall be fined 12 paṇas."[24] Even in such cases, a wife, concealing herself in her kinsman's house, forfeits her endowment. Her kinsman too loses his claim to the balance of the bride price.[24]

The wife's ornaments are sometimes pledged with the husband to ensure her return to him; he may forfeit these if the wife without his consent has gone to another village (*sthāpyābharaṇalopa*).[24] The wife's elopement or journey to places in the company of others is generally penal. However, she can go out to receive her maintenance or to unite with her husband. There seems to be a greater freedom of movement among the wives of actors, players, singers, fishermen, hunters, herdsmen, vinters and the like. Usually these persons move about with their women-folk.[24]

Apart from the duty of mutual company, Kauṭilya enjoins the duty of mutual service (*śuśrūṣā*) between the spouses. The husband should attend upon the wife and the wife upon the husband. Of course,

---

[23] *AŚ*. III. 4; *cf. KS*. IV. 1. 9.
[24] *AŚ*. III. 4.

the spouse, who has not attained the age of majority (16 years for boys and 12 years for girls), need not perform this duty. However, when an adult spouse fails to attend upon the other, the law prescribes a fine. For this offence a wife is liable to a fine of 12 paṇas and the husband 24 paṇas.[25]

Kauṭilya knows that there are good wives and bad. He believes that a good wife is above deceipt (*kuto hi sādhvījanasyacchalam*). The *Mahābhārata* and the *Smṛiti* works uphold an ideal of good wives and also denounce the fickleness of women in general. But Kauṭilya seldom makes such generalisations. Yet the *Arthaśāstra* shows that cases of marital infidelity are not rare. The ease with which spies or other designing persons are asked to tempt a spouse possibly indicates that matrimonial home is vulnerable. This might be the reason which leads Kauṭilya and *Smṛiti* writers to advise proper protection of the domestic life. Kauṭilya directs the state to protect the sanctity of *antaḥpura* or the hearth and home. Touching a brother's wife by hand is forbidden. The law prescribes punishment for defamation of married women.[26]

As we shall later see, there are detailed rules against adultery and incest. Jactitation of marriage is noted by Kauṭilya. A man might falsely claim another's wife or daughter-in-law as his own. This might lead to murder.[27] A wife murdering her husband is liable to be torn apart by a bull.[28] Cases of poisoning of the husband by the wife wilfully or through her folly are also mentioned in the *Arthaśāstra.*

In sum, while Kauṭilya recognises different factors underlying marriage, he advocates mutuality of rights and obligations between the spouse in some cases. Thus the husband has a duty to cohabit with his wife; he is punishable if he does not perform that duty. Likewise the wife has a duty to receive her husband; if she neglects to do so, she is superseded and deprived of her property. Under certain circumstances, however, either of them might refuse intercourse. Between the spouse desire for the sexual act is an important

[25] *AŚ.* III. 3.
[26] *AŚ.* III. 8.
[27] *AŚ.* V. 2.
[28] *AŚ.* IV. 11.

consideration. Mutual company is assured by the law. The wife is punishable if she deserts her husband; the husband might lose the wife for ever, if he deserts her. Mutual right of chastisement is permitted within certain limits. Mutual aid (*śuśruṣā*) is a legal duty, the breach of which is a punishable offence. No doubt a married woman's legal status is somewhat inferior to that of her husband, yet she is not absolutely helpless. As the *Arthaśāstra* shows, she is not a mere tool in the hands of her husband. With well-defined rights to property, she has, as we shall see later, some degree of economic freedom which enables her to play a respectable rôle in the drama of domestic life. Even the right to remarry, in certain contingencies, invests her with a sense of strength.

Chapter VI

ECONOMICS OF MARRIAGE

Marriage is not simply a partnership in sexual enjoyment. It has far-reaching economic consequences. It is also a joint enterprise of persons of different sexes for success in the business of life. Economic factors affect marriage when it comes of, continues and terminates. Modern scholars have tried to show how, in the social history of mankind, changes in the means of production are found to have left permanent impressions on the institution of marriage. Such impressions, however, cannot possibly be traced in the *Arthaśāstra*. But in this matter we should remember the warnings of Dr. E. O. James: "It does not follow, however, that history is an inevitable working of the economic process finding expression in particular forms of production, or that human relations can be reduced to the material conditions of life current at any given moment, as the Marxists contend."[1]

We have already noted Kauṭilya's view that sensuality (*kāma*) is to be satisfied without opposition to moral and economic considerations. Moreover, according to Kauṭilya, economics result in the acquisition of desired objects (*kāmaphalatvāt ca arthasya*). Inter-dependence of sensual and economic matters in human life is also desired by Kauṭilya. So in the *Arthaśāstra* economic factors are found to influence the institution of marriage in various ways.

A sense of property in women is a common characteristic in patriarchal societies throughout the world. Father has property in his daughter and he transfers it to the husband. A similar idea suggests itself in a passage in the *Arthaśāstra*.[2] "A man can have sexual intercourse with a girl who has not been received by him for the period of her seven menses after betrothal. He should not pay any damages to her father. The father loses his ownership over her for allowing

---

[1] E. O. James, *Marriage and Society*, p. 43.

[2] *AŚ*. IV. 12. A similar passage occurs in *Manu*. IX. 93.

her menses to go in vain"[3] (*saptārtavaprajātāṁ varaṇādūrddhvamalabhamānāṁ prakṛitya prakāmī syāt, na ca pituravahīnaṁ dadyāt ṛitupratirodhibhiḥ svāmyādapakrāmati*). Thus a father has 'ownership' (*svāmya*) over his daughter. Father loses this dominion, if he fails to discharge his duty to his daughter. The gift of the daughter (*kanyādāna*) for the purpose of marriage connotes the gratuitous transfer of this right to the bridegroom. In *Ārṣa* form of marriage the bridegroom gives a pair of kine. In the *Āsura* form, there is an out-and-out purchase of the bride upon payment of the bride-price (*śulka*) by the suitor. According to Kauṭilya the parents take the bride-price for the daughter (*tau hi śulkaharau duhituḥ*). In the approved forms of marriage, the father gives his sanction to the marriage, but in the unapproved forms, sanction of both the parents is required (*pitṛipramāṇāścatvāraḥ pūrve dharmyāḥ/mātāpitṛipramāṇāś śeṣāḥ*).[3] Kauṭilya contemplates a second category of bride price which probably comes from the sources other than the suitor; it goes to the bride (*dvitīyaṁ śulkam strī hareta*). The second category of *śulka* might include what a man is required to pay in some cases of relationship out-of-wedlock.[4] Thus, for sexual connection with a daughter of a courtezan, a bride-price valued at sixteen times the mother's fee is payable (*śulkam māturbhogaḥ ṣodaśguṇaḥ*). For a similar offence against the free daughter (*duhitaram adāsīm*), bride-price and ornmaents are to be given (*śulkamābandhya-dānam ca*). Where the bride-price has bcen paid by one for the engagement with a girl, any other man having a connection with her is required "to pay (back) the bride-price" (*śulkadānaṁ ca*).

The text also refers to the wedding gifts out of love (*prītyāropaṇam*). These also go to the bride.[5] In the Brāhma form of marriage, the father is required to bedeck the daughter (*kanyāmalaṁkṛitya*). Provisions for marriage (*naiveśanika*) are directed to be made at the time of partition. Sisters are to receive dowry (*prādānika*) and bachelor brothers, marriage expenses.[6]

Thus in some forms of marriage, bride-price or wedding gifts play an important role. Kauṭilya no doubt disapproves of the marriage

---

[3] *AŚ*. III. 2. Kangle refers to '*śulka*' in sacramental marriages too; *op. cit*. 152.
[4] *AŚ*. IV. 12.
[5] *AŚ*. III. 2.
[6] *AŚ*. III. 5.

by purchase, but he allows this mode to exist. During marriage too, money or money's worth is an important consideration. The husband has to foot the bills of household expenses (*bharma*). He has to make provisions for his wife's food and clothing (*grāsācchādanam*). If, however, the wife is a member of the father-in-law's household or stays separate, the husband is not responsible for maintenance (*śvaśura-kulapraviṣṭāyāṁ vibhaktāyāṁ vā nābhiyojyaḥ patiḥ*).[7] An able man, as we have already seen, has to maintain not only his wife and children but also parents, minor brothers, widowed sisters and daughters. Otherwise he is fined 12 paṇas. If he takes to asceticism without provisions for the maintenance of his wife and children, he is fined in the first amercement.[8]

A married woman is also entitled to her *strīdhana* or separate property. According to Kauṭilya, it is meant for emergencies (*āpadār-tham hi strīdhana*). It consists of (*a*) *vṛitti* (maintenance) and (*b*) *ābadhya* (ornaments). The former means investment not less than 2000 paṇas (*paradvisahasrā sthāpya vṛittiḥ*). There is no limit to the latter.

Kauṭilya imposes certain restrictions on the use of this separate property. "It is no guilt for the wife to make use of this property in maintaining her son, daughter-in-law, or herself whenever her absent husband has made no provision for her maintenance. In calamities, disease and famine, in warding off dangers and in charitable acts, the husband, too, may make use of this property. Neither shall there be any complaint against the enjoyment of this property by mutual consent by a couple who have brought forth a twin. Nor shall there be any complaint if this property has been enjoyed for three years by those who are wedded in accordance with the customs of the first four kinds of marriage. But the enjoyment of this property in the cases of *Gāndharva* and *Āsura* marriages shall be liable to be restored, together with interest on it. In the case of such marriages as are called *Rākṣasa* and *Paiśāca*, the use of this property shall be dealt with as theft."[9]

During marriage the husband acquires some right over the property of the wife, as the wife is entitled to maintenance from the husband.

---

[7] *AŚ*. III. 3.
[8] *AŚ*. II. 1.
[9] *AŚ*. III. 2.

We have also seen how the problem of money might strengthen the conjugal tie. The husband is not allowed to cast off his wife at his pleasure and take another, unless he pays her *śulka*, *strīdhana* and the price of supersession (*tasyātikrame śulkam strīdhanamartham cādhivedanikam dadyāt*).[10] Conversely, in the case of the desertion by the husband, the wife has to wait for a longer period if she is adequately provided with maintenance. After the lapse of such a period she is allowed to remarry.[11] The forfeiture of proprietary right is prescribed for preventing the wife from desertion (*niṣpatan*), elopement (*pathyānusaraṇa*) or other misbehaviours.[12]

Moreover, a spouse is liable for the debt of the other.[13]

Apart from the question of money, mutual aid, as we have also noted, is another result of marriage. Adult husband and wife are asked to attend to each other (*śuśruṣā*).[14] Megasthenes also expresses a similar view: "Some they marry hoping to find in them willing helpmate and others for pleasure and to fill their houses with children."[15] Children are assets to the household. As Megasthenes points out,[16] they do away with the necessity for slaves.

Upon the termination of marriage by death, there arise the mutual rights of inheritance. The widower in some cases inherits his wife's *strīdhana*. "On her death her property passes to her kinsmen (*dāyāda*). If the husband is alive and the wife is dead, then her sons and daughters shall divide her property among themselves. If there are no sons, her daughters shall have it. In their absence her husband shall take that amount of money (*śulka*) which he had given her and her relatives shall retake whatever in the shape of gift or dowry they had presented her."[17] The chaste widow, as we shall see, has a right to enjoy her husband's property (*patidāyam*).[18] We shall also see how Kauṭilya discourages the remarriage of the widow by providing for forfeiture of some of her proprietary rights.[18] In

---

[10] *AŚ*. III. 2.
[11] *AŚ*. III. 4.
[12] *Ibid.*
[13] *AŚ*. III. 11.
[14] *AŚ*. III. 3.
[15] *Meg*. 69.
[16] *Meg*. 100.
[17] *AŚ*. III. 2.
[18] Chapter VII, *infra*.

some cases fo divorce, either party has to return some properties to the other.[19]

Kauṭilya also mentions a special class of persons who make a living by using their wives (*strīvyavahāriṇām*) obviously for immoral purposes. They are mentioned along with actors, dancers, singers, players on musical instruments, buffoons, mimic players, rope-dancers, jugglers and wandering bards. The wives of these persons are classed with *gaṇikās* or courtezans.[20] The ordinary rules of conjugal morality are obviously not applicable to them. Their wives, it seems, even at the cost of chastity, help their husbands to earn their livelihood.

---

[19] *AŚ.* III. 3.
[20] *AŚ.* II. 27.

Chapter VII

THE WIDOW AND HER POSITION

The position of the widow in society has been highly controversial. Westermarck points out in his *The History of Human Marriage*[1] that her status has never been uniform. In some societies, both ancient and modern, she is even denied her right to survive her husband. "He often demands that the woman he chooses for his wife shall belong to him, not during his lifetime only, but after his death."[2] Again, some societies forbid her remarriage[3] or allow it only after the lapse of a certain period after her husband's death. According to some customs, she is required to lead a life of sorrow. Yet in some societies, her life is not overburdened with complex duties and strict taboos.

Such conflicting ideas are also to be found in the ancient Indian texts. Avoiding extreme views, Kauṭilya appears to take a liberal attitude with regard to the duties and status of the widow.

Although the Greek writers and later lawgivers mention[4] the cases of self-immolation (*satī*) of the widow, Kauṭilya is silent about it. In this he obviously follows the principal Smṛitis.[5] The Vedas hardly refer to it. It is "really foreign to the Epic, the cases which do happen to be found are rare exceptions and, undoubtedly belong at least in the greatest part to later revisions."[6] Many later writers condemn it. Some even prohibit it.[7] Jolly states: "The conclusion may be drawn from this that it was never a special Brāhmaṇical institution."

Even if the widow is not required to die, some principal Dharma-

[1] p. 124ff.

[2] *Ibid.*

[3] *Ibid.*, 127.

[4] Diodoros Siculus found this practice in vogue in the country of the Kathaians in the Punjab (*MC. I.* p. 279). Strabo also notices the practice in the kingdom of Sopithes. *MC. I.* p. 219, note 2.

[5] Jolly, *Hindu Law & Custom* (Eng. translation) pp. 148-51. Meyer, *SLAI.* 412. Kane, *HDS.* Vol. II. 10. Chap. XV. gives us a complete picture on this point.

[6] Meyer, *SLAI*, 412.

[7] Jolly, *op.cit.* 149, Meyer, *op.cit.* 413 note.

sāstras call upon her to lead a hard life, in other words, as it were, a death in life. For example, Manu states:[8] "A woman whose husband dies, should better (*kāmam*) waste her body by living upon pure flowers, roots and fruits, but she must not take even the name of another man. Till her death she must be patient, self-controlled and celibate and desire to follow the great code of devotion to one husband. Many thousand unmarried Brāhmin Brahmacārins have gone to Heaven without perpetuating the family (*akṛitvā kulasantatim*). On the death of her husband, the widow should stick to celibacy and, like those Brahmacārins, go to Heaven, although she is without a son." Manu here no doubt sets up an ideal for a widow to practise. He definitely enjoins upon her sexual continence but as regards other duties the advice seems to be optional (*kāmam*).[9] Kauṭilya speaks[10] of different types of widows. Some are devoted to piety (*dharmakāmā*) and maintain the purity of the husband's bed (*patiśayanaṁ pālayanti*). They correspond to Manu's ideal of widowhood. But Kauṭilya also mentions others who hanker after progeny (*kuṭumbakāmā*). Manu disapproves of this class of widows. Kauṭilya permits some degree of freedom to the widow. He allows her to lead an independent life, obviously free from the control of her husband's family. Thus, we read of a widow living a life of her own (*chandavāsinī*).[11] A special provision is made in the *Arthaśāstra* for the protection of such a widow. Any one forcibly violating her chastity (*prasahyādhicarataḥ*) is fined 100 paṇas.[12] Her honour is prized more than that of an ascetic woman. For, as we shall see, a man violating a female ascetic (*pravrajitā*) is fined 24 paṇas only. A widow appears to have a right to move about freely, for she might be employed as a spy of the itenerant type (*sañcārāḥ*).[13] She can have independent means of livelihood. She is employed by the

[8] *Manu.* v. 157-60.

[9] "As to the life of semi-starvation and wretchedness, in which it is argued that, according to the Śāstras, a Hindu widow, ought to live, that is a matter of religious or ceremonial observance rather than of law". Hurry Mohun Roy *vs.* Nayantara, 25 W. R. 474.

[10] *AŚ.* III. 2.

[11] Mm. Ganapati Sastri, however, interprets the expression *chandavāsinī* in a different way. He means by it "remaining taciturn without feeling lustful." Introduction to Vol. I., p. 9.

[12] *AŚ.* III. 20.

[13] *AŚ.* I. 12.

state not only as a spy, but also in the state textile factory.[14] The widow is allowed to have a direct approach to the governmental authorities for agitating her claims to inheritance or deposits.[15]

But in practice the ideal of chastity might not always be maintained by the widow. From the hypothetical cases of espionage mentioned by Kauṭilya, it appears quite possible that some widows might tempt men to fall in love with them. Thus Kauṭilya states: "(Rich) widows may dispute among themselves about the claim for inheritance or deposit and madden (*unmādayeyuḥ*) the leaders of non-monarchical groups (*saṁghamukhyān*)"[16] and "when the enemy is fond of wealth or women, the spies should tempt him with the help of rich widows or women of exquisite beauty and youthfulness who have been brought for the purpose of the (recovery) of deposits kept with a kinsman."[17] Thus, love affairs with a widow are not rare. But the Kauṭilyan law seeks to penalise the unapproved sexual intercourse (*jārakarma*) with widows as also with other married women even with their consent. Where such connections are not allowed by the law, the women, her paramour and the abettor are all chargeable with a criminal offence (*strīsaṁgraha*).[18]

Subject to certain well-defined limitations, Kauṭilya recognises a widow's rights to property and remarriage. His rules regarding these rights require a close scrutiny. Upon a careful analysis, it will appear that Kauṭilya's attitude towards the vexed question of the widow's status in society is not far removed from the orthodox view.

We have already seen that he allows the widow to earn and own

---

[14] *AŚ*. I. 23.

[15] *AŚ*. XI. 1; XIII. 2.

[16] *AŚ*. XI. 1.

[17] *AŚ*. XIII. 2.

[18] *AŚ*. III. 4. The *Mahābhārata* states that a widow is vulnerable, "Just as birds flock to a piece of flesh left on the ground, so all men woo (or try to seduce) a woman whose husband is dead" (Ādi. 160-72). Vātsyāyana includes a young widow among women who can be easily obtained for erotic purposes (*KS*. v. 1. 52). The Greek writers narrate the episode of Cleophis, dowager queen of the Assakenians in the Punjab, who charmed Alexander with her beauty and bore a son probably to him. "Queen Cleophis," writes Justin (*MC. I.* 322), "because she had prostituted her charity was thereafter called by the Indians the royal harlot." Argammes, King of Gangaridae and the Prasii, was reputed to be the son of a usurper and the widow of the murdered sovereign (*MC. I.* 22 & 282). The story is perhaps reflected in the fragment of Megasthenes (*Meg*. 80): "A woman who kills the king when drunk becomes the wife of his successor."

property. Kauṭilya also speaks of the rich widow (*āḍhyavidhavā*). But she is in a somewhat precarious position with regard to her wealth. Obviously, for taking advantage of her helplessness, a prince in emergency is advised to rob her of her properties.[19] Barring this exceptional case, the widow's proprietary right is protected by law. She is even allowed to enforce her rights of ownership before proper authorities. A mother, daughter and widowed sister are required to be maintained by every able man,[20] provided they, other than the mother, are not outcasts (*patita*).

A widow is ordinarily entitled to her ornaments (deposited with the husband's family) (*āsthāpyābharaṇa*), the balance of the bride-price (*śulkaśeṣam*), gifts made by her husband and father-in-law (*śvaśura patidattam*), and her *strīdhana*.[21] As regards the widow's right to her deceased husband's property (*patidāyam*), the text is somewhat difficult. It seems that a chaste widow is entitled to enjoy it. In the *Arthaśāstra* we are definitely told: "A remarried widow will forfeit her right to inheritance from the husband, but one devoted to piety will enjoy it" (*patidāyaṁ vindamānā jīyeta, dharmakāmā bhuñjīta*).[20] We also find that a widow can approach competent authorities for the recovery of inheritance and deposits (*dāyanikṣepārtham*). But in the list of heirs (*dāyāda*) mentioned in the *Arthaśāstra*[21a] her name is omitted. In the absence of heirs (*dāyāda*) the property left by a dead man escheats to the king (except in the case of a Śrotriya), but he is required to make a suitable provision for the endowment of the wife (*strīvṛitti*) (*adāyādakaṁ rājā haret strīvṛittipretakadaryavarjamanyatra śrotriyadravyāt*). The widow, it seems, is only entitled to use her husband's heritable property (*patidāyam*). She is not a *dāyāda* (or full heir). The fifth chapter of Book III speaks of such full heirs only.

The widow's proprietary rights depend in the main upon her chastity. If law and morals fail to keep her chaste, economic sanctions are imposed to encourage it. Even where Kauṭilya permits the remarriage of widows, he seems to discourage it by prescribing forfeiture of a large part of her proprietary rights. "On the death of her husband, a woman, desirous to lead a pious life, shall at once receive

---

[19] *AŚ*. I. 18.
[20] *AŚ*. III. 2.
[21] *AŚ*. II. 1.
[21a] *AŚ*. III. 5

not only her endowment and jewellery (*sthāpyābharaṇam*) but also the balance of *śulka* due to her. If after obtaining these two things she remarries another, she shall be caused to pay them back together (with interest on their value). If she is desirous of second marriage (*kuṭumbakāmā*) she shall be given on the occasion of her remarriage (*niveśakāle*) whatever either her father-in-law or her husband or both had given her...... If a widow marries any man other than of her father-in-law's selection (*śvaśuraprātilomyena vā niviṣṭā*) she shall forfeit whatever had been given to her by her father-in-law and her deceased husband. The kinsman (*jñāti*) of a woman shall return to her old father-in-law whatever property of her own she had taken with her while remarrying a kinsman. Whoever justly takes a woman under his protection shall equally protect her property. No woman shall succeed in her attempt to establish her title to the property of her deceased husband, after she remarries. If she lives a pious life, she may enjoy it (*dharmakāmā bhuñjīta*). No woman with a son or sons shall (after remarriage) be at liberty to make free use of her own property (*strīdhana*); for that property of hers, her sons shall receive. If a woman after remarriage attempts to take possession of her own property under the plea of maintaining her sons by her former husband, she shall be made to endow it in their name. If a woman has many male children by many husbands, then she shall conserve her property in the same condition as she had received from her husbands. Even that property which has been given her with full powers of enjoyment and disposal, a remarried woman shall endow in the name of her sons. A barren widow who is faithful to the bed of her dead husband may under the protection of her teacher, enjoy her property as long as she lives: for it is to ward off calamities that women are endowed with property. On her death her property shall pass into the hands of her kinsman (*dāyāda*)."[22]

From this long extract it appears that Kauṭilya allows remarriage but does not permit the widow to continue the enjoyment of the properties she has received as a gift through the husband or the father-in-law unless the father-in-law approves of the remarriage. She is also deprived of the *sthāpyābharaṇa* and the *śulkaśeṣa* which are also connected with the first marriage. She also loses her right to enjoy (*bhuñjīta*) the

---

[22] *AŚ*. III. 2 (Shama Sastry's translation).

property which has devolved on her from the first husband. Kauṭilya's attitude is quite logical. He does not allow such properties connected with her earlier marriage to be utilised by her during her next marriage. As regards her *strīdhana,* the benefit goes to her sons in the case of her remarriage. In any case, her second husband cannot utilise it (*pratipattā strīdhanaṁ gopāyet*).

In any event, the loss of valuable proprietary rights must prove a strong obstacle to a widow's remarriage.

Moreover, according to Kauṭilya, a widow who desires a progeny (*kuṭumbakāmā*) does not obviously fall within the category of pious (*dharmakāmā*) widow. This view seems to suggest some amount of moral disapprobation against her remarriage.

Again, the remarriage of a widow is hedged round by various restrictions. She has not the freedom of choosing a second husband up to her own liking (*yatheṣṭam*), which a wife, whether virgin or not, has in the case of her short desertion by the husband. Elsewhere we have seen how in the case of the wife of a man who has long gone abroad or taken to asceticism or died, the choice of the second husband is strictly confined to the husband's full brother, in his absence, his half brother, *sapiṇḍa* or other relations (*kulyam* or *tulyam*) in the order of mention. In other words, her choice of a second husband for marriage is confined to the circle of her first husband's family. But the wife, whose husband is alive but has left her for a short while (*hrasvapravāsinaḥ*), can, in some cases, marry according to her own choice (*yatheṣṭam*).[23] If this rule is not strictly followed, the sexual union between the widow and her lover (*jāra*) will amount to a criminal offence. Further, even when a widow's remarriage is allowed, a part of her proprietary right depends on the approval of the father-in-law. If she remarries against his consent (*śvaśura-prātilomyena*) she forfeits the gifts made by him and her husband.[24]

Lastly, with regard to sons by many wives, the rules of succession prefer the son of a virgin wife to that of a remarried woman.[25]

So we might conclude that Kauṭilya indirectly disapproves of the remarriage by the widow but allows it to take place within

[23] *AŚ*. III. 4.
[24] *AŚ*. III. 2.
[25] *AŚ*. III. 6.

well-defined limits. It is also possible for a widow to contract several marriages probably in succession and get sons by different husbands (*vahupuruṣaprajānāṁ putrāṇām yathāpitṛidattam*).[26]

Like most of the Smṛiti-writers, Kauṭilya mentions an inferior type of son, viz., *paunarbhava*. "The son of a remarried woman (*punarbhūtāyāḥ*) is *paunarbhavaḥ*." Kauṭilya does not clearly explain the word *punarbhūtā*. It is obviously the same as *punarbhū* mentioned in other sources. The ancient works assign different meanings to the word *punarbhū*.

Vātsyāyana includes a *punarbhū* in the list of *nāyikās* or lady-loves. He describes *punarbhū* as a widow, who, prompted by the frailty of the organs of senses, resorts to an accomplished and voluptuous man.[27] According to other authorities cited by Vātsyāyana, a *punarbhū* is not confined to widows only. "According to Bābhravīya, a woman who leaves her husband's house out of her own free will (outwardly) for her husband's worthlessness but (actually) hankering for another husband (is a *punarbhū*). Or, desirous of pleasure, she may marry again".[28] In Vātsyāyana's view, "sexual connections with a widow is neither approved nor disapproved but is meant for pleasure only."[29] From his descriptions of the life of a *punarbhū*, it appears that she is treated as a subsidiary wife only, not enjoying the status of a wife proper. But the *punarbhū* fully participates in the social and cultural life. "She should be devoted to social gatherings, drinking parties, garden parties and other entertainments."[30] She and her relations make it a point to secure such enjoyment from her new husband.[31]

Vasiṣṭha mentions two types of *punarbhūs*. "She who renounces the husband of her maidenhood and associates with another and takes shelter with his family (*kuṭumba*) becomes a *punarbhū*. She who renounces an impotent, ostracised (*patita*) or lunatic husband or whose husband is dead weds (*vindate*) another husband (*patim*) becomes a *punarbhū*."[32]

---

[26] *AŚ*. III. 2. Therīgāthā narrates the life-story of a thrice-married woman, although the former husbands were alive. (*Isidāsi-Therīgathā* XV.)
[27] *KS*. IV. 2. 39.
[28] *Ibid*. 40-41.
[29] *KS*. I. 5. 3.
[30] *KS*. IV. 2. 59.
[31] *KS*. IV. 2. 59.
[32] *Vasiṣṭha*, Chapter XVII. 19-20.

In spite of his strong disapproval of the remarriage of a woman, Manu is constrained to recognise *punarbhū* as a wife.[33] The son of a woman who remarries after being left by the husband or being a widow or out of her own desire (*svayecchayā*) and begets the son is called *paunarbhava*. "A woman who has no sexual connection (*akṣatayoniḥ*) or who having left her husband (for another) has returned to the former may have the ceremony (of marriage) again with the husband (*paunarbhavena bhartā*)." Thus, the author of *Manusmṛiti*, writes Mm. Kane, "probably only reiterates popular usage which was too much for him in spite of his own view (in V. 162) denouncing remarriage."[33] Nārada, Yājñavalkya and other *Smṛiti* writers give different classifications of a *punarbhū*.[34]

Nārada, Parāśara and Agnipurāṇa provide[35] that in five calamities a woman can remarry, viz., "when the husband is lost, or dead, becomes an ascetic, is impotent or *patita*." Commentators have made strenuous efforts to explain away the passage. But the practice of remarriage, although denounced, receives legal sanction in many of the principal *Smṛitis*.

We find Kauṭilya taking up a liberal attitude towards the widow. He does not prescribe the practice of her self-immolation. Although he mentions the pious life led by some widows, he is not hostile to those who live independently (*chandavāsinī*). He allows the widow to own property and earn her living. He even permits her to remarry, but puts some restrictions on her right of remarriage. Yet he strictly prohibits any licentiousness on her part.

---

[33] *Manu*. IX. 175-76; Kane, *HDS*. II. 612.
[34] Kane, *HDS*. Vol. II. 608-69 (*Nārada Strīpuṁsa*, v. 45). *Yāj*. I. 67.
[35] *Nārada*. (Strīpuṁsa v. 97); *Parāśara*. IV. 30 and *Agnipurāṇa*, 154. 5-6.

Chapter VIII

SONS AND FAMILY LIFE

Westermarck states: "The ancient Indo-European nations believed that a man's happiness in the next world depends upon his having a continuous line of male descendants whose duty it would be to make the periodical offerings for the repose of his soul."[1] De Coulanges too observes: "Every father, therefore, expected of his posterity that series of funeral repasts which was to assure to his manes repose and happiness. This opinion was the fundamental principle of domestic law among the ancients. From it followed, in the first place, this rule, that every family must perpetuate itself. It was necessary to the dead that the descendants should not die out."[2] The desire for progeny expresses itself in the hymns of the *Vedas*,[3] the ceremonials of the *Sūtras*,[4] in the anecdotes of the *Mahābhārata*[5] as well as in the *Smṛitis*.[6] Manu, however, wishing to enforce chastity upon a childless widow categorically states that many thousands of sages have gone to Heaven without progeny.[7] Kauṭilya also is prompted by the traditional ideas regarding the perpetuation of the race. Kauṭilya is fully conversant with the traditional doctrines of "funeral cakes (*piṇḍa*)" on which, it seems the succession to patrimony probably depends. "Sons or grandsons till the fourth generation from the first parent shall also have prescribed shares (*aṁśabhājaḥ*) in that property which is acquired by means of their undivided ancestral property; for the line (*piṇḍaḥ*) as far as the fourth generation is uninterrupted (*avicchinnaḥ*). But those whose line or genealogy from the first ancestor is interrupted (*vicchinnapiṇḍaḥ*, i.e., those who are subsequent to the fourth generation), shall have equal divisions."[8] Elsewhere, he gives the eldest son a special

[1] Westermarck, *Future of Marriage in Western Civilization*, pp. 22-23.
[2] Fustel De Coulanges, *The Ancient City* (Eng. translation), p. 61.
[3] Kane, *op.cit.*, 560-61.
[4] *Ibid.*
[5] Meyer, *SLAI.* 147-51.
[6] Kane, *ibid.*
[7] Manu. v. 157-60.
[8] *AŚ.* III. 5.

share in patrimony so that he may be freed from the noose of offering funeral libations (*pratimuktasvadhā pāśa bhavati*).[9]

Kauṭilya observes: "Wives are indeed for bearing sons" (*putrārthā hi striyaḥ*).[10] We have already seen how the husband is allowed to supersede a wife who is barren or bears only daughters or children who do not survive. In such a case, the husband is allowed to take another wife. This shows the imperative need of having sons. Even the king performs rites for obtaining a son (*putrīyaṁ karma*).[11]

In general, a son is preferable to a daughter. We have just now noted that the rites are performed for obtaining a son and a wife who gives birth to daughters only (*kanyāprasavinī*) is allowed to be superseded by her husband after twelve years. On the expiry of that period the husband is allowed to marry a second wife for obtaining a son (*tataḥ putrārthī dvitīyaṁ vindeta*).[12] Elsewhere, speaking of hostages, Kauṭilya states: "In a peace made with children as hostages, choosing between the son and the daughter, whoever gives the daughter gains advantages for the daughter is not entitled to succeed (to her father), is meant for others and causes troubles. But the son is not so."[13] Thus a daughter is said to cause troubles (*kleśa*) but the son is not.

In the *Arthaśāstra* a special care is required for a pregnant woman. Medical aids are provided for. The midwife attends to her. The state exempts the midwife from curfew rules[14] and the commodities required for confinement from tolls.[15] A pregnant woman gets free ferry service.[16] Criminal law exempts her from physical torture during pregnancy and one month after delivery.[17] The confinement seems to continue for ten days. For this purpose temporary structures are erected.[18] People, particularly women, says Aśoka, are used to celebrate several lucky rites at the birth of children.[19] Speaking of the birth of a prince,

[9] *AŚ*. III. 6.
[10] *AŚ*. III. 2.
[11] *AŚ*. V. 6.
[12] *AŚ*. III. 2.
[13] *AŚ*. VII. 17.
[14] *AŚ*. II. 35.
[15] *AŚ*. II. 21.
[16] *AŚ*. II. 28.
[17] *AŚ*. II. 28.
[18] *AŚ*. III. 8.
[19] *RE*. IX.

which might as well be true of a commoner, Kauṭilya states: "..... When the queen attains the age favourable for procreation, priests shall offer to Indra and Bṛihaspati the requisite oblations. When she is big with a child, the king shall observe instructions of midwifery with regard to gestation and delivery. After delivery the priests shall perform the prescribed purificatory ceremonials."[20] Discoursing on Brachmanes, Megasthenes too states:[21] "From the time of their conception in the womb they are under the guardian care of learned men, who go to the mother and under pretence of using some incantations for the welfare of herself and her unborn babe, in reality give her prudent hints and counsel. The women who listen most willingly are thought to be the most fortunate in their children". Speaking of physicians, Megasthenes records: "By their knowledge of pharmacy they can make marriage fruitful and determine the sex of the offspring."[22]

Craving for sons is so great that through legal fiction or otherwise various classes of sons are recognised by the *Arthaśāstra* as well as in the *Smṛitis*. These include sons conceived or born out of wedlock. These according to the *Arthaśāstra* are[23]:—

1. Aurasa — "Son begotten by the husband on his wife who has gone through all the required ceremonials" (*svayaṁjāta kṛitakriyāmaurasa*).
2. Putrikāputra — "Son of the appointed daughter".
3. Kṣetraja — "Son begotten on a wife of a person by another man, appointed for the purpose, and of the same *gotra* as that of the husband or of a different *gotra*."
4. Gūḍhaja — "Son secretly born in the house of relatives."
5. Apaviddha — "Son cast off by his natural parents and to belong to that man who performs necessary religious ceremonials to him."
6. Kānīna — "Son of an unmarried girl."
7. Sahoḍha — "Son of a woman married while carrying."

---

[20] *AŚ.* I. 17.
[21] *Meg.* 98.
[22] *Meg.* 102.
[23] *AŚ.* III. 7: for changing position of secondary sons, N. C. Sengupta, *Evolution of Ancient Indian Law* (TLL. 1950, Chap. VII).

8. Paunarbhava — "Son of a remarried woman."
9. Datta — "He who is given in adoption with water by both the father and the mother."
10. Upagata — "Son who either of his own accord or following the intention of his relatives, offers himself to be son of another."
11. Kṛitaka — "He who is appointed as a son."
12. Krīta — "He who is purchased."

There are mentioned various types of sons born of intercaste marriages.

The *aurasa* son is no doubt preferred by Kauṭilya. All the other types of sons are subsidiary. The son who is begotten by the father inherits both from him and his relations, but the son begotten by another man (*parajāta*) inherits from the adoptive father only and not from his relations.[24] According to the rules of succession, the son whose mother was a virgin at the time of marriage is preferred to one whose mother was not such.[25]

Mm. Kane has set out an excellent chart showing the relative position of these sons according to Kauṭilya and the principal Smṛiti writers.[26] Apart from the case of *aurasa* son, the relative status of the subsidiary sons as indicated in the Smṛitis appears to be highly confusing. Yet various kinds of sons can be grouped under four heads.[27] First, as regards the *aurasa* son there is no divergence at all. Secondly, *apaviddha*, *dattaka*, *upagata*, *kṛitaka* and *krīta* are acquired by gift or otherwise without any taint of illegality. Thirdly, *putrikāputra* is really a grandson by a daughter. He is adopted in the maternal grandfather's family pursuant to an agreement at the time of marriage. Fourthly, *paunarbhava* is the legal son of the man himself but as Mm. Kane points out "there is opprobrium attaching to 'him' as the mother contracted a remarriage (which was very much condemned by the Smritis)." Lastly, with regard to four kinds of sons only, viz., *kṣetraja*, *gūḍhaja*, *kānīna* and *sahoḍha*, a moral question might arise.

A *kṣetraja* is based on an ancient custom prevalent in the many countries of the world. It is reprobated by Āpastamba, Manu and

[24] *Ibid.*
[25] *AŚ.* III. 6.
[26] Kane, *HDS.* VOL. III. 645.
[27] *Ibid.* p. 649.

others and ultimately discontinued.[28] But the *Arthaśāstra* allows a son to be procreated by a man on another's wife by a special appointment. The wife is the field (*kṣetra*) and the procreator sows the seed (*bīja*) in her. Kauṭilya refers to the views of earlier lawmakers on the question of the paternity of the son. According to some,[29] the son belongs to the husband of the woman; while according to others,[30] he belongs to the procreator. But Kauṭilya holds that the son belongs to both. Yet he adds that in case the procreator has no aurasa son of his own, then the son raised by him on another's wife "will be son to both the fathers, offer funeral libations to both and take possession of the property (*riktha*) of both of them."[31]

The custom of levirate is allowed by the *Arthaśāstra*. By this method husbands who suffer from disabilities, social, physical or mental, get sons by legal fiction. Thus, Kauṭilyan law allows levirate in the case of married outcasts, eunuchs, idiots, lunatics, the blind and lepers, if their lines are likely to be extinct. Any relative may beget a son on the wife of such a person.[32] In the case of Brāhmaṇas, a *sagotra* or a *mātṛibandhu* is allowed to beget such a son.[33] Sons may also be raised on the queen[34] or a royal princess.[35] The great epic gives us many well-known cases in which sons are raised by this process in the royal family. The Smṛitis, however, prescribe strict rules to be followed by a man while he performs the act of procreating a son on another's wife.[36]

"As regards gūḍhaja, kānīna and sahoḍha", Mm. Kane rightly observes, "there is this to be said. They were the result of illicit connection, but some one had to maintain them, to bring them up and be their guardian. The Smṛitis when they assign these as the sons of the husbands of women of whom they are born are really providing for these matters of maintenance and guardianship . . . . .The very fact

[28] *Ibid.*, 655.

[29] The *Mbh.* gives us many examples of this view. Dhṛitarāṣṭra and his brother raised by appointment are treated as the sons of their mother's husband. Similarly, the Pāṇḍava brothers are known as Pāṇḍu's sons. S. Bhattacharyya, *Mahābhārater Samāj*, p. 27. He tells us that in the *Mbh.* there is no instance to support the contrary view.

[30] *Manu.* IX. 180 generally holds this view.

[31] *AŚ.* III. 7.

[32] *AŚ.* III. 5.

[33] *AŚ.* III. 6.

[34] *AŚ.* I. 27

[35] *AŚ.* V. 6.

[36] Kane, *HDS.* II. 601.

that the kānīna was assigned to the husband who married the girl shows that this was done because it was deemed that by marrying such a girl the husband condoned her past lapses. Similarly, in the case of sahoḍha, it was deemed that either the child must have been procreated by the husband himself before marriage or that he condoned the conduct of the wife. It appears to have been thought that when the husband (the party most concerned) did not openly object it was not open or allowable for any one else even by proof that the child was kānīna or sahoḍha to call for the abandonment of the child. Similar remarks apply to the gūḍhaja."[37] According to Yājñavalkya, the *kānīna* is to be under the guardianship of the father of the girl till she remains unmarried.[38] As is well-known, illegitimate children create a grave social problem. Westermarck observes: "The illegitimacy of birth affects the offspring even more than the mother. The death rate for illegitimate infants is very much higher than that for legitimate ones. . . . . Another result of them is the comparatively large number of criminals among children of unmarried parents, who grow up in so unfavourable circumstances. The way in which they have been treated in the Western world is a disgrace to its civilization."[39] He further states: "It is said that every healthy woman, married or unmarried has a right to be proud of her motherhood; that the taking of a husband should not be imposed on her as the price of her right to give birth to a child; that the social stigma attaching to unmarried maternity should be removed."[40] In the Soviet Union, it is reported, "there is no illegitimacy of birth, all children having exactly the same rights."[41] Kauṭilya and other ancient Indian lawmakers take a practical view by granting limited legal recognition to children born out of wedlock.

Although, in the *Arthaśāstra*, a son is found to be preferable to a daughter, the law makes ample provisions for her maintenance and marriage. She is no doubt under the dominion of the father. But, as we have seen elsewhere, the father loses this right for his failure to give her away in marriage at the proper time. We shall note later the daughter's right of inheritance from the parents. Kauṭilya even allows

[37] Kane, *op. cit.* III: 652-53.
[38] II. 129.
[39] Westermarck, *op. cit.* p. 128.
[40] *Ibid.* v. 129-130.
[41] *Ibid.* 129.

maidens to earn at the state textile factory. A *kanyakā* (small unmarried girl) is permitted to stay at home and send her products to the factory through maid servants.[42] As we shall see later, special provisions are prescribed by law for the protection of the chastity of a maiden.

According to Kauṭilya the wife has a right to maternity. Thus a woman whose husband is away may have to await his return for some time, yet there is no stigma (*apavāda*) if, meanwhile, she bears a child through some man of the same caste.[43] For procreation, the re-marriage of a deserted wife or a widow is allowed.[44]

Modern psychologists also hold that women in general feel a craving for motherhood. Westermarck quotes authorities: "According to Havelock Ellis, 'most people, certainly most women, feel at moments, or at some period in their lives, a desire for children'; and in women longing for a child 'may become so urgent and imperative that we may regard it as scarcely less imperative than the sexual impulse'. Van de Velde writes: 'To be a woman means to have the desire to become a mother both physically and mentally.' He admits that 'there are women, and presumably always have been women, although their number may be relatively very small, who feel such a strong antagonism to motherhood that they refuse to marry for this reason'; but he adds: 'The absence of maternal instinct in the modern woman is really nothing but a pose. The maternal instinct exists in spite of this, although there may be only one child. . . .'"

Although children are welcome, yet it appears from the *Arthaśāstra* that abortion is not unknown. It may be effected by striking or with medicine or undertaking hard work. The law prescribes fines of different degrees in such cases.[45] A woman murdering her child is required to be torn apart by bull, regardless of whether she is pregnant or not.[46]

Speaking of the kingdom of Sophites, Curtius Rufus records a strange custom: "Here they do not acknowledge and rear children according to the will of the parents, but as the officers entrusted with the medical inspection of infants may direct, for if they have remarked anything deformed or defective in the limbs of a child they order it

[42] *AŚ.* II. 23.
[43] *AŚ.* III. 4; *supra*, Chapter V.
[44] *Supra*, Chapter IV.
[45] Westermarck, *op. cit.*, p. 27.
[46] *AŚ.* IV. 11.

to be killed .... beauty in the children is a quality highly appreciated."[47] Strabo states that the inspection is made when the child is two months old.[47] The practice must have been a rare one as otherwise we would not have got many references to defective persons in the *Arthaśāstra*.

In the *Arthaśāstra* we get some idea of the picture of a joint family. It may include the wife or wives, children, parents, minor brothers, unmarried or widowed sisters. Every capable person (*śaktimān*) is required to maintain these relations, otherwise a fine is imposed on him.[48] Even a wife may have to maintain her son, daughter-in-law and herself, whenever her absent husband makes no provision for their maintenance.[49] A widow may marry another husband for maintaining her son (*putrabharaṇārtham vindamānā*).[50] An outcast, however, forfeits the right to maintenance. But the mother, even if an outcast, is an exception.[51] Kauṭilya is against desertion of the family. Again, between father and son, husband and wife, brother and sister, and maternal uncle and nephew, whoever abandons (*tyājataḥ*) the other (not being an outcast) is liable to punishment in the first amercement.[52] A person is also required to show deference (*aśriṇvato*) to his slaves (*dāsa*), pledged servants (*āhitaka*) and relatives (*bāndhava*). Otherwise the king is required to teach him a lesson (*vinayaṁ grāhayet*).[53]

It appears from the instances[54] cited by Kauṭilya that in some cases the noble ideal of family life advocated by him is likely to be violated. Thus, incited by designing persons near relations like father and son or two brothers might quarrel over some incestuous relationship. Likewise, brothers might fight over a share of the patrimony. The dispute might lead to murders. A son also might be instigated to kill his father. Of course, Kauṭilya prescribes capital punishment for such an offence. He also provides for death with torture for killing one's mother, father, son or brother. Even abuses (*ākrośa*) against these relations are sought to be penalised by cutting off the offender's tongue.[55]

---

[47] *MC. I.* 219.
[48] *AŚ*. II. 1.
[49] *AŚ*. III. 2.
[50] *Ibid.*
[51] *AŚ*. II. 1.
[52] *AŚ*. III. 20.
[53] *Ibid.*
[54] *AŚ*. V. 1.
[55] *AŚ*. IV. 11.

No wonder that Aśoka laments: "For a long time past, for many hundred of years, have ever increased......unseemly behaviour to relatives......"[56] By examples and precept, the great king tries to improve the morale in society. In this he seems to have pursued a course of conduct similar to that laid down by Kauṭilya. In several of his edicts Aśoka harps on seemly behaviour to relatives, hearkening to father and mother, hearkening to the aged, reverence to teachers, liberality and seemly behaviour towards friends, acquaintances and relatives, seemly behaviour to slaves and servants.[57] The great king claims that his efforts have proved a success. "As has not happened for many hundred years before, have now increased through King Priyadarśin—Beloved of the Gods' instructions in Dharma" these among other social and moral virtues.[58] Kauṭilya urges the king himself to maintain the infants, the aged, the diseased, orphans and women (barren or with sons).[59] The village elders are also called upon to improve the assets of infants till they reach majority.[52]

This ideal of Kauṭilya finds a happy parallel in Aśoka's edict. Aśoka creates a new class of government servants, Dhamma Mahāmātras. Their duties include works "among the Brāhmaṇs and Gṛihapatis who have become hirelings and among the helpless and the aged, for (their) welfare and happiness and (also) for the unfettering of those devoted to Dharma. They concern themselves with (money) grant for the unfettering or the release of (any one) who is bound with fetters, according as he is encumbered with progeny, is subject to oppression, or is aged."[60]

In short, Kauṭilya shows a great concern for progeny and family life. He advocates measures tending towards solidarity in the family. He boldly seeks to counteract the forces that undermine that solidarity. The state receives his directions to enforce laws and regulations which strengthen the family tie. As we have elsewhere noted, Kauṭilya does not share the orthodox Buddhists' contempt for family life. On the contrary, he upholds the ideal of a happy family which finds an apt parallel in the edicts of Aśoka the Great.

---

[56] *RE*, IV.
[57] Bhandarkar, *Aśoka*, p. 104.
[58] *RE*. III.
[59] *AŚ*. II. 1.
[60] *RE*. V. (Bhandarkar, *Aśoka*), p. 309.

CHAPTER IX

OUT OF WEDLOCK

Many societies, ancient and modern, permit extra-marital sexual relationship in some cases. Sexual gratification is not confined within the four corners of matrimony. James rightly observes: "All through the ages, as we have seen, sex has been one of the most disturbing elements in society, and unless it is sternly regulated it plays havoc with the social organism as well as with human personality at the most vital point. Therefore, it has never been possible to leave it to its own devices because a state of promiscuity would be a state of sexual and social anarchy involving jealousies and tensions destructive of all ordered and orderly family relationships, whatever measure of freedom may have been permitted in the pre-nuptial period. Latitude outside wedlock always has been balanced by restriction within the nuptial state, however widely this relationship may have been cast to include supplementary alliances, usually of a relatively temporary and subsidiary nature."[1]

In the *Arthaśāstra* some forms of extra-marital relationships are allowed to exist, while other forms are prohibited. From the ethical standpoint it is important to examine to what extent Kauṭilya permits some forms of sexual relationship out of wedlock and deprecates the other forms.

Pre-marital sexual intercourse on the part of a girl is allowed by Kauṭilya in two cases. First, where the father fails to get his daughter married after puberty. Then she is free to have sexual connection with an equal or, after three years, any man (*trivarṣa-prajātārtavāyāstulyo gantumadoṣa/tataḥ paramatulyo'pyanalaṁkritāyāḥ*).[2] In the case of her connection with a man of a different class, she must not have received any ornaments, possibly from her parents.[3] In this matter Kauṭilya's view finds a parallel in many orthodox law books.

[1] E. O. James, *Marriage & Society*, p. 146.
[2] *AŚ*. IV. 12.
[3] *Ibid.*

Vasiṣṭha,[4] Baudhāyana,[5] Manu,[6] Nārada,[7] and Parāśara[8] allows an unmarried girl to woo a mate upon the expiry of three years after her first period. Viṣṇu[9] will not wait even for three years. He writes: "If a maid in her father's house sees her monthly courses without having been dedicated (that is, married) she is to be looked upon as a *Vṛiṣalī*; he that takes her for himself without more ado lays no guilt on himself." Manu,[10] however, holds that a girl may remain unmarried till her death, if a suitable match is not available. But according to Nīlakaṇṭha,[11] this view of Manu is not meant to be taken literally. It may be observed that Kauṭilya in this context clearly allows intercourse even short of marriage.

Secondly, any man can have sexual relations with a betrothed girl who has not been given in marriage for a period of her seven menstrual cycles (*saptārtavaprajātām varaṇādūrdhvamalabhamānāṁ prakṛitya prakāmī syāt*).[12] In this case, the period of continence is much shorter than in the first case.

Psychological factors behind pre-marital intercourse is to be noted. One motive might have been to induce a father to get his daughter married. The orthodox lawmakers fix a charge of religious sin on the defaulting father. That is the sin of killing an embryo. In such cases, Kauṭilya, as we have seen, deprives the father of some pecuniary advantages connected with the daughter's marriage. Whatever might have been the real motive, the fact remains that pre-marital intercourse in the above two cases is not tabooed by the Kauṭilyan law.

As far as young men are concerned, apart from the rule as to celibacy during student-life, sexual continence does not appear to be compulsory. Moreover, the *āśrama* of a *brahmacārin* is confined to three upper castes only. The rule of sexual continence does not appear to apply to young men outside these castes; and probably there is no

---

[4] xvii. 71.
[5] iv. 1. 12f.
[6] *Manu.* ix. 90-91.
[7] xii. 25-27.
[8] vii. 6.
[9] xxiv. 41.
[10] *Manu.* ix. 89.
[11] Nīlakaṇṭha referred to in Jolly, *op.cit.* 122.
[12] *AŚ.* iv. 12.

liability if some other rules are not broken. Kauṭilya, however, speaks of *varadoṣa*[13] or defects of a bridegroom, but there is perhaps nothing to show that these defects include erotic experience prior to marriage. In fact, Vātsyāyana mentions, among the men who make a success of love, "a man capable of effecting sexual intercourse satisfactorily; a person disposed to caressing and fondling women."[14] Subject to the two exceptions mentioned above, Kauṭilya, it seems, indicates a double standard of pre-nuptial chastity for men and women. In practice at least, the problem of pre-marital connection is not so very important as marriage is likely to be contracted at an early age for both the sexes.

Apart from the permissible cases indicated above all other forms of pre-nuptial intercourse is penalised in the Kauṭilyan law.[15] Thus a man who violates an immature (*aprāptaphalā*) maiden (*kanyā*) of the same caste is to suffer heavy punishments. His hand is to be cut off or he is to pay a fine of 400 paṇas. If the unfortunate girl dies as a result of the offence, the offender suffers capital punishment. If the maiden is mature (*prāptaphalā*), her violator will have his first and middle fingers cut off or pay as fine two hundred paṇas in addition to compensation to the aggrieved father of the girl. But in case the gallant has received the consent of the virgin, the sentence is reduced, but both the lovers are liable to fine; the boy 54 paṇas and the girl 27 paṇas. This affair obviously takes place before the expiry of the above-mentioned periods of seven menstrual cycles or three years as the case may be, after which as we have seen, free love is allowed by law. A man who violates a girl who is engaged to another, in consideration of a bride-price (*paraśulkopadhāyām*), is punishable like a violator of an immature virgin of the same caste. In addition, he is to pay the bride price (*śulkadānaṁ ca*). Not only rape but abduction of a maiden is prohibited. For forcible abduction the fine is 200 paṇas. If the girl is decked with gold ornaments (*sasuvarnām*) the fine is doubled. If a body of men jointly abduct a girl, each of the culprits is punishable as deserved. Thus, it is clear that Kauṭilya does not generally encourage sexual relations with virgins. The punishment

13 *AŚ*. III. 15.

14 *KS*. VI. 1. 11. read with I. 5. 28-31.

15 *AŚ*. IV. 12.

for rape or abduction of a virgin is usually heavy. Only where both the parties consent, the punishment is appreciably reduced. There is no punishment at all, if the case falls within the two exceptions mentioned above. It should be noted that with regard to pre-marital intercourse by maidens, Kauṭilya is in general agreement with orthodox law-makers. For instance, Manu says: "If a maiden approaches a superior man, she shall not be made to pay a fine; if however, she courts an inferior man, she shall be kept confined in the house."[16] According to Manu, a man who cohabits with a willing maiden is fined only 200 paṇas, but otherwise his fingers are chopped off or he pays a fine of 600 paṇas.[17] In another place Manu speaks of capital punishment for the man who defiles an unwilling maiden.[18] Thus Manu prescribes heavier penalty for the man but no fine for the maiden. Nārada holds that there is nothing wrong in a man having intercourse with a willing maiden of the same caste but he has to marry her after having adorned and honoured her.[19] Kauṭilya, however, does not make marriage compulsory in such a case, but he recognises, as we have noted, *Gāndharva* marriage (by mutual compact), and *Paiśāca* marriage where the girl is obtained when she is asleep or drunken. But in these cases approval of both the parents of the girl is, according to Kauṭilya, necessary.[20] Kauṭilya even prescribes payment of bride-price (*śulka*) for the violated maiden. However, we have seen that a virgin wife is preferred to one who is not. One consequence of pre-marital sexual connection may be eventual pregnancy. We have already observed how the ancient Indian lawmakers including Kauṭilya solve the problem. They do not declare the sons of unmarried mothers as bastards. These sons are treated as subsidiary sons entitled to claim maintenance and enjoy other rights.[21]

Kauṭilya's attitude towards adultery is interesting. He does not penalise a married man having intercourse outside wedlock, provided he does not break some other law relating to sexual union. But a married woman is subject to stringent rules against adultery. Wester-

[16] VIII. 365.
[17] VIII. 367-68.
[18] VIII. 364.
[19] Nārada in *Vivādaratnākara*, p. 402 quoted in Jha's *Hindu Law in its sources*, Vol. I. For similar other extracts *vide* p. 494-500.
[20] *AŚ*. III. 2.
[21] *Supra*, Chapter VIII.

marck states: "The Indo-European nations in early times saw nothing objectionable in the unfaithfulness of a married man, whereas an adulterous wife was subject to the severest penalties. Until some time after the introduction of Christianity among the Teutons their law-books made no mention of the infidelity of husbands, because it was permitted by custom. The Romans defined adultery as sexual intercourse with another man's wife; on the other hand, the intercourse of a married man with an unmarried woman was not regarded as adultery."[22] In only a few cases does Kauṭilya excuse the extra-marital adventures of a married woman. First, where a wife is deserted by her husband even for a short time (*hrasvapravāsinām*), she may have a child by a man of the same caste. In that event, Kauṭilya says, she should not suffer from any stigma (*savarṇatśca prajātā nāpavādaṁ labheta*).[23] We have also noted the cases where a married woman is allowed to have a son by levirate.[24] Secondly, if a husband condones his wife's adultery, the offence is excused. Thus, Kauṭilya states: "If a wife whose husband is absent (*proṣitapatikām*) violates her chastity (*apacarantīm*), her husband's relative or employee should restrain her. Having been restrained, she should wait for her husband. If the husband condones (the offence), both (the wife and her paramour) should be released (*visṛijyetobhayam*). But if there is no condonation, the wife's ears and nose should be cut off and the paramour (*jāra*) should be killed."[25] In any event, it is a risky affair for the wife to indulge in extra-marital sexual connections, for if the husband does not condone the offence, serious consequences follow. In modern law, too, the husband's condonation takes away much of the gravity of adultery by a wife.

The third case of the permissible extra-marital connections mentioned in the *Arthaśāstra* seems to be based upon a peculiar custom rooted in the idea of salvage. Thus subject to some exceptions noted below a man who rescues a woman from some specified danger is allowed to enjoy her by mutual agreement. Kauṭilya states: "When a man rescues a woman from enemies, forests, or floods, or saves the life of a woman who has been abandoned in forests, forsaken in famine,

[22] E. Westermarck, *Future of Marriage in Western Civilization*, p. 67.
[23] *AŚ.* III. 4.
[24] Chapter VIII, *Supra.*
[25] *AŚ.* IV. 12.

or thrown out as if dead, he may enjoy her as agreed upon during the rescue. A woman of high caste, with children and having no desire for sexual enjoyment, may be let off after receiving an adequate amount of ransom. Those women who have been rescued from the hands of thieves, from floods, in famine, or in national calamities, or who, having been abandoned, missed, or thrown out as if dead in forests, have been taken home, may be enjoyed by the rescuer as agreed upon.

"But no such women as have been cast out under royal edict, or by their own kinsmen; nor such as belong to high caste, or do not like to be rescued, nor even those who have children, shall be rescued either for ransom or for their persons."[26] It is significant to note that a woman who does not consent, or who has children, or who is cast away by king's order or by her kinsmen cannot be enjoyed.

Another exceptional case concerns the wives of persons who use their womenfolk for earning livelihood (*strīvyavahārinām striyaḥ*).[27] Perhaps wanton women like *vandhakīs* and *kulaṭās* might be grouped with these women. Their cases are discussed in the next chapter.

Subject to a few exceptions, adultery by or with a married woman is sought to be suppressed by Kautilya. The orthodox law-makers like Vyāsa, Vrihaspati and Nārada recognise different grades of adultery (*saṁgrahaṇam*) starting from secret talks and flirtations to actual love-play and sexual connection. Likewise Kautilya prescribes punishments for misbehaviour by or with a married woman.[28] Details of such conduct have already been discussed. But a more serious offence is actual cohabitation in adultery. We have already noticed how the wife is to be mutilated and the paramour to suffer capital punishment, if the husband does not condone the offence. Elsewhere, it appears that Kauṭilya prescribes in the case of adultery a fine in lieu of mutilation. The woman is to pay 500 panas and the man 1000 paṇas. The same rule applies to abettors.[29] Thus the severity of the punishment for adultery is largely reduced.

---

[26] *AŚ.* IV. 12: According to a variant reading the last line of the text may be translated as: "But such a woman should be returned after obtaining a suitable ransom."

[27] *AŚ.* II. 27.

[28] *AŚ.* III. 2.

[29] *AŚ.* IV. 10.

Like the Smṛitis, the *Arthaśāstra* makes the severity of punishment for adultery or fornication depends largely upon the questions of incest and of caste.[30] Thus for an incestuous connection with the mother's sister or the father's sister or the maternal uncle's wife or the preceptor's wife, or one's own daughter, daughter-in-law or sister, the offender is to suffer emasculation and capital punishment. The consenting woman is punishable in the like manner.[31] In spite of severe punishments, cases of incest might be quite possible, for Kauṭilya speaks of some cases of this nature. Father and son or two brothers might quarrel with each other over incestuous relationship of one with the wife of the other.[32] Again, for violating an independent (*aguptāyām*) *Brāhmaṇa* woman, a *Kṣatriya* is punishable in the highest amercement, a *Vaiśya* forfeits all his belongings (*sarvasvam*) and a *Śūdra* is liable to be burnt in slow fire. A man who has sexual connections with a *Caṇḍāla* woman, is liable to be branded on his head and banished. If he is a *Śūdra*, he is to be degraded to the woman's caste. A *Caṇḍāla* who cohabits with an *Ārya* woman is liable to be killed and the woman's ears and nose to be cut off. A *Brāhmana* who violates the wife of a preceptor or elder (*gurutalpe*) is branded, exposed to public ridicule and banished or made to reside in mines.[33] It is no use continuing the examples any further.[34] It is quite clear that except in a few cases, Kauṭilya prescribes deterrent punishments for adultery. Yet, in practice, cases of incest and adultery, as it appears from the *Arthaśāstra*, are not rare. Kautilya gives us instances of intrigues with married women. Spies and agent-provocateurs are asked by him to take advantage of the resulting jealousy and scuffle.[35] Even a false charge of adultery in the family circle is likely to be believed readily.[36] The aggrieved husband might start a duel to vindicate his rights. A woman who makes a false charge of violation and in proof of it shows her own cloth coloured by the blood of another woman is liable to a fine of 100 panas. A man who makes such a false

[30] *AŚ*. IV. 13.

[31] *Ibid*. *Yāj*. III. 232 has a similar passage.

[32] *AŚ*. V. 1.

[33] *AŚ*. IV. 8.

[34] For penalties prescribed by the Smṛitis—Jha., *op.cit.* pp. 481-94. The severity of punishment depends on caste considerations.

[35] *AŚ*. XI.: V. 1 etc.

[36] *AŚ*. V. 1.

charge is equally punishable. According to Kautilya[37] adultery is proved by love marks, loveplays, expert opinion and the evidence of the woman concerned.

Punishments are prescribed not only for the principal offender but for abettors as well. Whoever gives aid or shelter to the offender in connection with the offence is required to be punished in the same manner as the principal culprit.[38] The State seeks to check offence against women. Thus for the abduction of another's wife or daughter, the gallant is liable to arrest at the ferry.[39]

Despite deterrent punishments prescribed in the Smṛitis, many exponents of the orthodox school, strangely enough, ask the husband to treat the adulterous wife with great leniency. As Mm. Kane points out: "The humane character of the legislation of the Indian sages is seen by the fact that even for adultery they do not allow the husband to drive the wife out of the house and to abandon her."[40] The learned author cites texts to show that adultery is a minor sin which can be atoned for by the wife's penance and she is usually entitled to starving maintenance in the meanwhile. On the other hand, the law against adultery was much more stringent in ancient Greece and Rome. As De Coulanges states: "At Athens the husband is allowed to kill the guilty one. At Rome the husband, as the wife's judge, condemns her to death. This religion was so severe that a man had not even the right to pardon completely, and that he was forced at least to repudiate his wife."[41]

Ordinarily a female slave or a slave's daughter falls an easy prey to the master's lust. Very often a slave woman (*dāsī*) is taken as concubine for her master. Kauṭilya, however, seeks to protect her virtue to some extent.[42] Thus, a master who violates a pledged woman (*āhita*) will forfeit the amount for which she is pledged (*mūlyanāśa-karam*). The nurse, maid servants, a female share-cropper (*ardhasītikā*), famale attendants (*upacārikā*) are manumitted (*mokṣakaram*) in case they are violated. A man who forces connections with his own pledged

[37] *AŚ.* IV. 12.
[38] *Ibid.*
[39] *AŚ.* II. 28.
[40] Kane, *HDS.* II. 571ff.
[41] Fustel De Coulanges, *The Ancient City* (Eng. trans.) p. 127; also *SLAR.* 30ff.
[42] *AŚ.* III. 13.

nurse (*āhitikā*) against her consent (*akāmā*) is punishable with the first amercement. If she belongs to some other man, the violator is punishable in the middle amercement. One who violates a virgin pledged girl (*kanyāmāhitikām*) or causes her to be violated by another, forfeits the amount of her price (*mūlyanāśa*), has to pay her bride-price (*śulkam*) and a fine twice that amount. A full-fledged slave woman (*dāsī*), it seems, can be enjoyed by her master. But if she has a child by her master, both mother and child are deemed to be freed from slavery (*svāminastasyāṁ dāsyāṁ jātaṁ samātṛikaṁ adāsaṁ vidyāt*). But if the slave woman continues to remain as a concubine in her master's household (*gṛihyā cet kuṭumbārthacintanī*) her mother, brother and sister are required to be emancipated. For abduction of a slave or slave woman, either mutilation of limbs or a heavy fine of 600 paṇas is prescribed.[43] No wonder a master seeks other means for avoiding the fruit of his indiscretion. Thus, we hear of causing abortion to a slave woman by medicine.[44] This is an offence punishable with the first amercement. Again, a man who violates his slave's or slave woman's daughter, herself a free-woman, has to pay a fine of 24 paṇas. He is also required to give the aggrieved girl her bride-price (*śulkam*) and ornaments (*ābadhya*). For violating a female slave whose ransom has been paid (*niṣkrayānurūpam*), a man is to be fined 12 paṇas and has to give her clothes and ornaments.[45]

It is quite clear that the chastity of a slave woman is not considered as precious as that of a free-woman. Nowhere was it so in the ancient or medieval world. But Kauṭilya's credit lies in granting her some protection against outrage by her master and other persons. On the contrary, if the mistress lives in lust with a slave, servant or a pledged man, both of them are to suffer castration and capital punishment.[46]

Another easy victim is a woman in captivity. The law specially prohibits rape of a captive, slave or hired woman in lock-up, the wife of a thief or a captive *Ārya* lady and the like.[47] If a convict rapes an *Ārya* female convict in the jail, he is required to be killed outright.

[43] *AŚ*. IV. 10.
[44] *AŚ*. III. 20.
[45] *AŚ*. IV. 12.
[46] *AŚ*. IV. 13.
[47] *AŚ*. IV. 9.

The public officer is liable to hang if he commits rape on an *Ārya* woman who has been arrested for untimely movement at night.

A woman working in the state textile factory is equally vulnerable. The *Arthaśāstra* prescribes special regulations for her safety. "Only so much light as is enough to examine the threads shall be kept. If the superintendent looks at the face of such woman or talks about any other work, he shall be punished with the first amercement."[48]

Likewise the policeman on duty is specially forbidden to rape slave women, free maid servants, house-wives (*kulastrī*) or female prisoners. Capital punishment is in store for him if he forces himself on a housewife (*kulastrī*).[49]

The *Arthaśāstra* permits two other forms of extra-marital alliances viz., prostitution and concubinage. The topics will be discussed in detail in the next chapter.

A controversy may very well arise as to the ethics of allowing sexual connections outside connubial relationship. Sociologists have traced their existence in many societies. It is not necessary to go into the details here. Even those who purport to ban such unions have not generally succeeded in living up to their professed ideals. Thus Westermarck observes: "The Christian attitude towards extra-matrimonial connections was fixed by the Church. While looking with suspicion even on the lifelong union of one man with one woman, she pronounced all other forms of sexual intercourse to be mortal sins. But in this, as in many other points of morals, there has always been considerable discrepancy between Christian doctrine and public opinion in Christian countries. The influence of the ascetic doctrine of the Church was in one respect quite contrary to its aspirations; the institution of clerical celibacy created a large class of people to whom illicit love was the only means of gratifying a natural desire, and this could hardly be favourable to the ideal of chastity. During the Middle Ages incontinence was largely an object of ridicule rather than censure, and in the comic literature of that period the clergy were represented as the great corrupters of domestic virtue. Whether the tenet of chastity laid down by the code of chivalry was taken

[48] *AŚ.* II. 23.
[49] *AŚ.* II. 36.

more seriously may be fairly doubted."[50] Even today, many civilized societies permit extra-marital sexual relationship in different garbs.[51] James, however, believes: "Extra-marital manifestations of 'love as an art', as Dr. Havelock Ellis conceives irregular intercourse and liaisons, undermine the biological, psychological and ethical foundations on which the family structure is built in human society, and when the 'unfettered delights' of free love have become exhausted, only the ruins of broken homes and spoilt lives remain on a scene of utter desolation."[52] On the contrary, Bertrand Russell observes: "Those who stimulate the appeals to harry prostitutes and those who secure legislation, nominally against the White Slave Traffic, but really against voluntary and decent extra-marital relations; those who denounce women for short skirts and lipsticks; and those who spy upon sea beaches in the hope of discovering inadequate bathing costumes, are none of them supposed to be the victims of a sexual obsession. Yet in fact they probably suffer much more in this way than do writers who advocate greater sexual freedom. Fierce morality is generally a reaction against lustful emotions, and the man who gives expression to it is generally filled with indecent thoughts—thoughts which are rendered indecent, not by the mere fact that they have a sexual content, but that morality has incapacitated the thinker from thinking cleanly and wholesomely on this topic."[53]

While modern authorities debate on the ethics of extra-marital relationship we may conclude by noting that Kauṭilya does not in fact encourage such relationship, but, as a man of worldly prudence, permits them to exist in some special cases.

---

[50] Westermarck, *Future of Marriage in Western Civilization*, pp. 130-31.

[51] Rattray Taylor points out: "English law does not specifically prohibit the performance of the sexual act between two consenting adults of opposite sexes, but not married to one another whether performed for gain or not." *Sex in History*, p. 307. "The law prohibits as incestuous (i.e., inchaste) sexual relations and *a fortiori*, marriage, between certain near relatives." *ibid.* p. 308.

[52] James, *Marriage & Society*, p. 164.

[53] Bertrand Russell, *Marriage & Morals*, pp. 288-89.

Chapter X

DAUGHTERS OF LOVE

"The real offence of the prostitute," observes Bertrand Russell, "is that she shows up the hollowness of moralistic professions. Like the thoughts repressed by the Freudian censor, she must be banished into the unconscious. Thence, however, as such exiles will, she wreaks an unintended vengeance."[1] But in Kauṭilya's *Arthaśāstra*, as in many other ancient works,[2] prostitution is a well-established institution, not wholly despised or surreptitious and in some cases, even approved and organized by the State. Scholars have traced its existence even in the *Ṛig-Veda*.[3] The *Mahābhārata* indicates its prevalence. So do the Jātakas. By the time of Kauṭilya, prostitution is raised to the status of an art (*Vaiśika-kalā*) which is studied and taught by experts.[4] Vatsyāyana mentions one Dattaka who wrote a special treatise on *Vaiśika*[5] at the request of the courtezans of Pāṭaliputra. It is possible that Kauṭilya has some such work in view.

It appears from the *Arthaśāstra* that prostitution is mainly urban in character. It is generally an adjunct to city-life. For, among the sources of royal income grouped under the head of fort (*durga*), Kauṭilya mentions *Veśyā* (prostitute), *Dyūta* (gambling) and *Surādhyakṣa* (Superintendent of wines).[6] The *Arthaśāstra* refers to a royal officer *Gaṇikādhyakṣa* (Superintendent of courtezans) who looks after prostitution organised and controlled by the state.[7] Kauṭilya also mentions prostitutes attached to the army.[8]

---

[1] Russell, *Marriage & Morals*, pp. 146-47.

[2] J. J. Meyer, *Sexual Life in Ancient India*, Chap. IX. Kane, *HDS*. Vol. I., Part I., Ch. XVI. Sternbach, *Gaṇikā-vritta-Saṁgraha. JAOS*. Vol. 71, "*Legal position of prostitutes*" Jolly, *Hindu Law & Customs*. R. Mehta, *Pre-Buddhist India.*

[3] *R.V.* I. 167. 4 quoted in Kane, *HDS*. Vol. I., Part I, Chap. XVI.

[4] *AŚ*. II. 27.

[5] *AŚ*. I. 1. 11.

[6] *AŚ*. II. 6.

[7] *AŚ*. II. 27.

[8] *AŚ*. X. 1; 3. Speaking of the prostitutes mentioned in the epics Meyer observes: "As so often in other literature, the strumpet is not only the camp's ornaments but

Megasthenes[9] mentions a class of overseers " to whom is assigned the duty of watching all that goes, and making reports secretly to the king. Some are instructed with the inspection of the city and others with that of the army. The former employ as their co-adjutors the courtezans of the city and the latter the courtezans of the camp." The ablest and most trustworthy men are "appointed to fill these offices." The *Arthaśāstra* confirms in material particulars the observations of the Greek envoy.

In the chapter on *Gaṇikādhyakṣa*[10] we get detailed particulars of prostitution organized by the state. *Gaṇikādhyakṣa* grants (*kārayet*) the status of *gaṇikā* (courtezan) to a deserving prostitute. The woman might be born in a courtezan's family or not. The requisite qualifications for the status are beauty, youth and artistic ability. (..... *rūpayauvanaśilpasampannāṁ sahasreṇa gaṇikāṁ kārayet*). *Gaṇikā* obviously is a high rank among public women. According to Vātsyāyana, "A prostitute (*veśyā*) who has good character, beauty and virtue (*śīla-rūpa-guṇānvitā*) and has progressed through the arts shall attain the title of *gaṇikā* and place in the public gathering."[11] In other words, she will no longer be hated as a common harlot. "She will always be worshipped by the king and extolled by gifted persons. She will be desirable, sought after (by people) and an object of notice."[12] We shall see how Kauṭilya makes special provisions for the training of a *gaṇikā* in various arts at the expense of the state.

A *gaṇikā* draws a state grant of 1000 paṇas probably for her establishment. The superintendent also appoints a *pratigaṇikā*,[13] presumably a deputy, enjoying half of the charges for the establishment

---

the ornament too of civic life, that lovely-coloured, scented flower that the city puts in its hair for all to see, when a festival or some other joyful event is being celebrated." *SLAI.* p. 268. It is significant that in some Jātakas the courtezans are described as *nagaraśobhanī* (ornaments of the city). Mehta, *PBI.* p. 294-7.

[9] *Meg.* 25.

[10] *AŚ.* II. 27.

[11] *KS.* I. 3. 20.

[12] *Ibid.*, 21. The *gaṇikā* has aptly been compared with the hetaira in ancient Greece. Of the latter it is said: "Many of them are distinguished by refined education and a wit quick at repartee; they know how to fascinate the most distinguished personalities of their time." Helbig quoted in Licht. *SLAG.*, p. 339. Portrait statues of such women were even kept in the Greek temples. (*ibid*). For ancient Rome, *SLAR.* pp. 57-59.

[13] Sternbach, *Legal Position of Prostitutes* according to Kauṭilya's Arthaśāstra, *JAOS.* Vol. 71. p. 26.

(*kuṭumba*). In the case of the death or desertion (*niṣpatita*) of a courtezan, her establishment descends to her sister or daughter whose duty it is to run it. Alternatively, her mother places the *pratigaṇikā*, the deputy, in her stead. In default of these successors, the establishment escheats to the crown.

The courtezans are classified in three grades on the basis of their attractiveness (*saubhāgya*) and ornaments. They draw accordingly, the state grants of 1000, 2000 and 3000 paṇas.

On the basis of their attractiveness, the superintendent engages them in holding the royal umbrella, vase and fan or attending upon the king seated on his royal litter, throne or chariot. Their presence heightens the colour and charm of the royal entourage. Ordinary slave girls (*dāsī*), however, attend to the king's personal comforts.[14] It seems that the courtezans (*gaṇikās*) generally associate with the king, when he has public contact; the slave girls (*dāsī*) cater to his private needs; while *rūpājīvās*, having beauty as their stock-in-trade, wait upon the royal wives.

According to Sternbach, "*gaṇikā* means only a government servant, similarly to any other government servant. . . . . Whenever the word *gaṇikā* is used in the text of Kauṭilya, it has this specific meaning and should not be confused with prostitutes who work on their own account." It seems, however, that the learned writer somewhat exaggerates the administrative status of the *gaṇikā*. She is no doubt paid and controlled by the state, with regard to her person as well as finances. She is also allowed to terminate her obligations (*niṣkraya*) to the state. Yet there is reason to believe that, subject to some governmental regulations, she is allowed to act on her own. The salary granted to her by the state is most likely in lieu of her personal services rendered to the king himself, for example, holding the royal umbrella, vase and so on. But in respect of her ordinary profession she is more or less free. Because of her threefold accomplishment, she enjoys special privileges from and undergoes special control by the state. There is no such privilege or control in the case of prostitutes of inferior types. A *gaṇikā*, according to the *Arthaśāstra*, is entitled to receive private patrons on payment of various fees.

According to Sternbach, *pratigaṇikā* is a "substitute *ganikā*, that

[14] *AŚ*. I. 21.

is a government servant with whom the contract was concluded for a short duration only, that is, for the duration of the leave of the *gaṇikā*, when she went abroad. She could become in the future a *gaṇikā*, but as long as she was only a *pratigaṇikā* she received only half of the salary of the *gaṇikā* for whom she substituted."[15] In other words, according to the learned author, it seems that her appointment is temporary. But it appears that she has a permanent status. She is very likely a deputy or a probationer under the *gaṇikā* and for her services she receives half the salary. The *pratigaṇikā* steps into the place of the *gaṇikā* when the latter dies or deserts or gives up (*niṣpatita*) her profession.

Kauṭilya's observations on the courtezan's association with the king have parallels in other ancient works. The Greek writers observe how the king is attended by courtezans at the palace, in the battlefield, on hunting expeditions and on various other occasions. Thus Curtius Rufus[16] writes of an Indian King: "amid the vows and songs of his courtezans he shoots the game enclosed within the royal park. . . . That no form of shameless profligacy may be wanting, he is accompanied by a long train of courtezans carried in golden palanquins, and this troop holds a separate place in the procession from the queen's retinue, and is as sumptuously appointed. His food is prepared by women, who also serve him with wine, which is much used by all the Indians. When the king falls into a drunken sleep his courtezans carry him away to his bed chamber, invoking the gods of the night in their native hymns." This luxurious splendour is characterised by the Greek writer as "corruption of morals". Megasthenes[17] also records: "The care of the king's person is entrusted to women, who also are bought from their parents." When the king sets out on a hunting excursion, he, observes Megasthenes,[18] "departs in Bacchanalian fashion. Crowds of women surround him. . . . The king hunts in the enclosures and shoots arrows from a platform. At his side stand two or three armed women. . . . Of the women, some are

---

[15] *Ibid.*, p. 28. The word *niṣpatita* does not seem to be connected with 'leave' as Sternbach thinks. It seems to mean 'desertion,' cf. *AŚ.* II. 4. where the word has the sense of unauthorised coming out or falling off.

[16] *MC. I.*, p. 189.

[17] *Meg.* 70.

[18] *Ibid.* 71.

in chariots, some on horses and some even on elephants and they are equipped with weapons of every kind as if they were going on a campaign."

The *Mahābhārata*, too, gives us colourful descriptions of prostitutes and their intimate connection with the royal splendour. "The Ādiparva (115·39) narrates how a *veśyā* waited upon Dhṛitarāṣṭra when his wife Gāndhārī was pregnant. In the Udyogaparva (30·38) Yudhisṭhira sends greetings to the *veśyās* of the Kauravas. Courtezans are described as going out to welcome Kṛiṣṇa when he came on a mission of peace to Kaurava Court (Udyoga, 86·15). When the Pāṇḍava armies are described as about to start for battle it is said that carts, markets and courtezans also accompanied them (Udyoga, 151·58)."[19] In the *Ramāyaṇa*, Rāma asks his younger brother Bharata if he is not satisfied with the courtezans (*gaṇikā*), horses and elephants.[20] The Jātakas, too, tell similar tales.[21] All these different sources tend to show that the ancient society did not generally consider the king's association with courtezans to be sinful or immoral.

As in the days of the *Mahābhārata*, *Arthaśāstra* mentions women accompanying royal troops. In the arrangement of camps in the battlefield, the king and his harem are placed at the centre.[22] Food and beverage for the army are made by women.[23] With these articles they stand behind and utter encouraging words to fighting men.[24] Army discipline, however, prohibits drinking, social gathering and gambling in the camp.[25] *Veśyās* (common prostitutes) obviously frequent the soldiers, for these women are required to spy upon military men.[26] Thus, whether in the palace or in the battlefield, public women are found to play colourful roles in the *Arthaśāstra*.

How are these courtezans recruited ? Some come from the family of courtezans (*gaṇikānvaya*),[27] some by purchase from their parents,[28]

[19] Kane, *HDS*. II. Ch. XVI. p. 636-37.
[20] *Rām*. II. 100. 50.
[21] Mehta, *PBI*. p. 294-97.
[22] *AŚ*. x. 2.
[23] *AŚ*. x. 3.
[24] *Ibid*.
[25] *AŚ*. x. 1.
[26] *AŚ*. v. 3.
[27] *AŚ*. II. 27.
[28] *Meg*. 70.

some by capture in warfare and some by way of punishment for adultery.

The *Arthaśāstra* throws some light on the *gaṇikā*'s private life. She has her own family (*anvaya*). Among her relations, her mother (*mātā*), sister (*bhaginī*), daughter (*duhitṛikā*) and son (*putra*) are mentioned. The mother exercises some sort of general supervision on the *gaṇikā*'s private affairs. The former is allowed to keep the latter's ornaments for safe custody and to substitute the *pratigaṇikā* in her place and stead in the case of the *gaṇikā*'s death or desertion. The mother herself might be an experienced woman. On the retirement of the *gaṇikā*, due to a fall in her good luck (*saubhāgya-bhaṅga*), she is placed in the position of a *mātṛikā*. The work might indicate the office of the matron as distinguished from the mother. The *gaṇikā*'s sister or daughter has a right of succession to her establishment (*kuṭumba*). The daughter enjoys special protection against assault.[29] A man forcibly assaulting a *gaṇikā*'s daughter has to pay a fine of 54 paṇas to the state and a *śulka*, sixteen times the mother's fees, probably to the aggrieved party (*gaṇikāduhitaraṁ prakurvataścatuṣpañcāśat paṇa daṇḍaḥ, śulkaṁ māturbhogaḥ ṣoḍaśaguṇaḥ*).[30] The word *śulka* usually means bride-price payable in connection with marriage. If the word is used here in this sense, it might connote a practice of marriage of the *gaṇikā*'s daughter. Vātsyāyana mentions[31] a form of marriage of such a girl. This form is, however, not an ordinary marriage but somewhat a ceremony of initiation of the girl in the mysteries of the profession. No reference, however, is made in the *Arthaśāstra* to the existence of a *gaṇikā*'s husband.

A *gaṇikā*'s son is bound down to the state, perhaps as a slave. From eight years of age, he is engaged in holding musical performance (*kuśīlavakarma*) before the king. A *gaṇikā* can acquit herself of her obligation to the state upon payment of 24000 paṇas. His son, too, can do so by paying 12000 paṇas. The price of liberty in the case of her son appears to be comparatively high. How can this sum be procured and what will be the status of the person after freedom (*niṣkraya*) is bought? The *Arthaśāstra* is silent on these points. The Jain

[29] *AŚ*. II. 27.
[30] *AŚ*. IV. 12.
[31] *KS*. VII. 1. 16-22.

writer, Hemachandra, records a tradition that King Nanda was the son of a barber by a courtezan.[32]

A *gaṇikā*, as suggested by the *Arthaśāstra*, has a choice in the selection of her callers, except in one case. When the king forces a companion on her, she has to accept him. In default, she is whipped a thousand times or has to pay a heavy fine of 5000 paṇas. Thus, a *gaṇikā*'s person is under the disposal of the king. Subject to this exception, law honours the desire of a *gaṇikā*. Thus, a person forcibly dealing with a *gaṇikā* against her will (*akāmāyāḥ*) is punishable with the highest amercement, while another confining a *gaṇikā* against her desire (*gaṇikāmakāmāṁ rundhato*) is ordinarily fined 1000 paṇas and in some cases even more. Once, however, a *gaṇikā* has accepted her fees, she is fined twice the amount of her fees, in case she shows hatred (*dviṣatyā*) for her lover. If she has accepted fees for allowing her lover the pleasure of residing with her (*vasatibhoga*), she is fined eight times the fees, in case she wrongfully refuses him (*apahāre*). Even in such cases, she can refuse a patron on account of his or her disease or his defects (*anyatra vyādhi puruṣadoṣebhyaḥ*). Conversely, if her patron does not pay her fees, he is fined eight times the amount. Thus, it appears that the contract between a *gaṇikā* and her caller is not void in law on the ground of immorality. Kauṭilya does not specifically state if a private person can place a *gaṇikā* in his exclusive keeping. Sternbach thinks: "*Gaṇikā* were also not allowed to become *avaruddhā*". But Kauṭilya's statement: "*gaṇikāmakāmām rundhato*" may suggest to the contrary that it is possible to keep (*rundhato*) with impunity a *sakāmā gaṇikā*. Even then she is subject to the overriding dominion of the king. She can be discharged (*niṣkraya*) of her obligations to the state only upon payment of 24000 paṇas.

A *gaṇikā* is entitled to own private property. Apart from the salary she receives from the state, she is entitled to ornaments (*alaṅkāra*), dress (*ābharaṇa*), moneys (*artha*), fees (*bhoga*), inherited properties (*dāya*), actual profit (*āya*) and prospective profit (*āyati*). She is also entitled to have slave women (*gaṇikādāsī*). The latter in her turn can be kept as a concubine (*avaruddhā*). In that case, she pays her mistress an amount equivalent to the monthly salary (*māsavetana*) plus 1 paṇa. There is also the *rūpadāsī* (beautiful maid servant), possibly attached to

[32] Hemachandra, *Pariśiṣṭaparvan*, VI. 232.

the *gaṇikā*'s household. It is the duty of the *gaṇikā* to inform the superintendent of her fees, prospective profit and paramours. The officer in his turn keeps a record of the *gaṇikā*'s fees, inherited property, actual profit, expenditure and prospective profit. He is also to stop her extravagance. Moreover, she is not fully competent to deal with all her properties. She cannot keep her ornaments in deposit (*nyāsa*) with anybody except her mother. For the sale or mortgage of her property (*svāpateya*), the *gaṇikā* has to pay a small fine of 50¼ paṇas. Thus, she seems to be a limited owner only. This restriction is perhaps necessary to prevent her from squandering away her fortune. Moreover, ornaments (*ābharaṇa*) constitute a portion of her stock-in-trade. On her death or desertion, her establishment (*kuṭumba*) descends to her sister or daughter or deputy (*pratigaṇikā*) and, in default of these successors, to the state. It is significant that the *gaṇikā*'s son does not appear to succeed to his mother's estate.[33]

According to Kauṭilya the state should look after these accomplished public women in their dark days. If she loses her attractiveness (*saubhāgya-bhaṅge*), a *gaṇikā* is made a matron (*mātṛikā*) possibly to guide the younger ones. A *gaṇikā*'s female slave (*gaṇikādāsī*) losing her

[33] Sternbach (*ibid.*, p. 34-35) observes: "The king paid a salary to *gaṇikā* but their income belonged to him." Again, ".... the *gaṇikādhyakṣa* fixed or determined the gifts (*dāya*), the gross receipts (*āya*), the gross expenditure (*vyaya*), the net income, profit (*āyati*)." Elsewhere, he translates '*āyati*' as expenditure. It is difficult to agree with the views of the learned author. The word *nibandhayet* used by Kauṭilya in this context appears to mean "should record" and not "fix or determine" as Sternbach seems to hold. The officer's duty is, it seems, to record the extent of wealth and expenses of the *gaṇikā*. Restrictions on her right of free disposition might have been directed against her improvidence. The text does not show that the *gaṇikā*'s income filled the royal coffers. The salary is paid to the *gaṇikā* probably in consideration of her personal services rendered to the king or at his behest. Her beauty, youth and accomplishment add to the royal splendour. Again, commenting on the restrictions on the *gaṇikā*'s power of disposition of her property, Sternbach states: "Both the above (Dr. Shama Sastry and J. J. Meyer) translate *svāpateya* by own property, that is the property of a *gaṇikā*. If we understand the context in this sense, than (*sic*) *gaṇikā* would not have any right to any property. Everything that they possessed would be used by them on a usufructual basis; they would have the right to use it as long as they lived, but would not be entitled to inherit it, since *gaṇikā* would not have the ownership over it. Such an understanding seems to be wrong, since we have a very clear ruling as to the right of inheritance of the property of the deceased *gaṇikā*" (*ibid*, p. 39). This criticism seems to be based on a misconception of the idea of ownership. The text "*Svāpateyam vikrayamādhānaṁ nayantyāḥ sapādapañcāśatpaṇo daṇḍaḥ*" merely prohibits the right of sale or mortgage. It does not suggest that the property is not heritable or disposable otherwise than by sale or mortgage. In other words, a *gaṇikā* is a limited owner without the powers of sale and mortgage.

power of entertainment (*bhagnabhogā*) is required to be employed in the king's storehouse or kitchen.[34]

The brothel, as depicted in the *Arthaśāstra*, is as usual a den of crimes. Offences may be by or against the *gaṇikā* and in some cases against her relations also. The *Arthaśāstra* mentions wrongs against the person or properties of the parties. As for wrongs done to the person of the *gaṇikā* or her relations we hear of grievous hurt, wrongful restraint, abduction, disfigurement of beauty, rape and causing death. Offences of abuse, assaults, and mutilation of ears are likely to be committed by either of the parties—the inmates of and the visitors to the brothel. Visitors run the danger of being murdered and their dead bodies might be burnt in the pyre or thrown into the water. Offences relating to the breach of contract have already been noted. Offences relating to the properties of the *gaṇikā* include theft of ornaments and moneys.

Various punishments are prescribed for these offences, according to their nature and the position or status of the victim (*sthānaviśeṣeṇa*). When a man has connection with a prostitute against her will or with an immature girl (*kumārī*), he is liable to be punished with the highest amercement. Likewise, causing hurt to the courtezan's mother, young daughter or a *rūpadāsī* is sought to be penalised.

Apart from *gaṇikās* or courtezans, the text mentions other categories of public women, viz:—

(*a*) *Rūpājīvā*—Literally, one who lives on her beauty. She seems to be a prostitute who does not have artistic accomplishments but possesses charm as her only stock-in-trade. She is required to pay two days' fees as tax to the state. A fine of 12 paṇas only is prescribed for forcible connection with

---

[34] Sternbach concludes: "Hence, *gaṇikā* who lost their beauty and popularity but were not too old had to receive another lower office where their income was lower; they had to become procuresses in the service of the king and, if they became very old and were completely incapable of rendering any service to the king either as *gaṇikā* or *mātṛikā*, they had to work in the storehouse or kitchen of the king where they received some kind of remuneration" (*ibid*, 36). This conclusion is not wholly correct. It seems to be based on the miscreading of "*Gaṇikādāsī*" as "*gaṇikā* or *dāsī*" as Sternbach does. The context clearly shows that by the word a female slave of a *gaṇikā* is meant here (*Gaṇikādāsī bhagnabhogā koṣṭhāgare mahānase vā karma kuryāt*: *aviśantī sapādapanamavaruddhā māsavetana dadyāt*). A *gaṇikā* seems to have been too much accomplished in various arts to be employed in stores or kitchen. On the contrary, her old slave can be a fit person for such prosaic jobs.

her,[35] whereas for a similar offence against a *gaṇikā*, the punishment imposed is higher. Apparently, *rūpājīvā* is below the rank of a *gaṇikā*, yet she is not a common prostitute, for a *rūpājīvā*, fresh from bath, wearing clean dress and ornaments, has access to the royal harem.[36] In national emergency she is required to pay half her fees to the state coffer.[37] She can be in the exclusive keeping of a man. Anyone else cohabiting with such a harlot is fined 48 paṇas.[38] *Rūpājīvā* and other women spies in the garb of wives might be used to help a captive prince escape.[39] She too has her *mātṛikā*. *Rūpājīvās* have special quarters in the city.[40] Vātsyāyana also mentions this type of harlots who trade upon their good looks.[41]

(*b*) *Rūpadāsī*—Woman who on account of her beauty seems to be employed in personal attendance.[42] She may be compared with a *vaṇṇa dāsī*, mentioned in the Jātakas in which the latter is found to serve under some *gaṇikā* or receive callers herself.[43]

(*c*) *Gaṇikādāsī*[44]—Female slave of the courtezan. She might cease to call at the house of her mistress and become a kept woman on payment of nominal fee. In the Jātakas[45] *gaṇikā* Sāmā of Benares was a favourite of the kings and had a train of five hundred female slaves (*vaṇṇadāsiyo*).

(*d*) *Mātṛikā*—The retired *gaṇikā*, generally engaged in training and looking after *gaṇikās*. *Mātṛikā* of a *rūpājīvā* might be employed in the state textile industry.

(*e*) *Kumārī*, *duhitṛikā*,—immature girls or daughters of *gaṇikā*. They are specially protected by law.[46] A man cohabiting

---

35 *AŚ*. IV, 13.
36 *AŚ*. I. 20.
37 *AŚ* V. 2.
38 *AŚ*. III. 20.
39 *AŚ*. VIII 17.
40 *AŚ*. II. 4.
41 *KŚ*. VI. 6.54.
42 *AŚ*. II. 27.
43 *Jātaka*, II. 380; III. 59-63, 69-72; III. 475-8.
44 AŚ. II. 27.
45 *Jātaka*, III. 59-63.
46 *AŚ*. II. 27.

with any such girl is required to pay a fine to the state and sixteen times her mother's fees as *śulka* or bride-price.

(*f*) A miscellaneous class comprising the wives of actors, dancers, singers, players on musical instruments, buffoons, mimic-players, rope-dancers, jugglers, wandering bards and persons who used their wives for a living (*strīvyavahāriṇām striyaḥ*) and harlots carrying their trade in secret.[47] Laxity in morals among women-folk of these professional groups is indicated in the *Arthaśāstra*. The laws relating to the *Gaṇikā* are said to apply to these loose women *mutatis mutandis*. The foreign artistes are required to pay five paṇas as tax to the state. Vātsyāyana includes *Naṭī* (actress) and *Śilpakārikā* (craftswoman) in the category of public women.[48] Elsewhere he mentions the wife of a musician or a dancer among women who can be had for the mere asking.[49]

Kauṭilya requires the state to make adequate provisions for the training of *gaṇikās, dāsīs* (slavewomen) and *raṅgopajīvinīs* (female artistes who live on entertainment). The state dominion (*rājamaṇḍala*) has to maintain the teachers for these women. The curriculum includes singing, playing on musical instruments, reading, dancing, stagecraft, writing, painting, playing on harp, flute and drum, thought-reading (*paracittajñāna*), preparation of scents and garlands, massage and the art of prostitutes.[50] Vātsyāyana gives us the well-known list of sixtyfour *kalās* or arts,[51] which may profitably be compared with the list given by Kauṭilya. Most of the topics mentioned by Kauṭilya are found in Vātsyāyana's list. But the former suggests basic training, e.g., reading and writing (*pāṭhya* and *akṣara*), while the latter provides for specialisation, e.g., *pustakavachanam* (reading from books in melodious tones), *kāvyakriyā* (composing poems), *akṣaramuṣṭikākathanam* (deciphering code-words). Vātsyāyana's list is more exhaustive. According to him, a knowledge of these arts will help a prostitute to attain the rank of a *gaṇikā*. His curriculum, however, is meant for all. Sometimes these

---

[47] *AŚ*. II. 27.
[48] *KS*. VI. S. 54.
[49] *KS*. V. 1. 51.
[50] *AŚ*. II. 27.
[51] *KS*. I. 3.

public women taught others in the arts.[52] The sons of courtezans are, according to the *Arthaśāstra*, made leaders of the artistes who live upon dancing and entertainment. The course of study mentioned in the *Arthaśāstra* obviously makes these women fit for the callings they undertake. It is significant to note that only three classes of public women are required by Kauṭilya to receive training at the expense of the state. Women, expert in all these attractive arts, no doubt, as Vātsyāyana also suggests, occupy coveted place in society. The Buddhist works tell us of famous *gaṇikās* Ambapāli, Sālāvatī, Sāmā, Sulasā and others who rose to a high position of honour through their intellectual and artistic accomplishments.[53] Politically, these accomplished women render much service to the state. They are part and parcel of the royal splendour. They attend to the king's person and pleasure. Some of them pay taxes to the state. In case of emergency, the state fleeces these girls or forces them to raise funds. From their circles, attractive spies are recruited. Versed in languages and signs, wives of the professional artistes are employed in detecting the wicked and murdering and deluding foreign spies.[54] On growing old, some of these women are employed in the royal storehouse, kitchen or the state textile industry.[55]

In addition to the organised prostitution under the control of the Superintendent of Courtezans, the *Arthaśāstra* mentions many women who indulge in unregulated liaison. Thus, we hear of:—

(*a*) *Puṁścalī*—a common whore who has connections with ordinary people. She is mentioned along with slaves and labourers. With no fixed fees, she might claim the price only on the proof of the marks of cohabitation. She is liable to forfeit her fee if she tries to squeeze money from her paramour or shows bad temper or insubordination.[56] Such a woman, herself a suspect,[57] is engaged by the government in watching the movements of suspects.[58]

(*b*) *Barmaids*—Often maids of exquisite beauty are employed

[52] *KS*. VI. 1.9
[53] Mehta, *Ibid.*
[54] *AŚ*. II. 27.
[55] *AŚ*. II. 23.
[56] *AŚ*. III. 13.
[57] *AŚ*. IV. 6.
[58] *AŚ*. IV. 8.

by barkeepers. The bars are provided with separate chambers, with seats and beds, furnished with scents, garlands, water and delicacies of the season. Persons appearing to belong to the high status (*Ārya*), aliens or denizens, are used to sleep there in a drunken condition. Barmaids in attendance are required by the *Arthaśāstra* to spy upon them and report to the barkeepers.[59] They might be compared with *Kumbhadāsī* mentioned in the Jātakas[60] and in the Kāmasūtra.[61]

(*c*) *Vandhakī*—housewife who turns into a whore. Often men live on her income (*vandhakīpoṣaka*). These men are required to pay special tax in case of national emergency and with the help of exquisitely charming and youthful women earn wealth for the state coffer.[62] They seem to associate with men of the upper strata. These men by devious means use women to stir up quarrel among leaders of non-monarchical states[63] and of armed forces.[64] They may be compared with *kulaṭā* and *svairiṇī*, both married strumpets, mentioned by Vātsyāyana.[65] The Nātyaśāstra describes a special type of play (*Prakaraṇa*) dealing with the exploits of depraved women of good family.[66]

(*d*) *Veśyā*—They are mentioned in the *Arthaśāstra* along with *kārukuśīlava* and spies. They are required to watch the conduct of soldiers.[67] The term seems to be generic.

(*e*) Women passing off as pious ladies (*Sādhvivyañjana*)—In their own house they receive callers. They often tempt traitors and cause them to be arrested and fleeced by the state officers.[68] These are opposites of *Prakāśa-vinaṣṭā* mentioned by Vātsyāyana.

---

[59] *AŚ*. II. 25.
[60] *Jātaka* v. 403; VI. 252.
[61] *KS*. VI. 6. 54.
[62] *AŚ*. v. 2.
[63] *AŚ*. XI. 1 (*Bandhakīpoṣakaḥ............strībhiḥ paramarūpayauvanābhiḥ saṁghamukhyān unmādayeyuḥ*)
[64] *AŚ*. XII. 2.
[65] *AŚ*. VI. 54.
[66] *NŚ*. XX. 63.
[67] *AŚ*. v. 3.
[68] *AŚ*. v. 2.

(*f*) *Devadāsī*—Kauṭilya mentions her only once in connection with women who find employment in the state textile factory. Kauṭilya provides that *devadāsīs* (literally, female slaves of the god) who have ceased to attend the temple (*vyuparatopasthānadevadāsībhiścha*) should be engaged in such a factory. Apart from their association with the temple, Kauṭilya does not mention the nature of work they are expected to do in the temple. They are mentioned along with matrons of prostitutes (*rūpājīvā mātṛikā*) and old royal slave-women (*vṛddharājadāsībhiḥ*).[69] This might suggest that the *devadāsīs* are likely to be loose women. Later literature shows that they were sacred prostitutes connected with temples.[70]

(*g*) Mendicant women (*Parivrājikā*)—Often of loose character, she acts as procuress or go-between. A man cohabiting with a *pravrajikā* is liable to a fine of 24 paṇas only, that is to say, twice the amount of fine for forcing himself on a harlot (*rūpājīvā*).[71] The nun submitting herself to the man is fined that small amount. The state often employs such women in nefarious activities. In return they get employment in the state textile industry.[72]

With regard to their relations with paramours, the prostitutes may be divided into two categories, viz. *avaruddhā* and the rest. *Avaruddhā* or a concubine is in the exclusive keeping of her lover. We have seen that a *rūpājīvā* and a *gaṇikādāsī* can be kept for exclusive companionship. The law protects such relationship by imposing a fine on the man other than the paramour for intercourse with an *avaruddhā*.[73] In the case of the other category, there is no such exclusive relationship.[74]

Kauṭilya's attitude towards prostitution is worthy of note. In the first place, his law recognises this institution and within proper limits, protects such an extra-marital relationship. Compact between a prostitute and her paramour is not void for immorality. The state

[69] *AŚ.* II. 23.
[70] Sternbach, *ibid.* p. 48.
[71] *AŚ.* IV. 13.
[72] *AŚ.* II. 23. For further details Chapter XI, *infra.*
[73] *AŚ.* III. 20.
[74] Dharmaśāstras of Yāj. & Nār. refers to *avaruddhā* & *bhujiṣyā*. Sternbach, *ibid.*, p. 49. Kane, HDS. II. 636-37.

organises a part of this profession and derives many advantages from it. Kauṭilya takes prostitution for granted. He neither approves nor disapproves of it. He seeks to minimise the dangers of violence, improvidence and the like inherent in it. Like a practical man, he tries to elicit as much good as possible out of prostitution and utilises it for the purpose of the state. He seems to designate the association with public women by the generic term *bāhya vihāra.* He does not ban it, but allows the chaste wife to correct her wayward husband by abusing or beating him within the limits fixed by law.[75] Vātsyāyana perhaps correctly expresses the general social attitude of his time towards prostitution. He observes: "To have sexual intercourse with courtezans and widows is neither approved nor prohibited as recourse to such acts is only for the sake of pleasure but not with śāstric objects."[76]

Even though prostitution is allowed to exist, the ancient writers seek to keep it within proper bounds. Thus, the Nāṭyaśāstra lays down:[77] "(In an act of the *prakaraṇa*) where a minister, head of the merchants' guild, Brāhmiṇ, priest, leader of the caravan stay in their family circle, no courtezan should be brought in there. When a person is in company of a courtezan there should not be (at the same time) his meeting with any respectable woman (lit. woman of good family), and while he is with a person of high family, no courtezan should meet him then. If out of necessity (lit. reason) there occurs a meeting of courtezans and respectable ladies in (any scene of) a *prakaraṇa* their language and manners should be kept undistorted." The courtezan in Bhāsa's Chārudatta expresses in soliloquy, "I am unworthy of being allowed entrance into the harem."[78] These passages show how the social etiquette seeks to keep prostitution at some distance from the respectable circles in society.

Lecky considers prostitution to be a safety-valve for the excessive force of passions. According to him, prostitutes protect the family "from the incursions of irregular passions." "Herself the supreme type of vice, she is ultimately the most efficient guardian of virtue. But for her the unchallenged purity of countless happy homes would be polluted...... She remains while creeds and civilizations rise

[75] *AŚ.* III. 3.
[76] *KS.* I. 53.
[77] *NŚ.* xx. 54-56, Ghose's translation.
[78] I. 26-38, quoted by Ghose, *NŚ.* p. LXXXV.

and fall, the eternal priestess of humanity, blasted for the sins of the people."[79] "Moralists," observes Bertrand Russell, "have denounced Lecky because his remark made them feel furious and they did not quite know why, but they have not succeeded in showing that what he said was untrue."[80]

In view of these observations of modern western thinkers, Kauṭilya's concern for the organization and control of prostitution through law becomes intelligible. If he cannot stop it, he can at best seek to sublimate it.

Even the orthodox Dharmaśāstras do not denounce prostitution in strong terms.[81] Manu forbids a Brāhmin to take food from a *gaṇikā*, a *puṁścalī* and a wife sheltering a paramour.[82] In the same list he includes people like doctors, dyers, vinters, goldsmiths, members of a *gaṇa* (non-monarchical groups) and so on. By taking food from such persons, a Brāhmaṇa is supposed to incur various sins. Manu also calls upon the king to bring skilful prostitutes (*nipuṇāḥ paṇyayoṣitaḥ*) under control.[83] Like Kauṭilya, Yājñavalkya and Nārada protect one's exclusive relationship with a concubine or kept woman.[84] Nārada further permits one's intercourse with a non-Brahmin wanton woman (*svairiṇī*), a common prostitute (*veśyā*), a female slave (*dāsī*), a woman who does not maintain the purdāh (*niṣkāsinī*), if they belong to a caste lower than one's own and are not kept mistresses of another man.[85]

Kauṭilya, however, goes a step ahead of these Dharmaśāstras by requiring the state to organize some important classes of prostitutes through a government officer.

---

[79] *History of European Morals*, Vol. II, p. 119.
[80] Russell, *Marriage and Morals*, p. 145.
[81] Kane, *HDS*. II. 638. Some Smṛitis prescribe penance for connection with a prostitute.
[82] *Manu*. IV. 209; 211; 216 cf Gautama. III. 6. 10.
[83] *Manu*. IX. 259.
[84] *Yāj*. II. 290; *Nārada Strīpuṁsa*, 78-79.
[85] *Nārada*, *ibid*., quoted in Kane, *HDS*. II. 1. p. 638.

Chapter XI

CELIBACY AND ASCETICISM

The history of Indian philosophy shows a recurring conflict between domestic and ascetic ideals. "From the early Vedic times," observes Dr. Radhakrishnan, "there had been in India ascetic tempers who had cut themselves adrift from the responsibilities of life and wandered free. We have seen in the Upaniṣads how in their love for the supreme, some 'relinquish the desire for children, the struggle for wealth, the pursuit of worldly weal, and go forth as mendicants.' The Brāhmaṇical codes recognised the right of those to sever themselves from the duties of life and the observance of rites."[1]

The ascetic ideal is further accentuated by the Buddhists. "Full of hindrances is household life, a path defiled by passion; free as air is the life of him who renounced all worldly things, ... let me go forth from a household life into the homeless stage."[2] This clarion call of the Buddhists attracted a host of followers, men and women, young and old, who readily cut off the bond of home life and sought for supreme happiness in the pursuit of monastic ideals. All of them, however, did not succeed. Some failed to persevere in the new environment and some could not live up to its high standard. In any event, the foundations of home and all that it stands for, were rudely shaken.[3]

The *āśrama* theory shows a via media between two extreme ideals of home life and hermitage. "Their (Brāhmaṇas') supreme genius for compromise and adjustment of differences probably led later to the formation of the wonderful theory of *Āśramas* or different stages of Āryan life."[4] Asceticism has its place in life, but at a proper time or on a suitable occasion. Kauṭilya, a firm believer in the *āśrama* ideal, is opposed to untimely asceticism.

---

[1] Radhakrishnan, *Indian Philosophy*, Vol. I, p. 435.

[2] *Tevijja Sutta*, 1. 47 quoted in *ibid.*

[3] Some instances of the chaotic conditions in society caused by untimely asceticism are to be found in Therīgāthā.

[4] *HCIP*. I. 493.

The householder, as we have seen, has a duty to marry (*vaivāhyam*). To this order belong the great mass of the people including the *Śūdras*. Father should get his daughter married. If he fails within the prescribed time, she is allowed to choose her own mate. Thus, in theory at least, marriage is the rule and celibacy the exception. A student (*brahmacārin*) is required to be a celibate. When his period of study is over, he is expected to marry and enter the stage of the householder. The *naiṣṭhika brahmacārin* is an exception to the general rule. He has to spend his whole life in the house of his teacher or the preceptor's son or with another student (*ācārye prāṇāntikī vṛittistadabhāve guruputre sabrahmacāriṇi vā*).[5] A student's duty includes complete sexual abstinence. In fact, the word *brahmacarya* is derived from him and connotes the duty of continence.

Upon retirement from the stage of a householder, a person enters that of a *vānaprastha* or forest recluse. He is required to observe chastity (*brahmacarya*), practise hard life, sleep on bare ground, keep twisted locks, wear deer skin, perform light religious rites and live upon wild food (*vanyaścāhāra*).[6] We do not learn from the *Arthaśāstra* if his wife goes with him into the forest. According to other sources, she might do so if she liked.[7] But abstention from sexual intercourse is a necessary duty.[8] The *vānaprastha* need not go far from the village. In fact, Kauṭilya allows him to settle in the countryside (*vānaprasthādanyaḥ pravrajitabhāvaḥ......nāsya janapadamupaniveśeta*).[9] In the last stage of the life's journey the *parivrājaka* or wanderer is required to control his senses (*saṁyatendriyatvam*), lead a solitary (*saṅgatyāga*) passive life in the forest, give up all rights to property (*niṣkiñcanatvam*), beg from different places and be pure in mind and body.[10]

From the economic point of view, all these three stages are non-productive; while the student and the wanderer depend upon alms

---

[5] *AŚ.* I. 2. Further details of the rights and obligations of the lifelong students are found in Kane, *HDS.* Vol. II, Part I. p. 375-76. Manu speaks with approbation of "many thousand unmarried Brāhmin *Brahmacārins* who have gone to Heaven without perpetuating the family" (V. 157-60).

[6] *AŚ.* I. 2 ; also Kane, *HDS.* Vol. II, Part II. Chap. XXVII.

[7] Kane, *HDS.* Vol. II, Part II, p. 918, 923.

[8] One possible exception is mentioned in Kane, *HDS.* II. 920.

[9] *AŚ.* II. 1.

[10] *AŚ.* I. 2 ; also Kane, *HDS.* II. Chap. XXVIII for similar duties mentioned in the Dharmaśāstras.

(*bhaikṣam*), the recluse gathers his food from the forest. Biologically, they do not contribute to the perpetuation of the race. The wanderer has also to fight the gregarious instinct (*saṅgatyāga*) and roam about in search of alms (*bhaikṣamanekatra*). He surrenders all rights to property. Society, obviously, cannot continue if all or substantially all run after such ideals. Following the *āśrama* theory Kauṭilya likes to place the non-productive and non-procreative elements within proper bounds in society. The state, as we have seen, is called upon to enforce the performance of one's own duties (*svadharma*) assigned by law.

Thus Kauṭilya regulates asceticism in different ways. He prescribes[11] the punishment of the first degree (i.e., a fine between 48 and 96 paṇas) for taking to asceticism without making provisions for the wife and children (*putradāramapratividhāya pravrajataḥ pūrvasāhasa-daṇḍaḥ*). Like punishment is prescribed for initiating a woman to asceticism. Even the senescent (*luptavyavaya*) requires approval of the civil judge (*dharmasthān*) before adopting asceticism. Otherwise he is to be restrained (*niyamyeta*). *Pravrajyā* can break up the marital tie. The wife of a *pravrajita* is asked to wait for seven menses or one year if she is barren or otherwise. After that period she is allowed to re-marry. Again, except the recluse (*vānaparastha*) following the approved order, ascetics are not allowed to settle in the countryside. The same rule applies to religious bodies (*saṁgha*) other than *Sajāta* (identified with the Buddhists). The reason is perhaps clear. These non-productive elements are probably not permitted to live upon the producers in the countryside. A special restriction is imposed on the heretical ascetics (*pāṣaṇḍas*) who are required to live with *caṇḍālas* in the neighbourhood of the cremation ground (*śmaśānānte vāsa*)[12] in the city. Only after proper enquiries (*avedya*) they (*pāṣaṇḍa*) are accommodated (*vāsayeyuḥ*) by the owners of religious houses (*dharmāvasathinaḥ*).[13] Even when they (*pāṣaṇḍa*) live in others' house (*paravāstusu*), they do not acquire any right by prescription.[14] The residents of *āśramas*

[11] *AŚ*. II. 1. The fine, however, is not very high. It is not clear if the initiation to asceticism, being opposed to law, is void. The senescent, however, is restrained possibly from taking to the order.

[12] *AŚ*. II. 4.

[13] *AŚ*. II. 36.

[14] *AŚ*. III. 16.

(*āśramiṇaḥ*) and heretical ascetics (*pāṣaṇḍa*) are to stay in a large area (*mahatyavakāśe*), without disturbing one another. The old residents are to make room for the newcomers. The ascetics (*pravrajita*) often move about. The state provides free ferry passes for them,[15] but during festive nights in the city, their movements are checked by the state officials who punish them in case of offence (*doṣato daṇḍyāḥ*).[16]

Despite the restrictions imposed by law and idealism, many ascetics enjoy wealth and comforts. Speaking of the *Udāsthita* spy, Kauṭilya observes,[17] "One who has taken to asceticism (or given up asceticism)[18] and has deep knowledge and purity is (called) an *Udāsthita*. He shall have enormous gold and disciples (*prabhūta hiraṇyāntevāsī*). With these, he shall start work on the land meant for *vārtākarma* (agriculture, cattle-breeding and trade). With the produce of his work, he shall provide all ascetics (*sarvapravrajitānām*) with food, clothes and shelter." In other words, this ascetic or ex-ascetic takes up the work of a wealthy *vaiśya*. Whatever might be his true colour, he purports to work solely for the maintenance of ascetics.

Monks of different sects like *muṇḍa* (the shaven-headed) (identified with the Buddhist and the like) and *jaṭila* (the mat-haired identified with the followers of Śiva) live with a large retinue of disciples in the neighbourhood of cities and sometimes play trick upon unwary believers.[19] Sometimes they even invite the king and his family to stay in their midst and enjoy feasts and festivities (*prekṣāpravahaṇapūrvaṁ vāstavyam*).[20] This seems to show that these monks do not abstain from popular pleasures. Heretical ascetics (*pāṣaṇḍas*) undoubtedly own properties which the prince and the king are advised to take in times of emergency.[21] Still Kauṭilya acknowledges even heretical ascetics to be holy men, if they own neither money nor gold (*ahiraṇya-suvarṇāḥ pāṣaṇḍās-sādhavaste*).

Kauṭilya's law, however, affords some protection to the pravrajitas. A respectable person who takes to *pravrajyā* does not lose

---

[15] *AŚ*. II. 21.
[16] *AŚ*. II. 36.
[17] *AŚ*. I. 11.
[18] Here the readings are different (*pravrjayā-pratyāvasita* or *pravṛjya pratyāvagrata*).
[19] *AŚ*. I. 11. also XII. 2.
[20] *AŚ*. XIII. 2.
[21] *AŚ*. I. 18; V. 12.

title to his goods kept in deposit with another. The owner can recover it.[22] Transactions by a *pravrajita* are invalid unless approved by the state officials.[23] The property (*riktha*) of a *vānaprastha*, *yati* and *brahmacārin* descends on the teacher, the disciple, the brother in faith (*dharma-bhrātṛi*) and fellow student in the order of mention. Except in certain offences they are allowed, in lieu of payment of fines, to perform religious services for the king and even holy heretical sages are allowed, in such cases, to fast and keep vows.[24] Thus, except perhaps in the case of *parivrājaka* who has to surrender property rights (*akiñcana*) other classes of ascetics appear to own properties. Some are undoubtedly rich men. Some have a large entourage. Some earn wealth by works, while others by receiving gifts and donations, not unoften by playing upon the credulity of the people. Crimes and depravity among ascetics are mentioned in the *Arthaśāstra*. The state is asked to keep a close watch on them. The officer in charge of the ferry arrests a novice or apostate from asceticism.[25] Police officers are directed to search for suspicious characters in the house of heretical ascetics.[26] *Tāpasas* are not allowed to give evidence in suit. While on a journey, the king is asked to keep a safe distance from a *pravrajita* and others.[27] Instances are cited where the king is killed while visiting an ascetic.[28] The royal harem is required to be closed to the *Muṇḍas*, the *Jaṭilas* and the like.[29] While punishment for minor crimes is commuted by performance of religious services, major crimes are not excused in their cases. The ascetics are punishable like ordinary persons for defamation, hurt, theft, assault and sexual offence (*pāruṣya-steyasāhasasaṁgrahaṇebhyaḥ*).[30] The text suggests that a fall from the noble ideal of true asceticism is not impossible.

---

[22] *AŚ.* III. 12.
[23] *AŚ.* III. 1.
[24] *AŚ.* III. 16.
[25] *AŚ.* II. 28.
[26] *AŚ.* II. 36.
[27] *AŚ.* I. 21.
[28] *AŚ.* XIII. 2.
[29] *AŚ.* I. 20.
[30] *AŚ.* III. 16; the epics and the Purāṇas contain some well-known stories of great sages like Viśvāmitra and others falling a prey to their passions. Mm. Kane cites later texts which seem to allow ascetics to have wives or concubines. *HDS.* II. 952ff. Some later writers quoted by him forbid *sannyāsa* in the Kali age. The depravity of many monks of Medieval Europe is mentioned in Lecky's *History of European Morals*,

The Greek account of Indian ascetics may be compared with the *Arthaśāstra* version. The Greek envoy seems to have made a confusion between different stages of life. But in substance his description of the ascetic life bears a close similarity to Kauṭilya's record. About Brachmanes, Megasthenes, inter alia states: "The philosophers have their abode in a grove in front of the city within moderate-sized enclosures. They live in a simple style and lie on beds of rushes or (deer) skins. They abstain from animal food and sexual pleasures, and spend their time in listening to serious discourse and in imparting their knowledge to such as will listen to them. After living in this manner for seven and thirty years, each individual retires to his own property where he lives for the rest of his days in ease and security."[31] The Greek envoy obviously confuses a *brahmacārin* with a *vānaprastha*. Elsewhere, he says, "They neither have wives nor beget children."[32] But he observes other Brāhmaṇas leading a different kind of life and begetting offspring on country women.[32] At another place, he speaks of philosophers, followers of Dionysos, observing certain Bacchanalian customs.[32a] "They observe also certain customs which are Bacchanalian. Thus they dress in muslin, wear the turban, use perfumes, array themselves in garments dyed of bright colours; and their kings, when they appear in public, are preceded by the music of drums and gongs." This reminds one of religious processions in modern India. About Śramaṇas, he says:[33] "Those who are held in most honour are called the Hylobioi. They live in the woods, where they subsist on leaves of trees and wild fruits and wear garments made from bark of trees. They abstain from sexual intercourse and from wine" and elsewhere,[34] "They clothe themselves with the bark of trees, subsist upon acorns, and drink water by lifting it to their mouth with their hands. They neither marry nor beget children." He also refers to physicians who are

II. 63-64. "The corruption had reached classes and institutions that appeared the most holy. The agapae or love feasts, which formed one of the most touching symbols of Christian unity, had become scenes of drunkenness and of riots . . . it had been common to find clergy professing celibacy, but keeping under various pretexts their mistresses in their houses . . . Virgins and monks often lived together in the same house, professing sometimes to share in chastity the same bed."

[31] *Meg.* 99.

[32] *Meg.* 122.

[32a] *Meg.* 97.

[33] *Meg.* 101.

[34] *Meg.* 105.

said to make marriages fruitful and determine the sex of the offspring and also to diviners and sorcerers.

The mania for asceticism is so great that even *vṛiṣalas* (śūdras) and women adopt it. Kauṭilya discourages this by providing that *vṛiṣala-pravrajitas* like the *Śākyas* (Buddhists) and the *Ājīvakas* should not be invited to dine on the occasion of pious or funeral ceremonies, otherwise the host should be fined 100 paṇas.[35]

Although Kauṭilya makes it penal to initiate women to asceticism (*pravrājayataḥ*), he mentions a large variety of women ascetics. To mention a few, *parivrājikā, muṇḍā, bhikṣukī* and *pravrajitā*. But most of them are painted in lurid colour.

Parivrājikā (who might be the female counterpart of *Parivrājaka* in the fourth stage of life) seems to have access to the harems of the king and his ministers. She is supposed to carry love messages, letters and presents from the king to the minister's wife,[36] and from the queen to the minister.[37] A shaven-headed (*muṇḍā*) female spy seems to have access to high society.[38]

A *Bhikṣukī* too might play the role of a go-between.[39] Thus these female ascetics are likely to adopt the roles of procuresses or messengers of love and thereby give vent to their repressed sexual cravings. Some (*Bhikṣukī*) are allowed to give shelter to a deserted wife.[40] Some mendicant women might succumb to the cravings of the flesh. For, the *Arthaśāstra* tells us the case of a female ascetic (*pravrajitā*) who voluntarily (*sakāmā*) submits to sexual intercourse.[41] In this case Kauṭilya prescribes a small fine of 24 paṇas for the woman and her lover. If the gallant forces a connection against her wish he alone is fined 24 paṇas. One should know that Kauṭilya prescribes a fine of 12 paṇas for forcibly enjoying a prostitute (*rūpājīvā*).[41] Chastity of a *pravrajitā* is looked upon as little more valuable than that, if any, of

[35] *AŚ*. III. 20; also *Yāj*. II. 241. Kane, *HDS*. II. p. 945.
[36] *AŚ*. 12. 2.
[37] *AŚ*. I. 10; *AŚ*. I. 12.
[38] *AŚ*. I. 12.
[39] *AŚ*. XI. 1.
[40] *AŚ*. III. 4.
[41] *AŚ*. IV. 12. Lecky writes on Medieval Europe: "Noble ladies pretending desire to lead higher life, abandoned their husbands to live with low-born lovers" *ibid.*, 64. Therīgāthā tells us how a nun practised incest with her own father, a fellow monk, whose identity she could not suspect. (*Uppalavaṇṇā-Therīgāthā*, XI. 64).

the public woman. It is also significant that a *pravrajitā* is employed in the state textile factory in the company of old female slaves of the king, retired female slaves attached to the temple (*devadāsī*), matrons of prostitutes (*rūpājīvā-mātṛikā*) and others.[43] It suggests that many female ascetics might possibly be of easy virtue. It is true that Megasthenes speaks of women philosophers who "abstain from sexual intercourse."[42] But the ideal is occasionally violated. Megasthenes refers to the dilemma of Brachmanes philosophers about their wives, for, either they would become depraved and divulge their secret or they would desert their husband if they (wives) became good philosophers.[44] Mahāmahopādhyāya Kane discusses various orthodox texts regarding female ascetics and concludes: "It must be said that the general trend of Hinduism is against women adopting the homeless or ascetic life."[45] In this respect the orthodox view seems to be reflected in Kauṭilya's measures against initiating women into the ascetic mode of life.

Yet it must be admitted that the ascetics, both male and female, are found to have a great hold on the mind of the people. They have easy access to persons belonging to different strata of society. An intelligent politician like Kauṭilya, naturally, seeks to recruit an influential army of spies from the order of ascetics.[46] In different garbs, viz., *pravrajitā*, *muṇḍā*, *jaṭila*, *tāpasa*, *pāṣaṇḍa*, *siddha* and the like, the spies of the monastic order roam the length and breadth of the country, amidst all walks of life, detect criminals, provoke possible offenders, stir up disputes, murder enemies and do all sorts of nefarious works for the furtherance of the ends of the state. Some of them are paid 1000 paṇas as salary. Brāhmaṇa, Buddhist (*muṇḍa*) and *Vṛiṣala* women ascetics (*parivrājikā*), and perhaps a widow desirous of earning a living, are appointed as *Bhikṣukī* spies.[47] They try to enter the royal harem and the minister's household. If they are stopped at the door, other spies inside the house are required to act in collaboration with them. From the types of services these *Bhikṣukī* spies are expected to

---

[42] *Meg*. 103.
[43] *AŚ*. II. 23.
[44] *Meg*. 100.
[45] Kane, *HDS*. II. p. 945.
[46] *AŚ*. I. 10, 11, 12, 13, 14, 16, 18; II. 35; IV. 4; XI. 1; XII. 4; XIII. 2, 3.
[47] *AŚ*. I. 11.

render, we can get a glimpse of probable exploits of these female mendicant spies. Thus in the *Arthaśāstra*[48] we find: "A mendicant woman, having captivated the wife of a seditious minister by administering medicines as excite feelings of love, may through that wife contrive to poison the minister." Elsewhere, acting as a go-between she is advised to make a false charge of adultery against the wife, daughter or daughter-in-law of a seditious chief with another such chief and cause a fatal duel between them.[48]

The picture of the ascetic life as painted in the *Arthaśāstra* is lurid indeed. It seems to reveal a pessimistic outlook of Kauṭilya towards asceticism in practice. Yet in the ideal of ascetic discipline in the stage of *Vānaprastha* and *Parivrājaka*, he definitely puts the standard high. He even admits that those heretical ascetics are holy men who do not covet money and gold. He asks the king to govern well so that even the *vānaprasthas* and the *parivrājakas* may not get angry.[49] At the same time he advises the king to see to it that the ascetics do not deviate from the path of morality. "The king shall, by awarding punishment, forbid improper conduct of ascetics (*pravrajyāsu*) for vice, overwhelming righteousness, will in the long run destroy the ruler himself."[50] Kauṭilya seems to expose the false prophets and warn the people of their machination. On the other hand, he is full of praise for ideal ascetics, even if heretical (*pāṣaṇḍa*). Different modes of leading ascetic life are also observed in the Greek accounts of two Indian philosophers, Kalanos and Mandamis or whatever might have been their real names. Various versions of their lives and philosophies have been left by the Greek writers. Strabo gives a short account as follows:[51] "He (Kalanos) was ruled by his passions and became a slave to the table of Alexander. He is on this account condemned by his countrymen, but Mandamis is applauded because when messengers from Alexander invited him to go to the son of Zeus, with the promise of gifts if he complied and threats of punishment if he refused, he did not go......Alexander expressed admiration of the man, and let him have his own way." According to Arrian,[52]

---

[48] *AŚ.* v. 1.
[49] *AŚ.* I. 3.
[50] *AŚ.* III. 16.
[51] *Meg.* 106-07.
[52] *Meg.* 116-17.

this 'Dandamis' lived at Taxilā along with his disciples and "not only refused to go himself, but prevented the others going......Alexander accordingly did not put forth his hand to violence knowing the man to be of an independent spirit. He is said, however, to have won over Kalonos, one of the sophists of that place, whom Megasthenes represents as a man utterly wanting in self-control, while the sophists themselves spoke opprobriously of Kalonos, because that, having left the happiness enjoyed among them, he went to serve another master than God." Kalonos was made an outcast from the society of the ascetics.[53] The life and teachings of 'Mandamis' offer an object lesson in the freedom of human spirit and the ideal of plain-living and high-thinking. "Know this, however, that what Alexander offers me and the gifts he promises, are all things to me utterly useless; but the things which I prize, and find a real use and worth, are these leaves which are my house, these blooming plants which supply me with dainty food, and the water which is my drink, while all other possessions and things which are amassed with anxious care, are wont to prove ruinous to those who amass them, and cause only sorrow and vexation, with which every poor mortal is fully fraught. But as for me, I live upon the forest leaves, and having nothing which requires guarding, close my eyes in tranquil slumber; whereas had I gold to guard, that would banish sleep. The earth supplies me with everything, even as a mother her child with milk. I go wherever I please and there are no cares with which I am forced to cumber myself against my will."[54] This philosophy of contentment and practice of material poverty set a standard for asceticism at its highest. "Dandamis," the Greek writes with compliments, "who though old and naked, was the only antagonist in whom he (Alexander), the conqueror of many nations had found more than his match."[53]

[53] *Meg.* 123 & 127.
[54] *Meg.* 125-26.

Chapter XII

ABNORMAL LOVE

While the normal relationship between different sexes is a common feature in the *Arthaśāstra*, various types of sexual aberrations are either mentioned or suggested by Kauṭilya. His attitude towards such perversions and perversities[1] reveals interesting ethical ideas and deserves a careful scrutiny.

"Sexual abnormalities are legion; numerous varieties and combinations of all kinds are found. For this reason, their classification is an extremely delicate matter.... Dr. Hesnard first of all makes a distinction between deviations of aim and deviations of object. The former include all pathological states characterised by the fact that the individual while seeking a normal object (a man a woman, or a woman a man) has only repugnance or indifference for the sexual act. He seeks to replace it by one of its derivatives, or rather by one of its constituent acts. For example, a male exhibitionist will find pleasure with a normal female partner, but he will do so not during the normal sexual act, but during one of its derivatives. It is the same with sadists and masochists: the object remains the same, but the aim differs essentially from the normal. On the other hand, in deviations of object the individual seeks the normal sexual aim but in conjunction with an object which normally would not produce excitement. As examples, we may mention homosexuality and zoophilia."[2]

This introduction to sexual abnormalities is a necessary guide to the study of such delicate matters cursorily mentioned in the *Arthaśāstra*.

When the sexual enjoyment is derived through an element of

---

[1] "Perversion is a deviation of tendency in a normal sexual impulse and can neither afford the individual any malignant pleasure nor appeal in any way to his desire for that which is forbidden; whereas perversity is a more or less abnormal quality in his character which impels him to evil for its own sake and to perform or wish to perform certain acts simply because they are forbidden." Dr. Hesnard quoted in *ESK*. 417.

[2] *ESK*. 417-18.

pain, either active or passive, psychologists name the phenomena as sadism or masochism. A sadist finds pleasure by inflicting pain and a masochist by undergoing it.

Modern psychologists might read Kauṭilya's aversion to sadism in his prohibition against forcible intercourse in opposition to the wishes of the unfortunate woman.[3] Kauṭilya also forbids forcible abduction of a girl (*prasahya kanyāmapaharato*) by a single man or several men in concert.[3] Force cannot be employed even against a courtezan (*akāmāyāḥ kumāryā vā sāhase uttamo daṇḍaḥ sakāmāyāḥ pūrvaḥ sāhasadaṇḍa*).[4] Again, a forcible enjoyment of a *rupājīvā* by a single man or several persons together is a punishable offence (*rupājīvāyāḥ prasahyopabhoge*)[5]. Veiled allusions to sadism might be traced in the offences of cutting off of ears (*karṇacchedana*), disfigurement of the beauty of a courtezan by cutting open wounds (*braṇavidāraṇena vā rūpamupaghnataḥ*), murdering public women and others connected with her.[6]

"Sadism finds a much clearer expression in certain forms of corporal punishment, and especially in flogging."[7] The *Arthaśāstra* prescribes flogging of a woman, sometimes publicly. Thus, for conversation in a suspicious place, she may be flogged or fined (*Paṇasthāne śiphādaṇḍaḥ*). A *caṇḍāla* is ordered to flog the defaulting woman five times on her each flank in the middle of the village (*Strīnāṁ grāmamadhye caṇḍālaḥ pakṣāntaraṁ pañcaśiphā dadyāt*).[8] A courtezan refusing to yield herself to a man at the command of the king is required to be flogged a thousand times or alternatively fined 5000 paṇas.[9] In any event, Kauṭilya allows commutation of flogging by payment of suitable fines.[10]

Physical torture, branding, mutilation of limbs by way of punishment might also be traced to an element of sadism. The *Arthaśāstra* describes such punishments too numerous to be set out here.[11] In

[3] *AŚ*. IV. 12.
[4] *AŚ*. II. 27.
[5] *AŚ*. IV. 13.
[6] *AŚ*. II. 27.
[7] *ESK*. 347.
[8] *AŚ*. III. 3.
[9] *AŚ*. II. 27.
[10] *AŚ*. II. 27; III. 3; IV. 2.
[11] *AŚ*. IV. 8, 11, etc.

prescribing these painful punishments, Kauṭilya professes to follow earlier writers[12] (*śāṣtreṣvanugatāḥ kleśaḍaṇḍā mahātmanām*). But in many cases he tempers down the rigours of punishment.[11]

Physical pain as a part of risky games might also be connected with sadism. The Romans are known to have enjoyed sadistic pleasures at the sight of mortal fight between men and wild beasts.[13] The *Arthaśāstra* mentions a class of fiery spies (*tīkṣṇa*). They are recruited from desperadoes who fight with tigers and elephants mainly for financial gains.[14] But in general Kauṭilya prohibits wanton destruction of animal life and directs the state officers to enforce regulations carefully.[15] Although Kauṭilya extols *ahiṁsā* as the common virtue to be followed by everybody,[16] he allows many exceptions to it. He praises hunting[16] but bans torture of various beasts and prescribes veterinary measures.[17] His law forbids bullfights. An unauthorised person castrating bulls or small quadrupeds is punishable in law.[18] A victorious king is likewise asked to forbid "slaughter of females and young ones as well as castration." Many of the measures advocated by Kauṭilya find parallel in the edicts of Aśoka.[19]

Castration of human beings is not unknown in the *Asthaśāstra.* It is ordinarily forbidden. But it is prescribed by way of punishment for incest.[20] The rule of 'tit for tat' applies in the case of wrongful castration (*Meḍhraphalopaghātinas-tadeva chedayet*).[21] The *Arthaśāstra* refers to a magical rite which is meant to make a man impotent (*apuruṣa*).[22]

The usual form of masochism is "found in men whose aspiration it is to be dominated by more virile women."[23] Masochists voluntarily

---

[12] *AŚ.* IV. 11.
[13] O. Kieffer, *SLAR.* Chap. II.
[14] *AŚ.* I. 12.
[15] *AŚ.* II. 26, 29, 31.
[16] *AŚ.* I.
[17] *AŚ.* II. 29.
[18] *AŚ.* III. 20.
[19] Mookerji, *Candragupta Maurya and His Times.* Appendix III. Dr. R. K. Mookerji also quotes Dīghanikāya condemning the games (*samājas*) in which elephants, horses, buffaloes, bulls, goats and rams fought (*ibid.* pp. 61-2). The Greek writers on India refer to bloody animal fights (*MC. I.* 280-81).
[20] *AŚ.* IV. 13.
[21] *AŚ.* IV. 11.
[22] *AŚ.* XIV. 3.
[23] *ESK.* 441. In the next two pages of the said work various instances of masochism may be found.

undergo various tortures and humiliations for perverse pleasures. The *Arthaśāstra* gives a few examples of this type of aberrations. Some of its punishments are directed against termagants. Thus, a courtezan is punishable for using harsh words (24 paṇas) and causing hurt (48 paṇas), but we do not read anything about the attitude of the poor paramour in these cases.[24] A wife is punishable for similar offences against the husband or for driving him out of the marital home at night or shutting the door against him or disobeying him.[25] But the text is silent about the mind of the unfortunate husband under such circumstances. It may very well be that some man will find pleasure in whatever his ladylove will do. For, a man devoted to his ladylove (*kāntāparam, kāntāpriya*) is not a rare figure in the *Arthaśāstra*.[26] Whatever might have been the actual state of affairs, it appears that Kauṭilya is not generally favourable towards conducts and practices which smell of sadism or masochism.

According to Havelock Ellis, exhibitionism is "an impulse to expose a part of the body, especially the genital region, for a sexual reason, either conscious or unconscious."[27] Kauṭilya, as we have already seen, does not allow a married woman to hold out her hair girdle, teeth or nail by way of flirtation.[28] Dalliance with the girdle (*nīvi*) suggests disrobement. Elsewhere we have noted Kauṭilya's attitude towards nudity.[29] Nudity even under the influence of drinks is deprecated.[30] Nakedness in a women is, as we shall see, probably discouraged.[31]

Pleasures derived from smutty talks and indecent sights are other forms of aberrations. But Kauṭilya does not allow actors, dancers and other artistes to entertain people by cheap stunts connected with copulation (*maithunāpahāne narmayeyuḥ*).[32] The law does not permit

[24] *AŚ*. II. 27.
[25] *AŚ*. III. 3.
[26] *AŚ*. IV. 6; VII. 5.
[27] *ESK*. 422.
[28] Chap. III. *supra*.
[29] Chap. XIV. *infra*.
[30] *AŚ*. VIII. 3.
[31] Chapter XIV. *infra*.
[32] *AŚ*. IV. 1; the pleasure in watching the sexual act being performed by others is variously called—voyeurism or scotophilia or mixoscopia. *ESK*. 418. *The Jain Pariśiṣṭaparvan*, VIII. 424 mentions the pleasure felt by heretical ascetics in peeping through the window into the harem.

satisfaction in watching sexual acts (*maithuna*) being performed by others.

"Of all deviations of object, the most widespread is unquestionably the 'love which dares not tell its name', homosexuality, as opposed to heterosexuality or love between individuals of different sexes."[33] Homosexuality has been traced back to the remotest times. Some Greek philosophers are known for their support to this type of love. They even place the love of young boys higher than normal love.[34] But Kauṭilya is definitely of a different view. He makes homosexuality penal. A man having sexual intercourse with another man (*puruṣamadhimehataśca*), is required to pay the first amercement (*pūrvaḥ sāhasadaṇḍaḥ*).[35] This fine ranges between 48 and 96 panas.[36] But lighter fines are prescribed for homosexuality among women. A woman having sexual connection (*prakartrī*) with another woman who desires such connection and belong to the same status has to pay 24 paṇas and the latter only 12 paṇas (*strī prakṛitā sakāmā samānādvādaśapaṇam daṇḍam dadyāt prakartrī dviguṇam*).[37] The text connotes mutual sexual passion between two women. But for her own pleasure a woman, ravishing an unwilling woman, is liable to pay 100 paṇas in addition to the payment of the bride price (*akāmāyāḥ śatyo daṇḍaḥ ātmarāgārtham śulkadānām ca*).[38] This passage seems to refer to a Lesbian who, prompted by her lust, forces herself on another woman who does not reciprocate the feeling. In this case the Lesbian not only pays a heavier fine but has to make a present of *śulka* (or bride-price) to the other. A woman deflowering herself becomes a slave to the king (*svayam prakṛitā rājadāsyaṁ gacchet*).[39] It is, however, clear that homosexuality whether between men or women is not considered to be a serious offence in the *Arthaśāstra*. Far more stringent punishments like death, branding,

[33] *ESK*. 448.

[34] H. Licht, *SLAG*. Chap. V.

[35] *AŚ*. IV. 13.

[36] *AŚ* III. 17. *Yāj*. II. 296 prescribed only 24 paṇas for the offence.

[37] *AS*. IV. 12. The *Mbh*. Anuśāsana 38, 22 refers to the Lesbian love.

[38] *AŚ*. IV. 12. The passage is differently interpreted by Dr. Shama Sastry, Gaṇapati Sastri and Dr. R. G. Basak. All of them read in it a reference to intercourse with a man. But the context seems to suggest the interpretation given above.

[39] *Ibid*. There is the same difficulty in interpreting this passage. Mm. Gaṇapati Sastri explains '*svayam prakṛitā*' as *svayaṁ kṛtayonikṣati*. If this interpretation is correct the text refers to masturbation by a woman. But why such severe punishment like slavery, even if under the king, is prescribed is not clear.

mutilation and the like are prescribed for many cases of heterosexual offences. Yet Dr. Basham rightly observes: "The erotic life in ancient India was generally heterosexual. Homosexualism of both sexes was not wholly unknown; it is condemned briefly in the law books and the Kāmasūtra treats of it but cursorily and with little enthusiasm. Literature ignores it. In this respect ancient India was far healthier than most other ancient cultures."[40]

Another sexual aberration is transvestism. "The patient who is afflicted by it identifies himself with the opposite sex just as much in his manner of dressing as in his ideals in general."[41] Havelock Ellis calls it eonism. Kauṭilya mentions persons moving about in the dress of the opposite sex (*pracchanna viparīta-veṣaḥ*).[42] Whether there is any sexual idea behind this mode of dressing oneself is not clear from the text. In any event mere wearing the clothes of the opposite sex is not punishable. Kauṭilya asks for punishment if there is offence (*doṣato daṇḍyaḥ*). Such persons move about in festal nights (*chārarātriṣu*). In modern times, "Quite a large number of persons seize every opportunity of going to a fancy dress ball in the clothes of the opposite sex. Many of these individuals themselves are not fully conscious that there is a sexual element in the pleasure that they get from dressing up."[43] This comment on modern practice might equally apply to the age of Kauṭilya.

In infantilism, an individual seeks an abnormal love object viz. a child.[44] In gerontophilia, a person seeks some one old. "It is the disproportion in age which here makes all the difference between the normal and the perverse."[44] Mere disparity in age between lovers does not appear to be offensive according to the *Arthaśāstra*. Kauṭilya, however, specially protects immature girls (*aprāpthaphalāṁ kanyām*). A man having sexual intercourse with an immature maiden belonging to the same caste will have his hand chopped off or pay a fine of 400 paṇas. If the maiden dies, he will suffer capital punishment.[45] Similarly, forcible abduction of a virgin (*kumārī*), whether reciprocating love or

[40] A. L. Basham, *op. cit.* p. 172.
[41] *ESK*. 461.
[42] *AŚ*. II. 36.
[43] *ESK*. 165.
[44] *ESK*. 469.
[45] *AŚ*. IV. 12.

not, is punishable.[46] The text, however, does not clearly refer to the age of the offender. The orthodox texts suggest a great disparity between the ages of the husband and wife. For instance, a husband of thirty years of age is required to marry a girl of ten.[47]

Necrophilia means "sexual predelictions for dead bodies".[48] The *Arthaśāstra* does not definitely mention this aberration. But it refers to magical rites dealing with dead bodies or parts thereof. For instance, "Having fasted for three nights, on the star of *Puṣyā*, prepare a round-headed pin (*śalākā*) from the branch of *puruṣaghātī*. Then having filled with ointment (*añjana*) the skull of any of the animals which roam at nights and having inserted that skull in the organ of procreation of a dead woman, one should burn it. Having taken it out on the day of the star of *Puṣyā* and having anointed one's own eye with that ointment one can walk invisible to others."[49] Psychologists might trace a sexual motif behind this magic. The insertion of the skull into the genitals (*yonau*) of the dead woman suggests necrophilia. Many other rites require working with human corpses, clothes of a dead man, the skull or bones of a dead man killed by a weapon or put to the gallows and the fat of roasted dead children in cremation grounds.[50] By way of punishment, the corpse of a suicide is required to be dragged on the highway.[51] The peculiar cult of defiling dead bodies might or might not have been rooted in sensuality. To an ordinary man, such practices are likely to be repugnant. Many other works throughout the world, however, refer to such nefarious practices.[52]

In fetishism, the pervert attributes an erotic value to some physical detail or peculiarity of the beloved or even to some inanimate object. A queer case of fetishism is mentioned in the *Arthaśāstra*. That is an erotic intercourse with an idol (*daivatapratimā gamana*). The ecstacy of religious attachment for the idol can very well lead to this sexual act. But Kauṭilya makes it penal and prescribes a fine of 24 paṇas.[53] A Brāhmaṇa, who has committed a rape, is required to be branded with

[46] *AŚ*. II. 271
[47] Jolly, *Hindu Law & Custom*, p. 126.
[48] *ESK*. 473.
[49] *AŚ*. XIV. 3 (Shama Sastry's translation).
[50] *AŚ*. XIV. 2; 3.
[51] *AŚ*. IV. 7.
[52] Chapter XIV. *infra*, note 40.
[53] *AŚ*. IV. 13.

the mark of the female genital. But this punishment may not be traced to fetishism. The use of human faece or urine or a woman's menstrual blood is required for certain magical rites described in the *Arthaśāstra*.[54] These objects might or might not have erotic symbolism.

Kauṭilya mentions zoophilia. "A senseless person who copulates with animals shall be fined 12 paṇas" (*maithune dvādaśapaṇaḥ tiryagyoniṣvanātmanaḥ*).[55] In this case too, he prescribes a light punishment.

Lastly, Kauṭilya refers to sexual intercourse with a woman against the order of nature (*ayonau*). He prescribes a fine of the first amercement to penalise this offence. The fine ranges between 48 and 96 paṇas.[56] The *Kāmāsūtra* devotes a chapter to the description of this practice.[57] It showers moral opprobrium on it. But Kauṭilya makes it illegal and penal. From the extent of fines he imposes, it appears that Kauṭilya considers this offence to be more heinous than zoophilia (12 paṇas), forcible intercourse with a prostitute (12 paṇas) or with a nun (24 paṇas), but equal in degree with homosexuality.

---

[54] *AŚ*. XIV. 3.
[55] *AŚ*. IV. 13.
[56] *Ibid.*
[57] *KS*. II. 9.

Chapter XIII

MORALS AND INCAPACITY, PHYSICAL OR SOCIAL

The rules of ordinary morality do not apply to extraordinary persons. People suffering from physical, social or other defects are usually governed by different standards of morality. Slaves, eunuchs, outcasts and the like occupy special positions in society. It is interesting to note how far the *Arthaśāstra* varies the common norms of morality to make it suitable for such persons.

Slavery was a universal institution in the ancient and the medieval world. But as Dr. Bandopadhyaya observes: "In regard to slavery, Kauṭilya's attitude stands apart as a glowing light of liberalism and humanity in a barbaric age, while his contemporary Aristotle was justifying slavery as a divine and a beneficent human institution not only sanctioned by nature but justified by the circumstances of social existence, he denounced it and strove to abolish it characterising it as a custom which could exist only among the savage Mlecchas."[1] Kauṭilya grants limited recognition to slavery and prescribes many rules for the welfare of the slaves. Dr. Ghoshal comments: "In the body of the Brāhmaṇical Smṛitis such wise and humane rules are in general completely absent."[2]

The existence of slaves in India has been traced to the Vedic age.[3] The Jātakas show that "the institution of slavery was so common that not only kings and wealthy people but the Brāhmaṇas and simple villagers and farmers also kept slaves in their families. The treatment of the slaves was generally speaking, humane and considerate. It, however, depended on, and differed according to the temperament and capacity of both the master and the slave. There is complete absence of legal right of the slaves in the stories. The right of the master over his slave seems, according to the prevailing custom, to

---

[1] Bandopadhyaya, *Kauṭilya*, p. 211.
[2] U. N. Ghoshal, *The Beginnings of Indian Histriography and other essays*, p. 98.
[3] Kane, *HDS*. II. 180.

have been absolute."[4] The Buddhists deprecate slavery but accept it as an institution.[5] Arrian on the testimony of Megasthenes writes: "The same writer tells us further this remarkable fact about India, that all the Indians are free, and not one of them is a slave. The Lakedaemonians and the Indians are here so far in agreement. The Lakedaemonians, however, hold the helots as slaves, and these helots do servile labour; but the Indians do not even use aliens as slaves, and much less a countryman of their own."[6] The Greek might have been struck by the unusual mildness of the system in vogue among the Indians[7] or prompted by some idealising tendency.[8] But slavery had, however, too deep-rooted an existence to be easily eradicated.[9] Kauṭilya boldly tries to stop sale or mortgage of children in some cases, to provide for compulsory manumission of slaves and to grant them a right to property and personal dignity.

According to Kauṭilya, slavery arises through sale, pledge, gift, judicial decree, capture in war, and birth.[10] A person in distress may offer himself, his wife and children as slaves to his rescuer, or may be allowed to pay for rescue only so much as experts deem fit.[11]

"Comparing the *Arthaśāstra* and the *Dharmaśāstra* rules on the subject of slavery", observes Dr. Ghoshal, "we are struck with the radical attitude of Kauṭilya which is based on his conception of the rights of the Aryan free man, not to say, those of the individual man."[12]

As regards slavery, the *Arthaśāstra* divides people under two groups, viz. Ārya and the rest. Kauṭilya states: "It is no crime for Mlecchas to sell or pledge their own offspring. But never shall an Ārya be subjected to slavery (*Mlecchānāmadoṣa prajāṁ vikretumā-dhātuṁvā na tvevāryasya dāsabhāva*)."[13] Although somewhat circumscribed, this ancient declaration of human rights deserves notice. It is not a hollow ideal but is

[4] Mehta, *Pre-Buddhist India*, pp. 209-10.
[5] U. N. Ghoshal, *ibid*, p. 91.
[6] *Meg*. 68.
[7] Rhys Davids, *Buddhist India*, p. 263.
[8] Jolly & Schmidt, *Introduction to AS*. p. 38.
[9] Bandopadhyaya, *Kauṭilya*, p. 211.
[10] *AŚ* III. 13. *Manu*. (VIII. 415) and *Nārada*. (V. 26-28) mention respectively seven and fifteen kinds of slaves.
[11] *AŚ*. III. 13.
[12] Ghoshal, *ibid*. p. 95.
[13] *AŚ*. III. 13. The principal Dharmaśāstras too condemn the practice of fathers selling their children into slavery e.g. *Yāj*. III. 236.

backed by the sanction of the state, for punishment awaits those who sell or purchase or abet the sale or purchase of an infant person by birth an Aryan (*āryaprāṇama-prāptavyavahāram*) and by caste *Brāhmaṇa, Kṣatriya, Vaiśya* or *Śūdra*. The mortgage of an Ārya is equally forbidden. Thus a relation selling or mortgaging him is fined 48 paṇas, 36 paṇas, 24 paṇas and 12 paṇas according as the child is a *Brāhmaṇa, Kṣatriya, Vaiśya* or *Śūdra* respectively. A stranger who sells or mortgages it, the purchaser and the witnesses are liable to suffer capital punishment in the case of a *Brāhmaṇa* and different degrees of fines in other cases. It is important to note that the *Śūdra* is here included in the category of an Ārya. The *Mahābhārata*, however, goes further. It states: "One should not sell a human being who is a stranger; how much more one's own children." How far this moral precept of the great epic is enforced, one cannot say. In any event Dr. Ghoshal rightly observes: "The general tendency of the *Smṛitikāras* is to emphasise the rights of the twice-born classes and specially the *Brāhmaṇas* to the exclusion of the *Śūdras*. To borrow a modern expression, while the *Arthaśāstra* insists, in the main, upon the principle of nationality, the *Dharmaśāstras* lay stress upon the principle of birth and social status."[14] He further states: "...the general tendency of the *Dharmaśāstra* was to eliminate or at least restrict the class of high-born slaves. It is apparently for this reason that the condition of the slave in the Smṛiti literature shows on the whole, as compared with the *Arthaśāstra*, a change for the worse."[15]

The *Arthaśāstra*, however, makes certain exceptions to the general rule that an Ārya cannot be reduced to slavery. Thus, (*a*) the mortgage of an Ārya is allowed in three cases, viz. (*i*) to tide over family troubles, (*ii*) to raise funds for payment of fines or satisfaction of judicial decrees, (*iii*) to recover forfeited properties (*kulabandhana tūryāṇāmāpadi*). But in such cases kinsmen owe him a duty to redeem him as soon as possible, specially if he is a young man or an able-bodied adult.

(*b*) The voluntary submission to servitude seems to have been allowed.

(*c*) Sale or mortgage of a slave by birth is not forbidden (*udaradāsavarjam*).

Not only does Kauṭilya restrict the extent of slavery, he also

[14] U. N. Ghoshal, *ibid.* p. 95.
[15] *ibid.* p. 97.

attempts to raise the status and personal security of the slaves. No longer is the slave dependent merely upon the temperament of the master as in the days of the Jātakas. The Kautilyan law is there to protect his interest. The slave is allowed by Kautilya to own personal property and enjoy a sense of dignity. Thus, Kauṭilya makes it penal to cheat him of his wealth (*vittāpahāriṇo*) or deprive him of his privileges as an Ārya (*dāsasyāryabhāva*), to employ a pledged slave to carry the dead or sweat, ordure, urine or the leavings of food (*pretaviṇmūtrocchiṣṭagrāhiṇām*), to hurt or abuse him or to violate a female slave.[16] A slave's personal safety and chastity are, thus, to a large extent guaranteed by law. We have already noted how the *Arthaśāstra* seeks to protect the personal honour of a slave girl, bond-woman and other maid-servants. The law forbids the employment of a slave below eight years of age in mean avocations against his will or the sale or mortgage of such a slave in foreign lands. The slave is permitted to enjoy various proprietory rights. A slave who has sold himself, a born slave and a bondman (*āhitaka*) can earn profits for themselves without detriment to their master's work. So do they inherit and enjoy properties from their ancestors. A slave's property goes on his death to his kinsmen and, in their absence, to the master. Manu and some other Smṛitikāras declare as a general rule that the wife, the son and the slave shall have no property of their own. They no doubt provide exceptions to this dictum in the cases of the wife and the son. But in the case of the slave the orthodox law-makers are somewhat hesitant.[17] Kātyāyana says that the only wealth that the slave can call his own is the price he gets for selling himself or a gift from the master.[18] Moreover, Kauṭilya makes various rules for the emancipation of the slave. The right to property no doubt helps the slave to earn his freedom. A born slave, a bondman and a slave who has sold himself can purchase their freedom upon payment of money for which they are sold or mortgaged. A person enslaved under a judicial decree can work his way to freedom. The failure to liberate a slave even upon receipt of an adequate consideration is penal.

---

[16] Nārada (*abhyupetyaśuśrūṣā*, 6-7), however, states that a *dāsa* may be employed to do impure works like cleaning filthy pits, touching private parts, taking up ordure and urine and the like. Mm. Kane, however, points out that Manu places a slave on the same level as one's son in the matter of corporal punishment. (*Manu.* VII. 299-300); *HDS* Vol. II. p. 182.

[17] Ghoshal, *ibid*, p. 100.

[18] Kātyāyana quoted in Kane, *ibid*.

On the violation of the chastity of a female slave, she is liberated. The sale or mortgage of a liberated slave is also forbidden unless he himself consents. A freeman taken captive in war (*āryaprāṇo dhvajāhṛitaḥ*) can gain freedom by work or half its equivalent in money (*karmakālānurupeṇa mūlyārdhena vā*). Thus, in the above cases the slaves can claim liberation as a matter of right and not as a matter of grace.

Kauṭilya prohibits manumission probably in three cases only, viz. (*a*) a person who has pledged himself once as a slave yet escapes (*sakṛidātmadhātā niṣpatitaḥ sīdet*), (*b*) a person who has been pledged twice by another and escapes (*dviranyenāhitakaḥ*) and (*c*) both these persons trying once to escape to a foreign kingdom (*sakṛidubhau paraviṣayābhimukham*). On the other hand, as Dr. Ghoshal clearly shows, the Smṛitakāras curtail the right of manumission to a great extent.[19]

The *Arthaśāstra* also recognises and protects a slave's family life. He is allowed to marry. His children ordinarily become slaves (*udaradāsa*). But a child of an Ārya who has voluntarily sold himself into servitude is taken to be an Ārya. Adequate provisions are directed to be made for the confinement of a pregnant slave woman. Without such provisions, sale or mortgage of such a woman is punishable with the first amercement. A pledged slave girl is allowed to marry. She is entitled to *śulka* or bride-price, if she is raped. Similarly, a man who defiles the daughter of his own male or female slave has to pay a fine to the state and an adequate nuptial fee (*śulka*) and jewellery (*ābadhya*) to the poor girl.[20] Mutilation of limbs or heavy fine is the punishment for those who abduct a slave possessed of gold.[21] Occasionally a slave-woman voluntarily surrenders herself to her master's lust. If she gets a child born of this union, both the mother and the child are set at liberty. Apart from Kātyāyana,[22] the orthodox lawmakers do not allow such a privilege to a slave-woman. According to *Arthaśāstra*, slaves, male or female, might be involved in erotic matters with their master or mistress or with a stranger. Kauṭilya disapproves such gallantry.

Dr. Basham characterises the humane regulations of the *Arthaśāstra* as "probably unique in the records of any ancient civilization".[23]

---

[19] Ghoshal, *ibid.* 101. Also Kane, *HDS.* II. 185.
[20] *AŚ.* IV. 12.
[21] *AŚ.* IV. 10.
[22] Kātyāyana, p. 723.
[23] A. L. Basham, *The Wonder that was India*, p. 153.

Dr. Atindra Nath Bose states: "But in the *Arthaśāstra's* time there were mleccha slaves who are summarily passed over, but who obviously outnumber the ārya slaves and for whom there was no mitigation."[24] This comment does not seem to be wholly correct. Although the Ārya slaves get some preference in the *Arthaśāstra*, many ameliorative measures apply to all the slaves irrespective of nationality.

Kauṭilya's humane law on slavery has far-reaching moral effects on society. It checks the tyrannical and ferocious spirit in the master and fills the slave with a sense of personal dignity. It enables him to have his own family and lead a normal sexual life. By penalising sexual crimes against a slave woman, it curbs depravity and enriches the moral tone in society. Its limitation upon the extent of slavery and recognition of the right to freedom directly encourage the growth of human values. In RE IX Aśoka declares that his law of piety includes the kind treatment of slaves (*dāsa*) and hired servants.

From early days, idiocy, lunacy, impotence, blindness and other physical defects have received special attention from lawmakers. In general the persons suffering from such defects are deprived of some social and legal rights.

Of the persons who suffer from physical incapacities, eunuchs occupy a peculiar position in society. We come across them on different occasions in the *Arthaśāstra*. Impotence can arise in various ways. Some are born impotent, some lose their potency naturally (*luptavyavaya*). Some might be castrated (*puruṣam apuruṣam*). In any event the *Arthaśāstra* makes some provisions for their livelihood. They find employment in the royal harem, where, not unusually, they act as spies.[25] The king is asked to employ hunchbacks, dwarfs, eunuchs and the dumb to work as spies in the inner apartments of his enemy (*antargṛihacarasteṣām kubja vāmana ṣaṇḍakāḥ*). Eunuchs (*varṣavara*) are required to test the purity of royal ladies (*avarodhanam*).[26] The king himself gives daily interview to eunuchs (*varṣavara*) among a host of other attendants.[27] A person who has lost his potency (*luptavyavaya*) is permitted to take up asceticism upon informing the civil judges.[28] Like the Smṛiti-writers,

[24] *IC.* IV. 1937-38, p. 438.
[25] *AŚ.* I. 12; also XII. 5.
[26] *AŚ.* I. 20.
[27] *AŚ.* I. 21.
[28] *AŚ.* II. 1.

Kauṭilya allows the impotent and other defective persons (or their defective children) to enjoy maintenance (*grāsācchādana*) only but no right of inheritance or share on partition[29] (*klībaścānaṁśāḥ*). The same rule applies to an idiot (*jaḍa*), a lunatic (*unmatta*), a blind man and a leper. But if they are married and their children (*apatya*) are not like them, the children inherit their (father's) share. A son raised by levirate upon the wife of any such incapacitated person is, however, entitled to inherit the father's share.

A charge of impotence is important from the legal and social angles. So, for making a false accusation of impotence, a person is to be fined 12 paṇas.[30] Impotence has important effect on marital rights too. It is quite possible for a person suffering from impotence or other defects to marry. The marriage does not become void *ipso facto*. Kauṭilya directs a wife to leave her husband if he is impotent (*tyājyaḥ klibo'pi vā pati*)[31]. Kauṭilya does not clearly state if the wife of an impotent person can remarry. A defective person who has married before he becomes impotent (*lupte prajanane*) is allowed to appoint a relative to beget a son for him on his wife.[32]

To enable these persons to live, Kauṭilya makes provisions for their maintenance and employment. Like the Smṛiti-writers, he does not allow these persons to inherit properties. But the father's defect does not deprive an able-bodied child from inheritance.

Marriage provides these persons with a chance of normal life But the case of an impotent person is peculiar. Even though his marriage does not appear to be void in the *Arthaśāstra*, his wife is required to forsake him (*tyājya*). Her desire for progeny is, however, allowed to be satisfied by the practice of levirate. Kauṭilya does not allow a man to cohabit with a lunatic or leprous wife, but a wife can approach an insane or leprous husband for having children.[33] Manu and Yājñavalkya[34] also allow an impotent person to marry. But according to them, if the wife is chaste, she is entitled to

---

[29] *AŚ*. III. 5, *Manu*. IX. 201-22 makes a similar provision.
[30] *AŚ*. III. 18.
[31] *AŚ*. III. 2.
[32] *AŚ*. III. 5. The Mitākṣarā on *Yaj*. II. 141, however, allows such levirate. Kane, *HDS*. III. 617.
[33] *AŚ*. III. 2.
[34] *Manu*. IX. 203; *Yāj* II. 142.

maintenance, but if she is unchaste or hostile to the husband's family, she is to be driven out. But *Mitākṣarā* allows even an unchaste wife to claim maintenance. Nārada, Parāśara and some other Smṛitikāras, as we have seen, even allows the wife of an impotent person to remarry.[35]

Another type of defect is social ostracism. From early days ostracism plays a significant part in enforcing the rules of social and moral conducts. A person who deviates from the approved path is in many cases degraded from his caste and thrown beyond the pale of society. All early works enlist a large variety of sins (*pātakas*) and great sins (*mahāpātakas*) which cause degradation from the social status. Mm. Kane, however, observes: "The commission of every sinful act did not make one patita as the word was technically understood. There were various grades among sins. . . . . The grave sins were differently enumerated by different ancient writers."[36] Grave sins causing degradation include the murder of a *bhrūṇa* (foetus), violating the wife of a *guru* (elder or teacher), drinking liquor, sexual connection by a woman with a male of a lower caste (but not adultery in general).[37] *Patita* or an outcast is a pathetic creature, overburdened with many disabilities. Ostracism has not only the social or religious sanction to back it, the state also comes to enforce it.[38] The *Arthaśāstra* does not give us many details of the sins and great sins which lead to ostracism. They fall within the province of the Dharma literature. The *Arthaśāstra* takes the practice of ostracism for granted and imposes legal sanctions to strengthen it. Kauṭilya's concise rules regarding outcasts have great bearing upon morals. According to the *Arthaśāstra* an outcast (*patita*) is deprived of some valuable social and legal rights. Thus, an outcast (*patita*) or his children (*patitājjāta*) are not entitled to inherit or claim a share on partition.[38] A *patita* and his children are also not entitled to any maintenance.[39] With regard to inheritance and maintenance, an outcast is in a worse position than the impotent or other defective persons. The latter may enjoy maintenance but the outcast cannot. Even his son is deprived of inheritance but the sons of the defective persons are not. Jayaswal suggests that Manu improves the position

[35] Chaps. IV. & VII *Supra*.
[36] Kane, *HDS*. III. 612.
[37] *Ibid*. IV. 68-76.
[38] *AŚ*. III. 5.
[39] *AŚ*. III. 5; II. 1,

of a *patita* by allowing the son of his body to claim inheritance.[40] The *Arthaśāstra*, however, makes an exception in the case of mother, for, even if she is an outcast, she is required to be maintained by the son.[41] A *patita* is also not allowed to give evidence in a court of law.[42] But the more dangerous effect of ostracism is the break-up of the social tie. One who does not abandon a *patita* within a year becomes himself a *patita*. No one is permitted to associate freely with the outcast in connection with sacrificial rites (*yājana*), teaching (*adhyāpana*) and sexual matters (*yauna*). The person having such connection for a year is also to be degraded. Similarly, any other person dealing with the last-mentioned outcast is also made an outcast (*Saṁvatsareṇa patati patitena samācharan/yājanādhyāpanādyaunāttaiścānyo'pi samācaran*).[43] If the outcast is already married his wife is required to leave him (*patitas-tyājyaḥ*).[44] Kauṭilya does not expressly state if the wife can take another husband. We have already seen some Smṛitis grant her such a right.

It is significant that Kauṭilya does not reiterate the dreadful *prāyaścittas* or expiations prescribed by the *Dharmaśāstra* writers. The *Arthaśāstra* is satisfied with some penalties which have a social or legal bearing. Yet Kauṭilya follows the *Dharmaśāstra* writers in providing for measures which tend to break up an outcast's social and family tie. An outcast stands alone on the verge of society; his wife is asked to leave him; his religious, intellectual and sexual life receives a rude shock through social non-cooperation; and his economic security is also endangered. Brooding over the moral sin he has committed, he leads his own solitary wretched existence. To strengthen the reign of morality, Kauṭilya, thus, recognises social ostracism and gives it a legal sanction.

---

[40] Jayaswal, *Manu and Yājñavalkya*, p. 272. Mm. Kane writes: "In the case of the patita even his son born after he committed a grave sin was held to be patita by most of the Smṛitis . . . . But in case of the daughter a difference was mercifully made." Kane, ibid. Vol. III. 616. She might be married by one without taking any property from her *patita* father.

[41] *AŚ.* III. 1.

[42] *AŚ.* III. 11.

[43] *AŚ.* IV. 7. Also *Manu.* XI. 180. Kane, *HDS.* III. 614. It seems that Kauṭilya grants one year's grace in such cases but the orthodox school enjoins immediate degradation.

[44] *AŚ.* III. 2.

Chapter XIV

THE CARE OF THE BODY

No investigation into the morals of a society may be complete without a proper appreciation of its general attitude towards the human body. With it are associated the psychological factors relating to modesty, luxury and a sense of shame.

Love of physical beauty is a common feature in the society depicted in the *Arthaśāstra*. People like very beautiful, young women (*paramarūpayauvanābhiḥ*)[1]. A prostitute is raised to the status of a courtezan if she has beauty, youth and artistic skill.[2] Her beauty is sought to be protected by law. Any one who disfigures her beauty (*rūpamupaghnato*) is punishable in law.[2] Beautiful barmaids also wait upon customers in wine shops.[3] Megasthenes too admits that the Indians have a high regard for beauty.[4] Some Greek writers record that in the kingdom of Sopithes people go so far as to kill ugly babies to keep up the standard of beauty.[5]

The care and culture of the human body, as the *Arthaśāstra* clearly shows, find favour with kings and commoners alike. According to Kauṭilya's view, the human body, it seems, is not an object of scorn. Physical exercise and beauty culture are quite popular with different sections of the people. Some degree of specialization too marks these fields, for among the spies, the *Arthaśāstra* mentions[6] experts trained in looking after the human body. Thus, we hear of *Snāpaka* (bather), *Saṁvāhaka* (massagist), *Kalpaka* (barber) and *Prasādhaka* (beauty culturist). These experts have an easy access to royal officers and other well-to-do people. Not rarely do women take up these professions. The slave women (*dāsī*) in the royal harem usually do the works of bathers, massagists and florists. Sometimes, under the

1 *AŚ.* v. 2; xi; 11. 2; 13.2.
2 *AŚ.* ii. 27.
3 *AŚ.* ii. .25.
4 *Meg.* 69.
5 *MC. I.* 279.
6 *AŚ.* i. 12.

direction of such women, specialists (*Śilpinaḥ*) attend to these works.[7] It is significant that the *Arthaśāstra* looks upon the care of the body as an art (*śilpa*). Indeed, among the various arts that courtezans, slavewomen and actresses are required to be taught at the public expense, we find[8] mention of *saṁvāhana* (massage) and *gandha-mālya-saṁyūhana-sampādana* (the arts of using scents and making strings of flower). Versed in these popular arts, they may easily reach the heart of their patrons. Megasthenes, too, informs us that the Indians avail themselves of every device to improve their looks.[9] Massage is a common form of physical exercise. Speaking of the manners of the Indians, Megasthenes writes:[10] "Their favourite mode of exercising the body is by friction, applied in various ways, but especially by passing smooth ebony rollers over the skin." Thus, massage is so common a luxury that King Candragupta, says Megasthenes, used to attend to his royal business in court "when he is to be rubbed with cylinders of wood. He continues hearing cases while the friction, which is performed by four attendants, is still proceeding."[11] Cleanliness is scrupulously cultivated. So, morning and afternoon baths are prescribed for the King.[12] Prostitutes (*rūpājīvā*) who attend the royal harem are directed to make their bodies clean by bath (*rūpājīvā snānapragharṣaśuddhaśarīrā*).[13] It is common for citizens to be attended by slaves at the time of bath. Sometimes the master may bathe naked. But law prohibits the master to compel pledged maid servants to wait upon him, while he is bathing without clothes on (*nagnasnāpanam*).[14]

The sense of modesty, thus, militates against nudity. Nudity, even under the influence of drink, appears to be deprecated.[15] Nakedness in women is obviously discouraged. The *Arthaśāstra* probably makes it criminal even for the husband to call his wife, 'naked' or 'fully naked' (*nagne, vinagne*). These words are regarded as offensive

---

[7] *AŚ.* I. 21.
[8] *AŚ.* II. 27.
[9] *Meg.* 69.
[10] *Ibid.*
[11] *Ibid.* 71.
[12] *AŚ.* I. 20.
[13] *AŚ.* III. 13. Manu does not allow one to bathe naked (IV. 45). So also Gautama. (IX. 67) and Baudh. (II. 3.6.24).
[14] *AŚ.* III. 13.
[15] *AŚ.* VIII. 3.

terms.[16] Even as a part of flirtation with persons other than her husband the suggestion of disrobement by a woman holding her girdle (*nīvi-grahaṇa*) is a penal offence.[17] In this respect Kauṭilya's view differs from that of the ancient Greeks about whom Rattray Taylor tells us: "They had no fears of nudity, and their spontaneous enjoyment of physical beauty did not stop short at the private parts."[17] Keifer, however, points out "the constant deprecation of nakedness which is preached throughout Roman literature,"[18] though in practice gymnasts and actors often appeared on the stage completely naked. "The Romans almost always took nakedness to be synonymous with indecency, impropriety."[18] But nudity is sometimes popular with the Indian sages. Plutarch reporting on the interview of the Greek philosopher Onesikritos with Indian sages states: "He tells us that one of these men called Kalanos ordered him with the most overbearing insolence and rudeness to take off his clothes and listen naked to his discourse otherwise he would not enter into conversation with him even if he came from Zeus himself."[19] Arrian refers to the Indian sages who "go naked, living during winter in the open air to enjoy the sunshine and during summer, when the heat is too powerful, in meadows and low grounds under large trees......"[20] Megasthenes speaks of a sect of philosophers among the Brahmins: "Throughout life they go about naked, saying that the body has been given by the deity as a covering for the soul."[21] These sages must have been exceptions. In general the *Arthaśāstra* shows a great demand among people for variety in dresses. Kauṭilya himself is not in favour of gaudy dresses (*uddhata-veṣatvam*) even for the king and his courtiers (*anujīvin*).[22] The latter are advised to avoid the royal, gaudy or funny dresses (*rājño veṣoddhatakuhakānāṁ ca*). As usual dress is an important item of gifts. A lover presents a dress to his ladylove through a messenger.[23]

---

[16] *AŚ.* III. 3. Manu prohibits one to look at a naked woman (IV. 53). So does *Yāj.* (I. 135). *Gautama.* (IX. 48), however, confines this restriction to the case of other men's wives (*para-yoṣitaṁ*).

[17] R. Taylor, *Sex in History*, p. 240. Licht, *SLAG.* 86-90.

[18] O. Keifer, *SLAR.* 148-49.

[19] *MC. I.* 315.

[20] *Meg.* 215.

[21] *Ibid.* 120-21.

[22] *AŚ.* I. 6; V. 4.

[23] *AŚ.* XI.

Speaking of the manners of the Indians in general, Megasthenes too records: "In contrast to the general simplicity of their style, they love finery and ornaments. Their robes are worked in gold and ornamented with precious stones and they wear also flowered garments made of the finest muslin. Attendants walking behind hold up umbrellas over them."[24]

Curtius Rufus describes ambassadors from the Sudracae and Malli states in the Punjab as wearing robes of linen and embroidered with in-wrought gold and purple.[25]

Although gorgeous dresses might have been common among well-to-do people, ordinary folk use simpler dresses, as Arrian's record indicates: "The dress worn by the Indians is made of cotton, as Nearchos tells us...... But this cotton is either of a brighter white colour than any cotton found elsewhere, or the darkness of the Indian complexion makes their apparel look so much the whiter. They wear an undergarment of cotton which reaches below the knee halfway down to the ankles and also an upper garment which they throw partly over their shoulders and partly twist in folds round their heads."[26] Curtius Rufus also writes: "They cover their persons down to the feet with fine muslin, are shod with sandals, and coil round their heads cloths of linen (cotton)."[27]

The whiteness of the dress may be ascribed to the washerman's art, of which the *Arthaśāstra* gives us some interesting details.[28] It is possible to make the clothes 'as white as jasmine flower' or attain the natural colour of their thread or 'whiter by removing their dirt' or 'as white as flowers' or 'as beautiful and shiny as lac, saffron or blood'. "Trustworthy persons," says Kauṭilya, "shall be judges in disputes regarding colour and experts shall determine the necessary wages."

The *Arthaśāstra* further furnishes us with information regarding variety of dresses. The weaver's craft produces linen, silk, woollen and other garments (*kṣauma-kauśeya-patrorṇā-kambala-dukūla*).[29] An organised state textile industry is found to provide occupation to many

[24] *Meg.* 69.
[25] *MC. I.* 248.
[26] *Meg.* 224.
[27] *MC. I.* 188.
[28] *AŚ.* IV. 1.
[29] *AŚ.* IV. 2.

persons including women.[30] Curtius Rufus writes of the Sibi people in the Punjab wearing skins of wild beasts.[31]

Apart from dresses, the Indians, as the *Arthaśāstra* indicates, used various other devices to beautify their looks.[32] Gold, silver, costly stones, pearls and jewels, scents, flowers and ornaments add to the charm of men and women alike. Curtius Rufus gives us a similar record: "They hang precious stones as pendants from their ears and persons of high social rank, or of great wealth, deck their wrist and upper arm with bracelets of gold. They frequently comb, but seldom cut the hair off their head. The beard of the chin they never cut at all, but they shave of the hair from the rest of the face, so that it looks polished."[33] Arrian also records, "The Indians wear also earrings of ivory, but only such of them do this as are very wealthy, for all Indians do not wear them. Their beards, Nearchos tells us, they dye of one hue and another, according to taste. Some dye their white beards to make them look as white as possible but others dye them blue; while some again prefer a red tint, some purple and others a rank green."[34] McCrindle comments on this statement: "Perhaps some of these colours were but transition shades assumed by the dye before settling to its final hue."[35] Arrian adds further: "Such Indians, he also says, as are thought anything of, use parasols as a screen from the heat. They wear shoes made of white leather, and these are elaborately trimmed, while the soles are variegated and made of great thickness, to make the wearer seem so much the taller."[34]

All these details go to show that the concept of the mortification of the flesh makes little impression on Kauṭilya's mind. It is true that he asks *Brahmacārins*, *Vānaprasthas* and *Parivrājakas* to lead a hard life. We have already noted their duties in detail. But such ideals are not meant for common people. For them Kauṭilya sets up an ideal of balanced living.

"The Dharmaśāstra writers," observes Mm. Kane, "generally condemn suicide or an attempt to commit suicide as a great sin."[36]

---

[30] *AŚ.* II. 23.
[31] *MC. I.* 232.
[32] *AŚ.* IV. 4.
[33] *MC. I.* 188.
[34] *Meg.* 225.
[35] *Meg.* 225.
[36] *Kane, HDS.* II. 924.

Kauṭilya states: "If a man or woman under the infatuation of love, anger or other sinful passions commits or causes to commit suicide by means of ropes, arms, or poison, he or she shall be dragged by means of a rope along the public road by the hands of a *caṇḍāla*. For such murderers as the above, neither cremation rites nor any obsequies usually performed by relatives shall be observed. Any relative who performs funeral rites to such wretches, shall either himself be deprived of his own funerals or be abandoned by his kith or kin."[37]

Like Kauṭilya, Vasiṣtha[38] and Manu[39] deprive a suicide the benefits of funeral rites. Kauṭilya even penalises a relative who ventures to perform the funerals of a suicide. Indignities are directed to be hurled upon the corpse of a suicide. Even the abettors are made to suffer similar punishments. Lecky tells us how the medieval Christian Church inflicted similar punishments and indignities on a suicide. He says: "......no religious rites should be celebrated at the tomb of the culprit and that no masses should be said for his soul...... the corpse was soon subjected to gross and various outrages...... it was dragged upon a hurdle through the streets, hung up with the head downwards and at last thrown into the public sewer or burnt or buried in the sand below high watermark or transfixed by a stake on the public highway."[40]

"In spite of this general attitude," states Mm.Kane, "exceptions were made in the smṛitis, the epics and purāṇas."[41] He cites passages to show that the penance of suicide is prescribed for various offences like the murder of a *Brāhmaṇa*, drinking spirituous liquor, for incest and for theft, although some lawmakers condemn such a penance. Suicide at holy places is also approved by some writers,[41] while others allow suicide at the end of the great journey (*mahāprasthāna*) to meet death.[41]

Megasthenes also speaks of the sect of philosophers who "regard death with contemptuous indifference.[42] His account of the death of Kalonos, an Indian gymnosophist, shows that the practice of religious suicide prevailed in India."[43]

[37] *AŚ.* IV. 7.
[38] Vasiṣṭha, 23. 14-16.
[39] Manu. v. 89.
[40] Lecky, *History of European Morals*, VOL. II. p. 22.
[41] Kane, 9. *Ibid.* pp. 924-26.
[42] *Meg.* 160.
[43] *Ibid.* 106.

Speaking of some philosophers, Curtius Rufus writes: "These think it glorious to anticipate the hour of destiny and arrange to have themselves burned alive when age has destroyed their activity, or failure of health has made life burdensome. They regard death if waited for as a disgrace to their life and when dissolution is simply the effect of old age funeral honours are denied to the dead body. They think that the fire is polluted unless the pyre receives the body before the breath has yet left it."[44]

Megasthenes notes diverse attitudes prevalent in India towards suicide. At one place he speaks[45] of "those most eminent for their wisdom, who when sated with life, seek death by mounting a burning funeral pile". At another place Strabo states: "Megasthenes, however, says that self destruction is not a dogma of the philosophers, but that such as commit the act are regarded as foolhardy, those naturally of a severe temper stabbing themselves or casting themselves down a precipice, those averse to pain drowning themselves, those capable of enduring pain strangling themselves and those of ardent temperaments throwing themselves into the fire. Kalonos was a man of this stamp."[46] Other Greek writers tell us how this sage who hob-nobbed with foreigners and later on fell ill, voluntarily died on the pyre in the presence of the Greek army, without betraying any sign of pain.

[44] *MC. I.* 190.
[45] *Meg.* 160.
[46] *Meg.* 106.

Chapter XV

PLEASURES OF THE MIND

According to Kauṭilya, hunting, gambling, copulating and drinking originate from desire (*kāmaja*). He discusses them under the heading *puruṣa vyasana*. The word *vyasana*, as we have seen, means "whatever leads one astray from the good" (*vyasyatyenaṁ śreyasa iti vyasanam*).[1] It includes extreme addiction (*prasaṅga*) to pleasures.[1] So it appears that mere pursuit of pleasure is not condemned but an excess of it.

The *arthaśāstra*-writers, as we have already noted, discuss the relative merits and demerits of various pleasures. Interesting comparisons are made between hunting and gambling, gambling and copulation, and the like. If we get over the schematisation involved in the discussion, the essential moral concepts behind the enjoyment of pleasure will come to light.

Thus, to Piśuna, gambling is preferable to hunting, as in the former there is a chance of victory for an expert, while in the latter there is fear from robbers, enemies, wild animals, forest fires, accidents, risk of getting lost, thirst, hunger and death. Every modern hunter too knows these hazards of sylvan adventures. But Kauṭilya gives us the other side of the picture. To him the merits of hunting consist in physical exercise, cure of phlegm, bile, fat and sweat, dexterity in marksmanship, insight into psychology and the like, whereas gambling means defeat for one party, misuse of well-earned money, ill-gotten gain, loss of wealth already won and physical ailment due to suppression of nature's call and hunger. Kauṭilya obviously prefers hunting to gambling.

Another theorist finds in gambling the loss of the sense of time and the neglect of social duties. Yet others see in it mutual hatred and dissension. Kauṇapadanta prefers the association with women to gambling, but Kauṭilya thinks otherwise.

---

[1] *AŚ*. VII. 1.

Vātavyādhi, another theorist, is a protagonist for drinking, for, he believes that, under the influence of liquor, enjoyment of pleasure increases, goodwill emanates to all and sundry, cordiality to associates; and the strain of hard work vanishes. But Kauṭilya enumerates the evils of drinking, as it means loss of sense, mental deficiency, lack of movement and modesty and impairment of learning, knowledge, vitality, wealth and freiendship; it leads one to the company of undesirable persons instead of the good. According to Kauṭilya and many others, drinking is the worst of vices.

Despite divergent views of ancient thinkers, the *Arthaśāstra* suggests the general popularity of hunting, gambling and drinking in society.

As the *Arthaśāstra* points out, hunting is a popular pastime with kings and commoners alike.

Kauṭilya gives us some details of the royal hunt. In the *Arthaśāstra* we hear of *abhayāraṇya*.[2] Certain beasts, birds and fish enjoy special protection. It is a serious offence to entrap, kill or molest protected games or hunt in the reserved forest. We have elsewhere noted how the king is associated with troops of armed women in the palace, who possibly accompanied him on the hunting excursion. Kauṭilya states: "With a view to acquiring efficiency in the skill of shooting arrows at moving objects, the king shall engage himself in sports only in such forests as are cleared by hunters and houndkeepers from the fear of highway robbers, snakes and enemies."[2] "The king's path shall on both sides be well-guarded by staff-bearers and freed from the presence of armed persons, ascetics and cripple."[2]

Almost echoing Kauṭilya, Curtius Rufus says of an Indian King: "His principal exercise is hunting; amid the vows and songs of his courtezans he shoots the game enclosed within the royal park. The arrows, which are two cubits long, are discharged with more effort than effect, for though the force of these missiles depends on their lightness they are loaded with obnoxious weight".[3] Megasthenes also gives us a similar description.[4] He narrates how the king used to leave the palace "to go to the chase, for which he departs in Bacchana-

[2] *AŚ*. I. 21.
[3] *MC. I.* 189.
[4] *Meg*. 71.

alian fashion. Crowds of women surround him, and outside this circle spearsmen are ranged. The road is marked off with ropes, and it is death, for man and woman alike, to pass within the ropes. Men with drums and songs lead the procession. The king hunts in the enclosures and shoots arrows from a platform. At his side stand two or three armed women. If he hunts in the open grounds he shoots from the back of an elephant. Of the women, some are in chariots, some on horses, and some even on elephants, and they are equipped with weapons of every kind, as if they are going on a campaign."

It is significant to note that the royal hunt is highlighted by its association with women,—according to Curtius Rufus, courtezans. If Megasthenes is to be believed, the hunt starts in a Bacchanalian fashion, the attraction of which the presence of women no doubt accentuates. Elsewhere, we have seen how trains of women accompany the army in an expedition. We can well-imagine that the fair companions of the king in excursions, military or hunting, are not all naïve and soft ladies of fashion, for the Greek writers tell us of valiant Indian women who fought the trained soldiers of Alexander with commendable bravery.

Regarding the royal hunt, Aśoka too confirms the other sources: "Kings used to set out on pleasure tours—on these (tours) hunting and other such pleasures were enjoyed."[5]

The old mode of hunting with forest-beaters, from *Māchāns* or *Howdāhs* is still common in India. Arrian in his Indika writes: "The Indians hunt all wild animals in the same way as the Greek, except the elephant......"[6] His description of the capture of wild elephants still holds good to a large extent. It is out of place to state the details of the elephant hunt but the significant fact is that both Arrian[6] and Kauṭilya[7] agree that young or diseased elephants are allowed to escape.

Although Kauṭilya eulogises hunting,[8] he denounces too much addiction to it, for this might lead to crimes.[9] At any rate, like other

---

[5] *RE*. VIII.
[6] *Meg*. 220.
[7] *AŚ*. I. 31.
[8] *AŚ*. VIII. 3.
[9] *AŚ*. IV. 6.

vices it might result in contempt and penury.[10] Asoka, however, stopped hunting and other entertaining sports.[11]

Hunting is a sport for some and profession for others. Like thieves, gamblers and artistes, the class of hunters is, according to Kauṭilya, undesirable (*anarthya*), whose company leads one to ignominy and ruin.[10] They usually move about with their womenfolk.[12] Kauṭilya seems to suggest some laxity in moral character among this nomadic class. According to the Greek writers, hunters and herdsmen form a distinct 'caste'. Thus Megasthenes states: "The third caste consists of huntsmen and hunters who alone (*sic*) are allowed to hunt and to keep cattle, and to sell draught animals or let them out on hire. In return for clearing the land of wild beasts and fowls, they receive an allowance of grain from the king. They lead a wandering life and live under tents."[13] and elsewhere, "Herdsmen, who neither settle in towns nor in villages, but in tents. By hunting and trapping they clear the country of noxious birds and wild beasts."[14] A similar record is left by Arrian.[15] The professional hunters probably came from the aboriginals, for we find that 'they are nomadic and live on the hills' and 'half-wild'.

The popularity of gambling can be traced to the Vedic and the Epic ages. It is too deep-rooted to be stopped altogether. Kauṭilya tries his best to bring it to the open and regulate it. The *Arthaśāstra*, therefore, mentions an officer to superintend gambling.[16] His duty is to localise (*ekamukham*) gambling; to stop foul play; to provide for a standard dice at a rental; and to furnish gamblers with a den, accessories and water for drinking. This control is meant to detect criminals who live through secret means, check deceipt and bring funds for the coffers of the state through fines, forfeitures of stakes, license fees, rentals and five-per-cent tax on the prize. The *Arthaśāstra* directs that through these officers all sales and pledges of articles in connection with gambling should be made. Kauṭilya holds that gamblers are all

---

[10] *AŚ*. VIII. 3.
[11] *RE*. VIII.
[12] *AŚ*. III. 4.
[13] *Meg*. 84.
[14] *Ibid*. 40.
[15] *Ibid*. 216.
[16] *AŚ*. III. 20.

false players (*kitava*). In the *Arthaśāstra* like rules apply to all wagers or competitions, except literary or artistic contests.

As the *Arthaśāstra* shows, drinking is quite common with all sections of the people. Curtius Rufus also records that 'wine was much used by all the Indians'. He describes how the courtezans served wine to the king who would fall into a drunken sleep.[17] In spite of moralizing, Kauṭilya himself is not a prohibitionist.

Through the Superintendent of Liquors Kauṭilya attempts to control drinking.[18] The sale of wine is also localised. Thus the sellers of wine have a special locality reserved for them in the plan of the city.[19] The state officer causes liquors to be manufactured by experts in the fort, the village and the military camps. He centralises or decentralises the sale of drinks according to the laws of demand and supply. Liquor shops are set up wide apart. The liquor manufactured in the village is not allowed to be taken out. The excise rules provide for the sale of liquor in controlled small quantities, lest workmen might forget their work in hand, the Āryas outstrip decency and the rowdies commit indiscreet acts. Only persons of known purity of character are allowed to take out liquor without restriction. Alternatively, customers may be compelled to drink at the bars only.[18]

The bar is properly furnished. It consists of many rooms with seats and beds and contains scents, flowers and water, comfortable for different seasons (*ṛitusukhāni*). Barmaids of exquisite beauty wait upon the customers. With the assistance of these lovely women the bar-keeper keeps a watch over strangers, citizens and foreigners. Drunken brawls are not uncommon.[20]

Apart from maintaining peace and decency in society, this control of the liquor trade helps the authorities to detect and capture thieves and spies, citizens or foreigners. The officers are also directed to arrest extravagant customers. The *Arthaśāstra* is in this respect borne out substantially by Megasthenes who informs us that the board of five at Pāṭaliputra "attend to the entertainment of foreigners. To these they assign lodgings and they keep watch over their modes of life by means of those persons whom they give to them for assistance".

[17] *MC. I.* 189.
[18] *AŚ.* II. 25.
[19] *AŚ.* II. 3.
[20] *AŚ.* XIII. 4.

The keeper of the bar is liable to pay fine and compensation, if a customer, while drunk, loses any property.

The *Arthaśāstra* mentions different varieties of liquor, manufactured or imported. Some are used for medicinal purposes. The state ordinarily restricts the import or manufacture of liquor but on special occasions (*kṛityeṣu*) restrictions are relaxed or withdrawn. In such cases, families (*kuṭumbinaḥ*) perhaps for their home consumption are allowed to distil white wine, *ariṣṭa* for medicinal purposes and other types of liquors. In certain festivities, community entertainments (*samāja*) and tours (*yātrā*) free distillation of liquor is permitted for four days. Even women and children are allowed to ferment liquor and its variety, *kiṇva*. In other cases the state collects license fee or excise duty.

From the regulations prescribed in the *Arthaśāstra* it appears that drinking is often part and parcel of popular rites and festivals. On the occasion of the birth of a son, marriage and funeral ceremonies, guests are treated with toasts (*naiṣecanika*).[21] Even Āryas or persons with reputation (*jñātaśaucha*) take to drinking. As in the *Smṛitis*, in the *Arthaśāstra* too, a *Brāhmaṇa* is prohibited from dirinking *surā*.[22] If he does so, he is liable to be branded with the sign of vintage and banished from the realm or sent to the mines for ever.[22] A similar provision possibly prompts Megasthenes to speak of prohibition in India. This prohibition, however, does not appear to extend to other kinds of wine like *medaka* (rice-wine). Married women, however, may drink intoxicants (*madya*) with the permission of their husbands.[23] According to Megasthenes, soldiers at peace time while away their hours in idleness and drinking;[24] but Kauṭilya tries to prevent indiscriminate drinking at military camps.[25] The crafty politicians are likely to take advantage of the common weakness for spirituous liquors.[26] Megasthenes also records "A woman who kills the king when drunk becomes the wife of his successor".[27]

The connection of drinking with religious rites can be traced

[21] *AŚ*. XI. 1.
[22] *AŚ*. IV. 8.
[23] *AŚ*. III. 4.
[24] *Meg*. 85.
[25] *AŚ*. X. 1.
[26] *AŚ*. XII. 4.
[27] *Meg*. 70.

back to the Vedic days. The tradition appears to continue even in this age as the *Arthaśāstra* suggests. Megasthenes perhaps hints at this tradition when he states that Dionusos (Siva) taught the Indians "the way to make wine as well as other arts conducive to human well-being".[28] Arrian in his Indika makes a similar statement. But Megasthenes is obviously misled when he states about the Indians: "They never drink wine except at sacrifices. Their beverage is a liquor composed from rice instead of barley...."[28a]. This observation seems to emphasise the religious aspect of drinking. On the contrary. moralists seek to belittle a drunkard, for Kauṭilya holds that one who performs a sacrifice and one for whose benefit it is performed may dismiss each other if the other drinks *surā* or is a husband of a *śūdra* woman, murderer of a *brāhmaṇa,* violator of a preceptor's bed, a receiver of condemnable gifts, a thief or a bad performer of sacrifices.[29] Thus, like the orthodox *Smṛitis*, Kauṭilya places *surāpāna* in connection with sacrifices in the same category as great sins.

Kauṭilya refers to vinters (*śauṇḍika*) whose status in society does not appear to be enviable. They are included in the list of undesirable persons (*anarthyam*). They appear to be lax in morals. Often they serve the state as spies and poisoners. A close association with them, says Kauṭilya, makes a person suspect in the eye of law and an object of ridicule in society. The vinters like hunters roam about with their women.[30] Kauṭilya curiously holds that too much association with women leads one to drinks.[31]

Professional entertainers, according to Kauṭilya, belong to a similar category. The *Arthaśāstra* gives us a long list of such artistes. Thus, we hear of actor (*naṭa*), dancer (*nartaka*), singer (*gāyana*), player on musical instruments (*vādaka*), buffoon (*vāgjīvana*) and bard (*kuśīlava*),[32] acrobats (*plavaka*), juggler (*saubhika*),[33] tap-dancer (*tālavachara*), foreign entertainers (*vāhirikas*),[34] troubador (*chāraṇa*),[35] *śilpin* and *śilpakārikā*.

[28] *Meg.* 36.
[28a] *Meg.* 68.
[29] *AŚ.* III. 14.
[30] *AŚ.* III. 4.
[31] *AŚ.* VIII. 3.
[32] *AŚ.* I. 12; II. 1; II. 2.
[33] *AŚ.* II. 27.
[34] *AŚ.* II. 3; 4; 27.
[35] *AŚ.* II. 27; III. 4.

Ordinarily, these professionals seem to be recruited from the *Śūdra* caste, for, according to Kauṭilya, the duties of a *Śūdra* include craftsmanship and entertainment (*kārukuśīlava-karma*).[36] Like hunters, herdsmen, fishermen and vinters, tapdancers and troubadors are found touring along the highway with their womenfolk (*prasṛiṣṭastrīka*).[37] According to Kauṭilya, it is no offence for women to follow such professionals. Their women seem to be of loose character and are often employed by their menfolk in secret prostitution (*strīvyavāhrinām*). These women, as we have already seen, are mentioned, with courtezans and controlled by the Superintendent of Courtezans.[38] It is not unlikely that the female artistes are recruited from trained prostitutes, slave girls and those who earn their livelihood by entertainment. Sons of prostitutes are trained to appear on the stage as chief actors. We have elsewhere seen how the state funds are employed for training up actresses along with courtezans and slave girls in various arts.[39] The wives of actors and others of the like profession are also taught various languages and signs.[40] The teachers thus try to make them cultured ladies at the state expenses. For this class of women serves the ends of the state in various ways as spies, assassins, taxpayers and emergency tax-collectors.[41] For instance, the *Arthaśāstra* tells us how *plavaka*, *naṭa*, *nartaka* and *saubhika* induce their women, young and exquisitely beautiful, to tempt the leaders of non-monarchical states into lusty adventures and bring them to their doom.[42] These professionals again are expected to help a hostage to escape from the foreign prison.[43]

The royal entertainers receive pay from the state coffer. But it must be admitted that in the grades of pay, the artistes and musicians are placed very low. Thus, artistes (*śilpavantaḥ*) and trumpeters (*tūrya-kāraḥ*) draw 500 paṇas, musicians (*kuśīlavaḥ*) 250 paṇas, skilled artisans (*kāru-śilpī*) 120 paṇas, the maximum pay for Prime Minister, Minister, etc. being 48,000 paṇas.[44] The court bard (*māgadha*) how-

---

[36] *AŚ.* I. 3.
[37] *AŚ.* III. 4.
[38] *AŚ.* II. 27.
[39] *Supra.* Chapter X.
[40] *AŚ.* II. 27.
[41] *AŚ.* II. 27, V. 3.
[42] *AŚ.* X. 1.
[43] *AŚ.* VI. 17.
[44] *AŚ.* V. 3.

ever, draws 1000 paṇas. Teachers of music receive for public service honorariums varying between 1000 paṇas and 500 paṇas.[44] The artistes entertain the king with performances, from which safety rules ban weapons, fire and drinks.[45] They are specially protected by the laws of defamation[46] and criminal regulations concerning theft.[47] Sportive kings patronize artistes and craftsmen.[48] So do the leaders of non-monarchical states.[49]

Kauṭilya is very much conscious of the general laxity of morals among the artistes. He connects the vice of drinking with music and other arts.[50] Treachery and crimes are often found among artistes. Like traders and craftsmen, artistes are known as "thieves though not in name" (*corān acorākhyān*).[51] The law seeks to stop them from oppressing countrymen (*deśapīḍanāt*).[51] Experts fix their fees and charges.[52] Professional entertainers are not allowed by the state to disturb works in the villages (*naṭanartakagāyanavādakavāgjīvanakuśīlava vā na karmavighnaṁ kuryuḥ*).[52] So in the rainy season, when the cultivators are busy in the fields, the artistes are required to rest and are not allowed to tour.[53] Artistes, local or foreign, are subject to license fees (*prekṣāvetana*) and taxation.[54] In cities, they live in distinct localities.[55] The law forbids them to accept gifts exceeding proportion or to take recourse to flattery. They ordinarily have freedom in entertaining people. But law and decency prevent them from producing cheap stunts relating to locality, caste, family religion and copulation (*kāmaṁ deśa-jātigotra-charaṇa-maithunā-vabhāsena narmayeyuḥ*).[56]

Yet life is not without entertainments. In cities, curfew passes are granted to persons going to a theatrical performance passed by the censor.[57] The entire community in a village is expected to

[45] *AŚ*. I. 21.
[46] *AŚ*. III. 18.
[47] *AŚ*. 10.
[48] *AŚ*. VIII. 4.
[49] *AŚ*. XI.
[50] *AŚ*. VIII. 3.
[51] *AŚ*. IV. 4.
[52] *AŚ*. III. 13; II. 1.
[53] *AŚ*. IV. 1.
[54] *AŚ*. II. 27.
[55] *AŚ*. II. 3 & 4.
[56] *AŚ*. IV. 1.
[57] *AŚ*. II. 36.

organise and participate in public shows (*prekṣā*). "Any person who does not co-operate in the work of preparation for a public show shall, together with his family, forfeit his right to enjoy the show. If a man who has not co-operated in preparing a public play or spectacle is found hearing or witnessing it under hiding, or if any one refuses to give his aid in a work beneficial to all, he shall be compelled to pay double the value of the aid due from him."[58] It is significant that Kauṭilya connects public shows (*prekṣā*) with works of social welfare. Indeed, these spectacles are used for propaganda and other purposes. In times of national emergencies the state is required to organise charity performances, rites and festivities for raising funds.[59] Aśoka utilised these shows for preaching morality (*Dharma*). Thus he used to show the populace aerial chariots, elephants, balls of fire and divine bodies and spectacles connected with the Buddhist religion.[60]

Not all shows and sports are meant for universal presentation. Some are restricted only to the male and some to the female (*strī-prekṣāvihāra* and *puruṣa-prekṣāvihāra*). Shows are held both in day time and at night. A wife without her husband's permission is not allowed to witness any such show, otherwise she is liable to fine.[61] The shows are not always peaceful for we hear of rowdyism in them (*prekṣā-kṛityotsaveṣu*).[62]

Of common festivities we hear of sports (*vihāra*), tours (*yātrā*), community gatherings (*samāja*), entertainments (*utsava*) and garden parties (*pravahaṇa*) in the *Arthaśāstra*. The king participates in the festivities, only when they are policed by special groups. Attended by trustworthy bodyguards, the king also visits saints and ascetics. Aśoka takes pride in his visits to holy places. The king is to protect the beauty of the villages (*grāmaśovā*),[63] but halls (*śālā*) for rest or amusement are not allowed to be constructed in the villages.[64] Cities have their pleasure parks and the zoo for housing beasts, birds and wild animals.[65] The latter is maintained by the state funds. At the fringe of a forest

[58] *AŚ*. III. 10.
[59] *AŚ*. V. 2.
[60] *RE*. IV.
[61] *AŚ*. III. 3.
[62] *AŚ*. V. 1.
[63] *AŚ*. III. 10.
[64] *AŚ*. II. 1.
[65] *AŚ*. II. 6.

or in game-houses (*krīḍā-gṛiha*), lovers meet.[66] Women also take part in games (*krīḍā*). For this purpose married women are to take the permission of their husbands.[67] There are feasts at garden parties (*pravahaṇa*).[68] People enjoy themselves with great abandon in pleasure groves and other places of recreation.[63] Wine flows freely in festivities (*utsava-samāja-yātrā*).[69] The state organises *yātrā* and *samāja* for raising funds in emergencies.[70] These festivities have such a hold on popular imagination that a conqueror is advised to devote himself to the national and religious gatherings, entertainments and sports of the conquered country (*deśa-daivata-samājotsava-vihāreṣu ca bhaktimanuvarteta*).[71] According to Megasthenes, Bacchanalian fashion is well-known in the palace.[72] We have already noticed royal procession (*yātrā*) with music and pomp. Megasthenes even mentions some philosophers "as live on the mountains are worshippers of Dionysos ... They observe also certain customs which are Bacchanalian".[73] Kauṭilya too speaks of ascetics with a large retinue purporting to entertain the king and the royal family in some festivities (*pravahaṇa*).[74]

Kauṭilya suggests that some festivities have religious association (*daivata-samājotsava-vihāreṣu*).[75] The presence of *devadāsī* (temple dancers) has already been noticed.[76]

But there are other festivities purely secular in character. Possibly these are condemned by Aśoka. He tells us how the kings of yore used to set out on pleasure tours (*vihāra-yātrā*) when they indulged in hunting and like pleasures,[77] but the great monarch initiated *dharma-yātrā* or tours of morality.

In *RE I* he prohibits *samāja*, for he sees many evils associated with it. He, however, speaks with approbation only of one type of *samāja*—one inculcating moral excellence. Reading the said edict as a

---

66 *AŚ*. xi.
67 *AŚ*. iii. 4.
68 *AŚ*. xiii. 4.
69 *AŚ*. ii. 25.
70 *AŚ*. v. 2.
71 *AŚ*. xiii. 5.
72 *Meg*. 71, 111.
73 *Meg*. 97.
74 *AŚ*. xiii. 2.
75 *AŚ*. xiii. 5.
76 *AŚ*. ii. 23.
77 *RE*. viii.

whole it seems that in an ordinary *samāja*, large number of animals used to be killed, perhaps for a feast. But the great king restricted animal-slaughter considerably. Kauṭilya also advises a victorious king to restrict animal-slaughter.[75] His provisions in this behalf are somewhat similar to those in the Aśokan edicts.[78]

[78] Mookerji, *Candragupta Maurya & His Times*, Appendix III. pp. 243-44.

Chapter XVI

COURT LIFE AND MORALS

Part I

The King and the Royal Family

In every state the morals of the ruling class exercise a great influence on the moral life of the ruled. The conduct of the ruler and his associates sets an example and tends to cast a spell on the popular mind. It is, therefore, important to note how the *Arthaśāstra* depicts the moral life of those in charge of the government.

The luxury and splendour of Indian monarchs have all along been proverbial.

The king's life is, as usual, twofold—private and public. However, it is difficult to demarcate the two parts, for one is linked up with and influenced by the other.

At the head of the royal household stands the king. An ideal king, according to Kauṭilya, must undergo a broad education in various arts and sciences,[1] conquer his senses (*indriyajaya*),[2] avoid others' wives and properties, devote himself to the maintenance of law and order[3] and strive diligently for the welfare of his subjects. He must be an example of propriety and good conduct for all people. Dr. Basham remarks: "The *Arthaśāstra*, despite its advocacy of every dishonest expedient for the acquisition and maintenance of power, puts the kingly duty in simple and forceful language, setting an ideal such as few ancient civilizations can boast of."[4]

In his elaborate discourse on the sources of sovereignty Kauṭilya sets up a noble ideal of monarchy and enlists the high moral qualities that a king should possess. Kauṭilya harps on the necessity of an

---

[1] *AŚ.* I. 5.
[2] *AŚ.* I. 6.
[3] *AŚ.* I. 2.
[4] A. L. Basham, *The Wonder that was India*, p. 89.

ideal king's magnetic personality, intellectual acumen, spirit of enthusiasm and deep-rooted self-possession. Thus Kauṭilya elaborates these qualities as follows: "Born of a high family, godly, possessed of valour, seeing through the medium of aged persons, virtuous, truthful, not of a contradictory nature, grateful, having large aims, highly enthusiastic, not addicted to procrastination, powerful to control his neighbouring kings, of resolute mind, having an assembly of ministers of no mean quality, and possessed of a taste for discipline—these are the qualities of an inviting nature.

"Inquiry, hearing, perception, retention in memory, reflection, deliberation, inference and steadfast adherence to conclusions are the qualities of the intellect.

"Valour, determination of purpose, quickness, and probity are the aspects of enthusiasm.

"Possessed of a sharp intellect, strong memory, and keen mind, energetic, powerful, trained in all kinds of arts, free from vice, capable of paying in the same coin by way of awarding punishments or rewards, possessed of dignity, capable of taking remedial measures against dangers, possessed of foresight, ready to avail himself of opportunities when afforded in respect of place, time, and manly efforts, clever enough to discern the causes necessitating the cessation of treaty or war with an enemy, or to lie in wait keeping treaties, obligations and pledges, or to avail himself of his enemy's weak points, making jokes with no loss of dignity or secrecy, never brow-beating and casting haughty and stern looks, free from passion, anger, greed, obstinacy, fickleness, haste and back-biting habits, talking to others with a smiling face, and observing customs as taught by aged persons—such is the nature of self-possession."[5]

In the enumeration of the personal qualities of an ideal monarch Kauṭilya is in no sense inferior to the orthodox Smṛitikāras. By way of comparison we may cite one example. Yājñavalkya writes: "A king should have great energy, should be generous, mindful of past (good or bad) turns done by others, dependent on those who are advanced (in austerities, knowledge and experience), possessed of a disciplined mind, endowed with an even temper (in good or bad luck), born of a

[5] *AŚ*. VI. 1. (Shama Sastry's translation).

noble family (on both sides), truthful, pure (in body and mind), prompt in action, of strong memory, not mean-minded, not harsh (in words or acts), observant of the rules of dharma (as to *varṇas* and *āśramas*), free from vices, talented, brave, clever in concealing secrets (or according to Bhāruchi and Aparārka 'clever in scenting the secrets of his enemies'), guarding the weak points of his state, well-taught as regards logic, the science of government, the science of wealth and the three Vedas. He should be forbearing towards Brāhmaṇas, straightforward towards his friends, wrathful towards his enemies, and should be (kind) like a father towards his servants and subjects."[6] Kauṭilya also holds up the paternal ideal of monarchy (*piteva anugṛihṇīyāt*)[7]. Aśoka asserts: "All men are my children" (*sabe munise pajā mamā*).[8] Mm. Kane shows how the long list of kingly qualities set out by Śaṅkha-likhita and Kāmandaka agrees with that in the *Arthaśāstra*.[9]

But he must be a strong man, indeed, who can get over the corroding influence of royal luxury, splendour and power. Kauṭilya himself is conscious of the danger. He asks the king to give up lust, hot temper, greed, vanity, insolence and overjoy. Apart from stating the general precepts, he cites examples of the monarchs of old, who paid the penalty for greed, lust and other follies. So, we hear of Bhoja Daṇḍakya, who perished with his state and relations for making lascivious attempt on a *Brāhmaṇa* girl; of Karāla Vaideha for lust, and of various other kings for different vices.[10] Conversant with the erotic propensities of kings, Kauṭilya suggests means to bring about their downfall by pandering to their lust. Thus, dressed as a beautiful rich widow, the ancient Mata Hari, is called upon to present her plaint to the king sitting in judgment and tempt him into her snare and his doom.[11]

An ideal king must be busy the whole day and night. His daily routine is full of activities. The *Arthaśāstra* gives us useful details of a model routine.[12] Twenty-four hours are split up into two parts, one

[6] *Yāj*. I. 309-11, quoted in Kane, *HDS*. III. 44 and also *Mbh.* Santi. 118, 16-23.
[7] *AŚ*. II. 1.
[8] *SRE*. I.
[9] Kane, *ibid.* pp. 45-46.
[10] *AŚ* I. 6; cf Manu. VII. 41-42; Kane, *ibid.* p. 53 gives parallel passages in the *Mahābhārata, Kāmandaka, Śukranītisāra* and other works (pp. 60-61).
[11] *AŚ*. XIII. 2.
[12] *AŚ*. I. 19; Kane, *ibid.* (pp. 60-61) gives us parallel references.

for the day and the other for the night. Each part again is divided into periods, an hour and a half each. A short summary of the king's activities in these periods is instructive:

Day:

1. receiving guards and checking finances;
2. attending to the affairs of the city and the country peoples;
3. bath, food and study;
4. receiving revenue and meeting superintendents;
5. despatching writs, meeting council of ministers and hearing secret information;
6. favourite entertainment;
7. superintending the army in its four branches;
8. considering military plans with Commander-in-Chief; at the end of the day offering the evening prayer.

Night:

1. receiving secret emissaries;
2. bath, food and study;
3. entering the bed chamber amid music;
4. 5. } sleep;
6. rising with music and recalling *śāstric* injunction and contemplating on the day's duty;
7. considering administrative measures and sending out spies;
8. attending to spiritual matters, physicians, cooks and astrologers, etc., entering into court.

Daṇḍin laughs at a similar time-table, as it makes royalty a heavy burden.[13] But this heavy programme, however, can be altered according to the capacity of the king. For Kauṭilya states "or the king may divide the parts of day-time and night-time according to his capacity (*ātmavalānukūlyena*)".[14] It is significant to note that in the ideal routine only few hours are spared for the king's personal matters and enjoyment.

That this picture of a hard-working Indian king is not a mere figment of imagination is borne out by the Greek envoy. Megasthenes

[13] *Daśakumāracarita Ucchāsa,* VIII.
[14] *AŚ.* I. 19.

writes of Candragupta[15]: "The king leaves his palace not only in time of war but also for the purpose of judging causes. He then remains in court for the whole day, without allowing the business to be interrupted, even though the hour arrives when he must need attend to his person—that is when he is to be rubbed with cylinders of wood. He continues hearing cases while the friction, which is performed by the attendants, is still proceeding. Another purpose for which he leaves his palace is to offer sacrifices; and third is to go to the chase." "The king may not sleep during the day-time." Aśoka the Great also speaks of his active life. "This therefore I have done, namely that at all hours and in all places whether I am eating or I am in the closed female compartments, in the inner chamber (*garbhāgārā*), with the stud (*vraja*), on horseback (*vinīta*) or in pleasure orchards, the reporters may report people's business to me."[16]

Curtius Rufus, however, tells another story about the Indian kings: "The luxury of their kings or as they call it, their magnificence, is carried to a vicious excess without a parallel in the world.

"When the king condescends to show himself in public his attendants carry in their hands silver censers, and perfume with incense all the road by which it is his pleasure to be conveyed. He lolls in a golden palanquin garnished with pearls, which dangle all around it, and he is robed in fine muslin embroidered with purple and gold. Behind his palanquin follow men-at-arms and his bodyguards of whom some carry boughs of trees, on which birds are perched trained to interrupt business with their cries. The palace is adorned with gilded pillars clasped all around by a vine embossed in gold, while silver images of those birds which most charm the eye diversify the workmanship. The palace is open to all comers even when the king is having his hair combed and dressed. It is then that he gives audience to ambassadors and administer justice to his subjects. His slippers being after this taken off, his feet rubbed with scented ointment."[17] Curtius Rufus then describes the hunting and other excursions of the king in the company of courtezans, which we have noticed elsewhere.[18] The

[15] *Meg.* 70-71.
[16] *RE.* VI.
[17] *MC. I.* 188-89.
[18] *Supra.* Chap. X. and Chap. XV.

version of the royal life as given by Curtius Rufus may very well be true. In the epics and historical records we have many instances of profligate kings. On the other hand, the account of an ideal monarch given in the *Arthaśāstra* and confirmed by Megasthenes and Aśoka may equally be true. In every age and country there may be good kings and bad. Kauṭilya himself cites several instances of bad kings. But Curtius Rufus is certainly wrong in holding that the Indian kings are guilty of 'vicious excess without parallel in the world'. The history of monarchy throughout the world is replete with instances of royal luxuries and vices. To cite a few examples, Licht quotes an ancient writer who relates the case of a Persian king and his harem of three hundred women. "They slept during the day that they might be awake during the night which was spent by lamplight with singing and music and in cohabiting with the king. These women of the harem also accompanied him when he went hunting."[19] History knows much about the erotic adventures of Alexander himself. Justin openly accuses Alexander of illicit intercourse with the dowager Indian Queen of Massaga.[20] The gross perversities of many Roman Emperors are too well-known to be recounted here. We can safely conclude that the *Arthaśāstra* is speaking of an ideal of monarchy which might have been realised to a great extent in the lives of the early Maurya emperors.

The *Arthaśāstra* sheds light on the private life of the king. According to Kauṭilya, the king's life should not be devoid of pleasure. The king should enjoy life without detriment to moral and economic considerations. The *Arthaśāstra* wants the king to practise celibacy (*brahmacharya*) up to sixteen years of age and then to marry (*brahmacaryyaṁ cāṣoḍaśādvarṣāt ato godānaṁ dārakarma ca*).[21] The king may take more than one wife. Aśoka, in fact, had at least two wives. The second wife was named Kāruvākī. In addition, the *antaḥpura* or *avarodhana* undoubtedly consists of a number of concubines and courtezans. Aśoka mentions his harem (*olodhana*) and those of his brothers and also the residences of his sisters, located in the capital as well as in outlying towns.[22] Aśoka's second queen Kāruvākī probably had lands

[19] Licht, *SLAG.* 10-11.
[20] *MC. I.* 322.
[21] *AŚ.* I. 5.
[22] *RE.* IV.

at the outlying town[23] of K uśāmbī. The *Mahāvaṁśa* refers to another queen of Aśoka, living at Vediśā (Besnagar).[24] *Divyāvadāna* refers to two other queens, Tiṣyarakṣitā and Padmāvatī. Mahāvaṁśa speaks of the traditional 'sixteen thousand women' of the Aśoka's palace who were made to surround an honoured guest.[25] Kauṭilya also mentions royal harem and pleasure-nooks both within and outside the palaces (*bāhyāvyantara vihārarakṣāsu*).[26] These are guarded by competent officers. The *Kāmasūtra* provides: "Being adorned with jewels a king should pay a visit to the zenana in the afternoon and see all the ladies well-decked and assembled in a common place. The king should allot to them suitable palaces and honours at the proper time and according to their status and should pay loving attention to them and treat them with pleasant conversation full of jokes. Then he should see and treat the concubines (*punarbhūs*) in the same manner. He should then visit the courtezans (*veśyā*) accommodated in the zenana and also actresses. There should be separate apartments for these women in order described above. The chamber maid accompanied by the servants and the respective consorts should report to the king, after he has arisen from the midday nap, whose (of which consorts) turn of union (*vāsaka*) the day is, whose turn has passed and which of them has bathed after her menses...."[27].

The royal harem stinks with an air of suspicion and concealed dangers. The *Arthaśāstra* mentions detailed precautions against palace intrigues. Provided with many compartments, enclosed by parapet and a ditch, furnished with delusive chambers, underground rooms, secret doors, passages and hollow pillars, the harem is sought to be made proof against snake, fire and poison.[28] Women's compartments are provided with medicines and herbs useful in midwifery and diseases. Guards under the command of *Antarvaṁśika* (harem chief) stand on watch between two compartments. Aśoka mentions a minister in charge of affairs of women-folk. The officer is called *Strī-Adhyakṣa-Mahāmātra.*[29] According to Kauṭilya, a minister who has passed the

[23] Minor *PE.*
[24] *Māhāvaṁśa.* v. 85; xx.
[25] *Ibid.*
[26] *AŚ.* I. 10.
[27] *KS.* IV. 2. 75-80.
[28] *AŚ.* I. 20.
[29] *RE.* XII.

'love-test' may find employment in the royal harem. It is interesting to note that *Antarvaṁśika* is a highly paid officer. According to Kauṭilya, he draws 24,000 paṇas, second in rank in the matter of pay to the Prime Minister, Chief Priest, Commander-in-Chief, the Crown Prince, the Queen and the Dowager Queen who receive 48,000 paṇas each.[30] With spies in various garbs, old men and eunuchs watching the inmates including the palace guards, the harem is sealed off from inside. Ascetics, buffoons and public prostitutes are not allowed to go in. Only the prostitutes (*rūpājīvā*), clean, fresh from bath, wearing dresses and ornaments, attend the harem. Even the queen's relations have no right of ingress into it except in the cases of illness, pregnancy or death. Vātsyāyana too observes: "No woman of the palace should be allowed to go out of the palace nor any outsider to enter it except those who are known to be of good character."[31] According to Kauṭilya, before meeting the king, even the queen has to submit to body-searches by old maid servants. The proof of personal purity must be established before the king could touch any woman. Kauṭilya cites a number of instances in which the king was surprised by assassins in the harem, "for hidden in the queen's chamber, his own brother slew king Bhadrasena; hiding himself under the bed of his mother the son killed king Kārūśa; mixing fried rice with poison, as though honey, his own queen poisoned Kāśīrāja." Similarly, many other queens slew their husbands with poison painted on an anklet or coated on a gem or her zone or a looking glass or with a weapon hidden under her tuft of hair.[32]

Kauṭilya's apprehension for the personal safety of the king is justified by other sources.

Both Curtius Rufus and Diodoros Siculus refer to the episode of an eastern queen who fell in love with a lowborn person, a handsome barber, advanced him in the court circle, murdered or caused to be murdered her first husband, the reigning king, and, finally, set up the paramour on the throne.[33] She was the mother of Agrammes, ruler of Prasii and Gangaridae. The Jain traditions record a similar story.

---

[30] *AŚ.* v. 3.

[31] *KS.* iv. 2. 83.

[32] *AŚ.* i. 20; also *Kāmandaka.* vii. 51-54; Kane, *HDS.* V. iii. 845 for parallel passages.

[33] *MC. I.* 222, 282.

They describe Nanda as the son of a barber by a courtezan.[34] The *Divyāvādāna* reports that Aśoka kept a close watch on his harem. Once a royal lady (*antaḥpurikām*) gossipped with a prince. Both were beaten to death at the king's order.[35] The *Mudrārākṣasa* also confirms the tradition of intrigues and palace revolutions. The orthodox *Smṛitis* also advise the king to follow the rules of 'safety-first' much in the lines of Kauṭilya. According to Manu, "Only women devoted to him and well-examined and found safe as regards their dress and ornaments should be allowed to touch him when fanning or bathing him or applying perfumes to his body."[36] Even the *Mahābhārata* states that the king should trust nobody (*viśvasecca na kasyacit*), not even his sons (*putreṣvapi hi rājendra viśvāso na praśasyate*).[37]

Kauṭilya himself is fully aware of the possibility of lapses on the part of royal ladies, when he suggests that the spy should spin out a story of the queen's love for a minister. That the fabrications are likely to be believed suggests the probability of such incidents. Conversely, when, according to Kauṭilya, the minister's wife is likely to have liaison with the king, who might send her love-letters and presents to invite her into the harem, the luckless husband will merely fret and await his opportunity to take revenge.[38] A story of a confidence trick is suggested by Kauṭilya.[39] Dressed as a merchant, a spy is to pick up friendship with a beautiful personal maid of the queen, feign love with the new sweetheart, give her presents and jilt her with an ulterior motive. Another spy is to give her love-charm to regain her lover who in his turn purports to yield to the woman. Prompted by the immediate success of the love charm, the maid naturally conveys its efficacy to her royal mistress. The queen in her turn seeks to repeat the performance on the king. This time the poisoned charm kills the king. The *Divyāvadāna* narrates the legend of Prince Kuṇāla and his stepmother, Queen Tisyaraksitā, which indicates palace intrigues.[40] A similar legend finds place in the Jain *Pariśiṣṭaparvan*.[41] Here the step-

---

[34] *Pariśiṣṭaparvan*. VI. 232.
[35] *Divyāvadāna*. 377.
[36] *Manu*. VII. 219.
[37] *Mbh*. Śānti. 85. 33, 34.
[38] *AŚ*. XII. 2.
[39] *AŚ*. XII. 2.
[40] *Divyāvadāna*. 407-10.
[41] IX. 14-34.

mother wanted to sponsor the claim of her own son to the throne. Both *Pariśiṣṭaparvan*[42] and *Mudrārākṣasa*[43] record the tradition of the death of Candragupta's ally, Parvataka (or Parvata), through his contact with poison-maid (*viṣa-kanyā*). As a safeguard against poison, *Pariśiṣṭaparvan* states: "On Cāṇakya's order, the food of Candragupta was mixed with a gradual dose of poison, so that in the end even the strongest poison had no effect upon him. Once the queen Durdharā who was big with child was dining with the king, when Cāṇakya came upon them. Observing that the poison almost instantly killed the queen, he ripped open her womb and extracted the child. He had been nearly too late; for already a drop (*bindu*) of the poison had reached the boys head, who, from this circumstance, was called Bindusāra."[44]

No wonder that the *Arthaśāstra* provides for special protection of the king even from his near and dear ones.[45] Food and drink offered to the king are first tested for detecting poison. Women attendants offering scents, garlands, dress and other personal requirements to the king touch them by their eyes, arms and breast to vouchsafe their purity.

Manu also warns the king against poisoning. "The king should partake of food that is well-examined and prepared by servants that are trustworthy, that know the proper times (for dining), that cannot be won over, and over the food spells destroying poison should have been muttered. He should fix up in all that he partakes medicines that are antidotes against poison and should always wear gems that work against poison."[46] He cannot even sleep in peace, for Megasthenes states: "By night he is obliged to change his couch from time to time, with a view to defeat plots against his life."[47] In spite of all such restrictions for personal safety, the king's life is obviously not without pleasures and amusements. Subject to the safety-first measures, the kings take part in processions, journeys, entertainments, religious visits and other activities which bring him in contact with the people.[48]

The queens are part of a polygynous household. They are placed

---

42 VIII. 326-29.
43 Act. I.
44 VIII. 436-445; also Jacobi's introduction, p. 62.
45 *AŚ*. I. 20; 21.
46 *Manu*. VII. 217-18.
47 *Meg*. 70.
48 *AŚ*. I. 21.

in different ranks. Often, as we have seen, they take part in palace rivalry and intrigues. On violation of their chastity, the culprit (*antaḥpurapradharṣaka*) is required to be killed by placing burning fire on his head and hands.[49] Often ministers or other influential personages might be tempted to have an illicit liaison with a queen. Perhaps, she might take the first step through a go-between. To avoid this danger Kauṭilya forbids a king or a queen personally to play with the matters of heart in love-tests of ministers.[50] While on a royal tour, it is quite possible, as Kauṭilya suggests, that a queen might approach a minister at his residence for nocturnal adventures.[51] In the matter of succession to the throne, dowager queens might urge the cases of their respective sons. In these contests, the ministers play important parts. Occasionally, the queen might act as regent or herself ascend to the throne.[52] The episode of Queen Cleophis indicates that a kingdom might be ruled by a dowager queen. Megasthenes refers to Pandae in the extreme south of India, "as the only race in India ruled by women. They say that Hercules having but one daughter, who was on that account all the more beloved, endowed her with a noble kingdom. Her descendants rule over 300 cities...."[53] "The Pandean nation is governed by females, and their first queen is said to have been daughter of Hercules." These references, however, have been interpreted to mean the existence of matriarchy in South India.

Next in importance to the queen and other royal ladies are the prince and the princess. Often they are many in number. With no hard and fast rules of succession, princes are likely to have ambitions of overthrowing their father and ascending the throne. "Princes, like crabs, have notorious tendency of eating up their begetter," said Bhāradvāja quoted in the *Arthaśāstra*. So the text provides an elaborate discussion as to the means of protecting the king from the ambition of his son. Kauṭilya quotes the opinions of earlier *arthaśāstra*-writers who enjoin many devices like secret punishment, restraint, captivity inside the kingdom or outside it or residence with maternal relations. The pros and cons of these devices are discussed by the *Arthaśāstra*. One

[49] *AŚ*. IV. II.
[50] *AŚ*. I. 10.
[51] *AŚ*. V. 1.
[52] *AŚ*. I. 6.
[53] *Meg*. 150-51.

politician Vātavyādhi is reported to have prescribed a vicious remedy: "Princes may be suffered to dissipate their lives by sensual excess (*grāmyadharma*) inasmuch as rebelling sons do not dislike their indulgent father." "This," says Kauṭilya in contradiction, "is death in life, for no sooner is a royal family with a prince or princess given to dissipation is attacked, than it perishes like a worm-eaten piece of wood." Another politician Āmbhīya is reported to hold: "Any one of the class-mate spies may allure the prince towards hunting, gambling, liquor and women and instigate him to attack his own father and snatch the reins of the government in his own hands. Another spy shall prevent him from such acts." Kauṭilya strongly deprecates this depraved view and says: "There can be no greater crime or sin than making wicked impressions on an innocent mind" (*mahādoṣamabuddhabodhanamiti*).[54]

Kauṭilya gives us details of the ceremonies connected with the birth of the prince. "When the prince attains the necessary age, adepts shall train him under proper discipline," writes Kauṭilya. In keeping with his balanced view of life, he wants to set a high moral ideal before the prince. He attempts to save him from various vices in which royal children generally indulge; these are women, wine, gambling, hunting and ruthless ambition. Thus he states: "When under the temptation of youth he turns his eyes towards others' women, impure women under the disguise of Āryas shall, at night and in lonely places, terrify him; when fond of liquor, he shall be terrified by making him drink such liquor as is adulterated with narcotics (*yogapāna*); when fond of gambling, he shall be terrified by spies under the disguise of highway robbers; and when desirous of attacking his own father, he shall under the pretence of compliance, be gradually persuaded of the evil consequences of such attempt. . . ."[55] "When a prince is possessed of good and amiable qualities, he shall be made commander-in-chief or installed as heir-apparent." Mm. Kane rightly observes: "This symposium shows how the problem of the king's safety against bad princes taxed the ingenuity of all ancient writers on *Arthaśāstra* and how Kauṭilya advocated the only reasonable course possible."[56] Kauṭilya even favours the practice of raising a son

---

[54] *AŚ*. I. 17.
[55] *Ibid.*
[56] Kane, *HDS*. III. 83.

on the queen by another person. He emphatically states, "But never shall a wicked, though an only, son be installed on the royal throne."[57] In exceptional cases, however, even a wicked prince or a princess, a pregnant queen or even a child begotten on the princess by a man of same caste is allowed by Kauṭilya to be set upon the throne.[58]

The *Arthaśāstra* prescribes a wide syllabus for the education of a prince.[59] During his student life he has to study diverse subjects. "He shall observe celibacy till he becomes sixteen years old. Then he shall observe the ceremony of tonsure (*godāna*) and marry". Discipline is the keynote of royal tutelage. "In view of maintaining efficient discipline, he shall ever and invariably keep company with aged professors of sciences in whom alone discipline has its firm root."

The *Arthaśāstra* gives us the details of the adventures of a disinherited prince.[60] He might repair to the forest. He might flee his father's kingdom and contract marriage with the daughter of an influential personage in a neighbouring state. He might gather wealth by hook or crook, including intimacy with and murder of rich widows. He might adopt various disguises, biding his time. Spies or his mother, natural or adoptive, might reconcile him with his father. Otherwise, the father might by devious means cause him to be killed; alternatively, "he may be caught hold of at night by employing women equal to the occasion or by use of liquor or on hunting and brought back (to the Court)."

Often in the royal harem, a foreign prince, princess or women of high ranks or other persons are kept as hostages.[61] Kauṭilya mentions various modes of their escape. Dancers, actors, singers, players on musical instruments, buffoons, courtbards, swimmers, courtiers, prostitutes and female spies in the garb of wives help the prince in his escape.[62]

Kauṭilya's account of the private lives of the king and his near relations shows that the ideal of good living is placed at a high level. The king is personally required to be a model of perfection,

---

[57] *AŚ. ibid.*
[58] *AŚ.* v. 6.
[59] *AŚ.* I. 3.
[60] *AŚ.* I. 8.
[61] *AŚ.* VI. 3, 17.
[62] *Ibid.*

virtuous, self-controlled, taught in various arts and sciences and always devoted to the good of the subjects. Being a practical thinker, Kauṭilya knows the problems of court-life, its intrigues and treacheries. He, therefore, asks the king to take adequate precaution for his personal safety. With regard to the princes, Kauṭilya definitely sets a higher moral norm than his predecessors quoted by him. Kauṭilya believes in education and discipline as the best precaution against moral laxity. In the tussle between the king and his disinherited son, Kauṭilya no doubt advocates some measures which may very well be questioned by moralists. But these are extreme measures, a necessary part of the game of politics. Necessity for these dubious measures may not arise at all if Kauṭilya's advice regarding education of the prince is followed scrupulously.

PART II

STATE EMPLOYEES

With regard to ministers and other government servants, Kauṭilya's ideal is similarly high. According to Kauṭilya, "Sovereignty is possible only with assistance. A single wheel can never move" (*sahāyasādhyaṁ rājatvam cakramekaṁ na vartate*).[1] So the king has to depend upon his ministers (*sacivān*). They must combine theoretical knowledge with practical acumen.[2]

In the selection of ministers and other officers the *Arthaśāstra* asks the king to exercise great care. The *Arthaśāstra* gives us many interesting details of the intellectual and moral qualifications of an ideal officer of the state. "Native, born of high family, influential, well-trained in arts, possessed of foresight, wise, of strong memory, bold, eloquent, skilful, intelligent, possessed of enthusiasm, dignity and endurance, pure in character, affable, firm in loyal devotion, endowed with excellent conduct, strength, health and bravery, free from procrastination and ficklemindedness, affectionate, and free from such qualities as excite hatred and enmity—these are the qualifications of a ministerial officer (*amātyasampat*)."[3] Kauṭilya mentions various examinations to test the character of the officers. These throw an interesting light on the question of morals. Assisted by his chief minister and *purohita*, the king is to conduct the tests for examining *amātyas*, in four important matters, *viz.*, religion, money, love and fear.[4] Temptations are offered to the *amātyas* in these matters to see if they can resist them or not. Of these, the love allurement deserves special mention. "A woman spy under the guise of an ascetic and highly esteemed in the harem of the king, may allure each minister (*mahāmātra*) one after another, saying, 'The queen is enamoured of thee and has made arrangements for thy entrance into her chamber;

---

[1] *AŚ*. I. 7.

[2] *AŚ*. I. 8.

[3] *AŚ*. I. 9, Kātyāyana gives similar qualifications (IV. 35-38).

[4] *AŚ*. I. 10.

besides this, there is also the certainty of large acquisitions of wealth.' If they discard the proposal, they are pure." In any event, the test indicates the inherent weakness of a large royal harem. A secret erotic liaison between a minister and a royal lady is not an impossible affair.

A pass in the religious test secures for the candidate a judgeship in civil and criminal courts; in the money test, the post of revenue collector or chamberlain; in the love test, the office for protecting the king's ladies in and outside the court (*bāhyāvyantaravihārarakṣāsu*); and in the fear test, the post of personal officer of the king (*āsannakāryeṣu rājñaḥ*).

A pass in all the tests makes the candidate a *mantrin* or minister.

If a candidate fails in all the tests, he may still be engaged in some minor governmental job requiring bodily exertions.

The inherent danger in offering temptation does not escape the attention of Kauṭilya. For, it might corrupt the pure for ever. " . . . Nor shall he vitiate the pure, like water with poison. Sometimes the prescribed medicine may fail to reach the person of moral disease; the mind of the valiant, though naturally kept steadfast, may not, when once vitiated and repelled under the four kinds of allurements, return to and recover its original form." So Kauṭilya enjoins that the king and the queen should never personally take part in offering temptations but rather ascertain the character of the officers through organised espionage.

Kauṭilya advises the royal officers (*anujīvī*) to avoid all complications with women, pimps and undesirable persons like professional artistes.[5]

Kauṭilya knows that "the life of a man under the service of a king is aptly compared to life in fire; whereas fire burns a part or the whole of the body, if at all, the king has the power either to destroy or to advance the whole family, consisting of sons and wives of his servants." So Kauṭilya advises: "Self-protection shall be the first and constant thought of a wise man."[5]

The officer is expected to be a good thought-reader. He should not try to contradict the king openly for his moral lapses but should employ the method of pleasant persuasion. "He may even keep silent, but should never describe what is hateful." "He shall follow the king in his pursuits after hunting, gambling, drinking and sexual pleasures.

[5] *AŚ.* v. 4.

Ever attending upon the king, he shall by flattery, endeavour to arrest his fall into evil habits and save him from the intrigues, plots and deceptions of his enemies."[6] The high dignitaries of the state often participate in the palace intrigues. Bhāradvāja quoted by Kauṭilya advises them to aspire to the throne. But Kauṭilya contradicts him and observes that they should not do such an immoral act (*adhaɪmiṣṭham*).[7] Kauṭilya, moreover, is not tolerant towards wicked ministers (*duṣyamahāmātra*), courtiers (*ballabha*) and other dignitaries (*mukhyas*), if they cause harm to the state (*rājyopaghātinaḥ*). They are to be ruthlessly punished. As they wield influence, open punishment may be risky. In such a case, Kauṭilya does not hesitate to prescribe secret murders (*upāṁśudaṇḍa*) to do away with them.[8] The ethics of the measures prescribed by Kauṭilya have been discussed in the next chapter.

Apart from oppression of the people and participation in palace intrigues, the state officials, as we have seen, might be involved in affairs of the heart. Some public officer might possibly carry on with the queen or other royal ladies; with the wife, daughter or daughter-in-law of another minister;[9] with the wife of even his own father, brother or son;[10] and more commonly with public women[11]. Kauṭilya obviously deprecates such adventures, but is prompt to take advantage of them for the furtherance of the ends of the state. The king might, according to Kauṭilya, provoke a wicked minister to indulge in such affairs and ultimately bring about his ruin.

According to the *Arthaśāstra*, in court life as well as in public life, espionage plays a very significant role. The *Arthaśāstra* devotes a large space to its organisation and work.[12] It is not within our province to give full details of the organisation and exploits of the spies as mentioned in the *Arthaśāstra*. We should only refer to some facts about them as may have some bearing on the question of morals in society.

Spies are recruited from various spheres of life; they come from

[6] *AŚ*. v. 5.
[7] *AŚ*. v. 6.
[8] *AŚ*. v. 1.
[9] *Ibid.*
[10] *Ibid.*
[11] *AŚ*. v. 4.
[12] *AŚ*. i. 11-14; v. 1. 2; xi; xii. 2, 3, 4, 5; xiii. 1, 2.

different castes, sexes (male, female or eunuch), intellectual and artistic classes, various professions and callings, merchants, traders, ascetics and prostitutes. Thus we get different types of spies in the *Arthaśāstra*, for example, 'crypto-student, recluse, householder, merchant, ascetic, classmate, firebrand, poisoner and mendicant woman'. They keep watch in their respective fields. For the overriding purposes of the state, no amount of fraud and deception is beneath them. In general, they seize upon the credulity and weakness of their fellowmen and discover secrets for the benefit of the state. Neither religious scruple nor moral principles deter them from pursuing the ends of the state.

Directly under the king are the last four classes who roam about everywhere, in private residence, fields and forests, schools, shops and amusement halls, cities and suburbs, forts and army camps, home and foreign territories. They watch princes and royal officers, citizens and foreigners in their public and private activities. Servants, entertainers and other persons who frequent private households collect private information.

Apart from collection of news, these trained personnel are employed in various state services, *viz.* killing traitors, dividing enemies, raising funds for the state, carrying on publicity and propaganda for the state and what not. Many of them tempt men and women in the matters of the heart. Eros finds a boon companion in some. Keepers of harlots cause beautiful young women to ensnare leaders of the armed forces to cause dissensions in the army. Astrologers and mendicant women rouse the ambition of the minister and his wife for seizing the royal throne.

Strict moralists always question the ethics of espionage. The Encyclopaedia Britannica observes: "The clandestine character of espionage lays it open to objection from the moral point of view, and espionage is, in fact, often practised by persons of undesirable character. As Montesquieu says, 'Spying might perhaps be tolerable if it were done by men of honour; but the infamy which invariably attaches to the agent is a criterion of the infamy of practice.' Individuals have taken the view that by practising espionage they were performing a necessary service to their own country."[13]

---

[13] *Encyclopaedia Britannica*, 14th Edition, ESPIONAGE.

Whatever might be the moral consideration, the fact remains that espionage is an accepted institution in politics. In the modern age we have different types of espionage—private, political, diplomatic and military. The same authority gives us instances of secret agents in Europe who "penetrated into all strata of society, gained the confidence of conspirators, sometimes acted as agents provocateurs and sent in reports which varied in value according to the intelligence and character of the agent. They were and still are of considerable assistance to their governments . . . . " Again, "Acts of espionage are recorded in the Bible and by classical authors such as Xenophon and Caesar. Organised espionage did not however exist until the 17th century under Cromwell in England and Richelieu in France."

It is important to note that Kauṭilya has the political sagacity to provide for a well-knit organisation of spies. His methods of espionage find support in modern examples. The same modern authority states: "In obtaining information, spies either act for themselves or bribe other persons who have access to the information which they require. In this, money and women's wiles both play an important part as is shown by all the spy trials which have taken place at various times." In the *Arthaśāstra* too money and women are prominent in matters relating to espionage.

Even the orthodox works harp on the importance of espionage. Manu[14] asks the king to employ five classes of spies (*pañcavarga*) which have been interpreted by Medhātithi and Kullūka to mean "kāpaṭika, udāsthita, gṛihapati, vaidehaka and tāpasavyañjana". These are some of the types of spies mentioned in the *Arthaśāstra*. Manu also directs the king to employ spies (*cārān*) in war time.[15] The epics again refer to the system of espionage. "Kings see through the spies (*cāraiḥ paśyanti rājānaḥ*)",[16] says the *Mahābhārata*. Megasthenes too speaks of their organised existence. According to him the spies or overseers form a distinct class. They are connected with the courtezans of the city and of the camp.[17] Aśoka mentions *pativedaka* or informers who have direct approach to the emperor even in his private apartments.

[14] *Manu*. VII. 154 & 184.
[15] *Ibid.*
[16] *Mbh.* Udyoga, 34. 34.
[17] *Meg.* 41, 85.

We might profitably quote the observation of Mm. Kane on this point. "One need not feel surprised at the machinery of espionage that Kauṭilya so elaborately describes. All governments in modern times keep themselves informed of the activities, views and resources of their opponents. We know also how the Indian Police, in order to catch offenders against the Prevention of Gambling Act or other similar Acts, employ agents with marked coins or notes and draw in their net unsuspecting people."[18] The learned scholar is rightly supported by Dr. Basham who remarks: "The ancient Indian secret service has incurred much criticism, some of which is not wholly fair. Probably no government at any time has been able to function without such secret agents of some sort, if only honest detectives for the suppression of crime, and every ancient civilization had its spies, though perhaps not so thoroughly organized as in the system of the *Arthaśāstra*."[19]

---

[18] Kane, *HDS*. III. 131.
[19] A. L. Basham, *The Wonder that was India*, p. 122.

Chapter XVII

PUBLIC LIFE AND MORALS

Kauṭilya has been bitterly criticised for his supposed indifference to the use of 'immoral' means for political purposes. With the ends of the state in view Kauṭilya prima facie seeks to set at naught the very ideals of marriage, family life and other social and moral virtues which he advocates in ordinary cases. Many suggest his comparison with Machiavelli who, according to Sabine, "offers an extreme example of a standard of morals, one for the ruler, another for the private citizen."[1] It is necessary to find out to what extent Kauṭilya allows the state to flout the ordinary rules of law and morality, chiefly relating to marriage and family life, for promoting political ends.

Many Indian thinkers, orthodox or otherwise, have in the past enunciated the doctrine of four means (*upāyas*) or expedients of state policy. These are *sāma* (conciliation), *dāna* (making gifts), *bheda* (causing dissensions) and *daṇḍa* (punishment). This doctrine is well-known to Kauṭilya as also to Manu and other orthodox thinkers.[2] Kauṭilya goes even further and makes permutations and combinations of these expedients.[3] Yet like orthodox thinkers Kauṭilya is primarily in favour of peaceful methods of conciliation, gifts or dissensions, and, failing these, as the last resort, punishment. For instance, discussing the contented and the discontented elements among citizens, Kauṭilya observes: "Honours and rewards shall be conferred upon those that are contented, while those that are disaffected shall be brought round by conciliation, by gifts or by sowing dissension or by punishment."[4] "The greater the contentment of such persons the more shall be the honour shown to them while those who are disaffected shall be ingratiated by rewards or conciliation; or dissension may be sown against them so that they may alienate themselves from each other. . . Failing this measure, they may be so employed in collecting fines

[1] Sabine, *A History of Political Theory*, p. 341.
[2] Kane, *HDS* III. 171-2; *Manu.* VII. 109 *Yāj.* I. 346.
[3] *AŚ.* IX. 7.
[4] *AŚ.* I. 13.

and taxes as to incur the displeasure of the people. Those who are inebriated with feelings of enmity may be put down by punishment in secret or by making them incur the displeasure of the whole country."[4] Similar rules are also prescribed in connection with foreign policy.[5] Manu also says that for the prosperity of one's kingdom *sāma* and *dāna* are preferred, but if the king's antagonists do not yield to him by the employment of the first three *upāyas*, then he may bring them round by *daṇḍa*, and that *daṇḍa* is to be employed as the last resort, since victory is not certain.[6] The great epic also has similar provisions.[7]

So it appears that even the orthodox thinkers do not discard *bheda* and *daṇḍa* as means to be pursued by the state. Like Kauṭilya, Manu states that the king should protect the good and kill the bad people (*hanyācca paripanthinaḥ*).[8] *Divide et impera* has ancient traditions throughout the world.

While the orthodox writers like Manu do not give us detailed methods of causing dissension and awarding punishment as matters of the state policy, Kauṭilya's work is full of many such details. We have a full contingent of secret murders, poisoning and other devious means suggested by Kauṭilya. Many methods of causing dissensions have important bearing on morals too. For state purposes Kauṭilya seeks to utilise the moral weakness of people. With that end in view he does not in some cases hesitate to break up the family loyalty or marital fidelity. Thus for suppressing wicked officials by secret means he advises the secret agents employed by the state to incite a son to kill his wicked (*duṣya*) father; a brother to quarrel with another for a share of the patrimony or a near relation to kill another on a charge of incest.[9] For dividing the leaders of the corporations, Kauṭilya wants the spies to stir up jealousy about family and social status; to excite sexual cravings of the leaders with the help of beautiful widows and prostitutes; to induce the leaders to abduct or rape the wife, sister, daughter or daughter-in-law of a poor man; or to make a jealous husband fight another person over a got-up erotic affair with the wife.[10]

---

[5] *AŚ.* v; ix; vii. 14; xi. 1.
[6] *Manu.* vii. 108-9; 198-200.
[7] *Mbh.* Udyoga. 150; Sānti. 69. 23.
[8] *Manu.* vii. 110.
[9] *AŚ.* v. 1.
[10] *AŚ.* xi.

Apart from taking advantage of the sexual weakness, Kauṭilya does not hesitate to advise the state to derive profit out of religious beliefs and credulities of the people. Thus, the superintendent in charge of idols (*devatādhyakṣa*) is directed to arrange for various tricks regarding idols and fleece the believers.[11] The shamans and medicine-men are asked to administer poison to undesirable persons who might have faith in their drugs.

One, however, must not forget that even the orthodox works mention similar tricks and devious methods for causing dissension and death. The *Mahābhārata* has some well-known instances, *viz.* burning of *Jatugṛiha;* Bhīma, dressed as Draupadi, meeting Kīcaka and so on. The *Viṣṇudharmottara* refers to secret punishments.[12]

Once the necessity for *bheda* and *daṇḍa* is recognised, it is probably a question of expediency as to how the methods are to be applied. As we have already seen, Kauṭilya does not usually run after *bheda* and *daṇḍa* involving all such devious means.

With regard to secret punishments (*upāṁśudaṇḍa*) Kauṭilya solemnly states: "A king in the interest of righteousness may inflict punishment in secret on those courtiers or confederacy of chiefs who are dangerous to the safety of the kingdom and who cannot be put down in open daylight."[13] So Kauṭilya lays down strict conditions for adopting the extreme step.

Again, regarding the exaction of wealth from citizens in an emergency, Kauṭilya observes: "measures such as above shall be taken only against the seditious and the wicked, and never against others" (*evam duṣyeṣvadhārmikeṣu ca varteta netareṣu*).[14] With regard to foreign policy also, harsh methods, according to Kauṭilya, are required to be applied only when peaceful methods fail. Goodhart observes: "If our basic premise is grounded on the view that all men are wicked and are not to be trusted, then we shall get a peculiarly warped moral law. I think that this explains the extraordinary conclusions reached by Machiavelli and Hobbes. Thus in the eighteenth chapter of *The Prince*, Nicolo Machiavelli discusses 'The way princes should keep

[11] *AŚ.* v. 2.

[12] II. 146, quoted in Kane, *HDS.* III. 173. Similar provisions are also found in the South Indian Kural of Tiruvalluvar. *HCIP.* II. 325.

[13] *AŚ.* VI.

[14] *AŚ.* v. 2.

faith' and he reaches the conclusion that they should not do so if it is against their interest. 'If men were entirely good this precept would not hold but because they are bad, and will not keep faith with you, you too are not bound to observe it with them.' If it is true that men are bad then his conclusion that there is no duty to keep faith with them is perfectly reasonable. The result is that morality disappears and only force remains."[15] Sabine also restates Machiavelli's view: "Since the ruler is outside the group, or at least in a very special relation to it he is above the morality to be enforced within the group."[16]

But Kauṭilya's vision is not blurred by pessimism about human nature. To him all men are not bad. As a practical politician, he knows the common fact that some men are good and some bad. So he warns the king against taking recourse to secret punishments and extortions of wealth in the case of good, virtuous men. In general the *Arthaśāstra* requires the king to be very careful in awarding punishment of whatsoever nature. If he inflicts an unjust punishment, he himself will have to pay the *Brāhmaṇas* thirty times the amount of the punishment measured in money and to undergo a penance.[17] So, in Kauṭilya's theory at least, the king is not above the law. Kauṭilya's concern for the state is not really meant for the personal gain or power of the king. His ideal is the welfare state. He boldly asserts: "In the happiness of the subjects lies the happiness of the king; in the welfare of the subjects lies his welfare. In personal pleasure does not lie the king's welfare but whatever pleases his subjects he shall consider as good." (*prajāsukhe sukhaṁ rājñaḥ prajānāṁca hite hitam / nātmapriyaṁ hitaṁ rājñaḥ prajānāṁ tu priyaṁ hitam*).[18]

In the basic approach to morality Kauṭilya and Machiavelli sharply differ. Machiavelli says: "Therefore it is unnecessary for a prince to have all the good qualities I have enumerated, but it is very necessary to appear to have them. And I shall dare say this also, that to have them and always to observe them is injurious and that to appear to have them is useful; to appear merciful, faithful, humane, religious, upright, and to be so, but with a mind so framed that should

[15] A. L. Goodhart, *English Law and Morals*, p. 34.
[16] Sabine, *ibid.* p. 341.
[17] *AŚ.* IV. 13.
[18] *AŚ.* I. 19.

you require not to be so, you may be able and know how to change to the opposite."[19] Thus Machiavelli openly advises the prince to cultivate a habit of deception. In enumerating the good qualities of the king nowhere does Kauṭilya say that the king should simulate those virtues.[20] Machiavelli further states: ".. let the prince have the credit of conquering and holding his state, the means will always be considered honest, and he will be praised by everybody; because the vulgar are always taken by what a thing seems to be and by what comes of it; and in the world there are only the vulgar . . ."[21] But unlike Machiavelli, Kauṭilya does not justify the principle of any means against anybody. As we have seen, Kauṭilya clearly forbids the application of the devious methods against the good and virtuous people. In connection with foreign policy, Kauṭilya advocates duplicity and appeals to arms, when peaceful methods fail. In this view of morality Kauṭilya, we have seen in the chapter on *Relativity of Morals*, does not fundamentally differ from the orthodox moralists in ancient India.[22]

We might, therefore, conclude that Kauṭilya grants only a limited approval to the 'immoral' actions in public life, but that is done not for the personal aggrandizement of the king but for the ultimate benefit of the people. In his justification, we quote Croce: "But the truth is that if, at a time when the moral conscience was at its greatest clarity, the performance of these actions proved necessary (necessary, of course, not to satisfy one's own lust for power or other private ambitions or passions, and not because of the habit of brutality and evil-doing, but for the sacred protection, for the development, or for the rebirth of the fatherland) these actions can be neither a breach of promise, nor murder, nor any kind of roguery or wickedness; just as the 'magnanimous lie' of which Tasso speaks could not be a 'lie', exactly because it was 'magnanimous', except as a poetic metaphor."[23]

---

[19] Machiavelli, *The Prince*, p. 139. Also Kangle, *op. cit.* pp. 269-73.
[20] *AŚ.* VI. 1.
[21] *Op. cit.* p. 140.
[22] Chapter II. *Supra.*
[23] B. Croce, *Politics & Morals*, p. 9.

Chapter XVIII

MORALS IN NON-MONARCHICAL STATES

Scholars have accepted the existence of non-monarchical states in ancient India. Their antiquity is in dispute. Some find references to them in the Vedic texts and Pāṇini's grammar. The Buddhist and the Jain works clearly show that such states functioned in many parts of India. The Great Epic states some important features of these states. The Greek writers testify to their existence. The rise and fall of non-monarchical states have received attention from several well-known scholars.[1]

Kauṭilya speaks of two classes of corporations (*saṁghas*), viz. one following agriculture, cattle-breeding, trade and military professions (*vārttāśastropajīvinaḥ*) and the other living on the epithet of king (*rājaśabdopajīvinaḥ*). To the first class belong the Kṣatriya guilds of Kāmboja, Surāṣṭra and other places. According to Dr. Majumdar, these are guilds which take up the profession of arms and have "sometimes an independent political career."[2] To the other class belong the Licchavikas, Vṛjikas, Mallakas, Madrakas, Kukuras, Kurus and Pāñcālas. "The list of corporations given above is indeed suggestive. It includes Vṛjikas, Licchavikas and Mallakas in the east, the Kurus and Pāñcālas in the centre, the Madrakas in the north-west and the Kukuras in the south-west, of northern India .... That they possessed considerable power is admitted by Kauṭilya himself when he says that to a king the acquisition of the help of corporations is better than the acquisition of an army, a friend or profit."[3] Dr. Basham believes: "The *Arthaśāstra* probably refers ironically to the martial arrogance and practical ineptitude of the republics when it states that the members of seven named tribes 'make a living by their title of *rājā*'."[4]

Kauṭilya's policy towards these groups is clear from his own

---

[1] K. P. Jayaswal, *Hindu Polity*. R. C. Majumdar, *Corporate Life in Ancient India*. R. K. Mookerji, *Local Government in Ancient India*.

[2] R. C. Majumdar, *ibid*. p. 249-50.

[3] *ibid*. pp. 252-53.

[4] A. L. Basham, *The Wonder that was India*, p. 97.

observations.[5] "By means of conciliation and gifts, the conqueror should secure and enjoy the services of such corporations as are invincible to the enemy and are favourably disposed towards himself. But those who are opposed to him, he should put down by sowing the seeds of dissension among them and by secretly punishing them."

Kauṭilya devotes a whole chapter to the method of overthrowing these corporations by diverse means. The chapter throws some light on the morals of the people living in the non-monarchical states. According to Dr. Majumdar, the corporation has a general assembly and its executive (*mukhya*) officers are subordinate to it.[6] Dr. Shama Sastry, however, translates the word *mukhya* as the chief of the corporation.[7] But it appears that there are several *mukhyas* in the corporation. Dr. Majumdar shows that the members of the assembly are called *rājās* and "one can be imprisoned or rejected only by the orders of the assembly." The democratic nature of the constitution is hinted at by Kauṭilya.[8] He advises the leaders to be virtuous and self-controlled and to pursue a policy which finds favour with the people.[9] But, as the *Arthaśāstra* seems to suggest, these noble ideals are more often violated than observed. Kauṭilya mentions a number of hypothetical cases to show how the aggressive king may sow the seeds of dissensions among these states. From these brief references it is possible to form some idea of the moral life in these non-monarchical states.

The chief weakness of these corporations consists in factionalism and internecine strife.[10] Foreign powers seek to foment dissessions among the ruling class and take full advantage of their vices. Thus vanity, a false sense of dignity and social status, ambition, greed and lust bring about their speedy downfall. These vices lead to duels, fights among factions, slaughter of men, women and children, the destruction of cattle and goods, poisoning, murder and treachery.

---

[5] *AŚ.* XI. 1. The *Mbh.* Śānti. 107 also tells us that disunion brings ruin upon the *gaṇas*; disunited they fall an easy prey to the enemies; spies bring troubles to them; secrecy of counsel should be maintained.

[6] Majumdar, *op. cit.*, 251.

[7] *AŚ.* Shama Sastry's translation, pp. 457 and 458.

[8] Majumdar, *op. cit.* 252.

[9] *AŚ.* XI. 1.

[10] *AŚ.* XI. According to Gautama Buddha quoted by Dr. Majumdar "the essence of the strength of a corporation lies in the unity of its members," p. 253. The *Mahābhārata* also states: "The destruction of the *gaṇas* is mainly due to dissensions" (Śānti, 107. 8, also 14).

The chiefs find pleasure in matters intellectual and artistic. They take part in disputations on matters of knowledge, arts and entertainment probably under the guidance of experts (*vidyāśilpadyūtavaihārikeṣu*). These pursuits often end in childish brawls (*vālakalaha*). Many chiefs take pleasure in gambling, wine and prostitutes (*veśaśauṇḍikeṣu*). Gambling brings about their downfall.[11] Keepers of prostitutes often procure for them women of exquisite beauty and youthfulness. "Keepers of harlots or dancers, players and actors may, after gaining access, excite love in the minds of the chiefs of corporations by exhibiting women endowed with bewitching youth and beauty. By causing the woman to go to another person or by pretending that another person has violently carried her off, they may bring about a quarrel among those who love that woman; in the ensuing affray, fiery spies may do their work and declare: This has been killed in consequence of his love." Thus it appears that professional artistes like *plavaka*, *naṭa*, *nartaka* and *saubhika* with their beautiful women find enthusiastic patrons among the chiefs and these women often stir up jealousy among them. Female entertainers find in them gallant companions. Wine is distributed in gallons as a part of nativity, obsequies or marriage. "On the occasions of any affray, spies under the guise of vinters, should, under the plea of the birth of a son, of marriage or of the death of a man, distribute as toast (*naiṣecanika*) hundreds of vessels of liquor adulterated with the juice of madana plant." Social dignity plays an important part in society. Some *kulas* (families) are held in higher regard than others. Interdining and intermarriage (*ekapātre vivāhe*) occasionally become controversial. Claims to prominence by a family or an individual might lead to disputes.[12]

Caityas and temples are sacred places where solemn agreements are entered into and deposits accepted. The faith of the people in ascetics and mendicant women leads to occasional dangers. Here again the ascetic administers love charm to the wife to enable her to control the husband. "A spy, under the garb of an ascetic, may apply to a lover such medical ointments as are declared to be capable of captivating the beloved woman and as are adulterated with poison."

---

[11] *AŚ.* VIII. 3.

[12] The *Mbh.* (Śānti. 107. 28) states: "Quarrels in families ignored by the old men of the family, destroy the '*gotras*' and thereby create dissension among the *gaṇas*."

The mendicant woman acts as a go-between carrying or professing to carry love letters and presents from a chief to another chief's wife. When the scandal comes to light, serious trouble crops up. A mendicant woman may tell a chief who is fond of his wife: 'This (another) chief, proud of his youth, has sent me to entice your wife; being afraid of him, I have taken with me his letter and jewellery (for your wife); your wife is free from sin; secret steps should be taken against him; and I am very anxious (about your success).' Astrologers stir up a chief's ambition or lust. "A spy, under the guise of an astrologer, may describe to a chief the destiny of a maiden who is at the point of being married to another, and say: 'This man's daughter deserves to be the wife of a king and will bring forth a son destined to be a king; purchase her with all your wealth or seize her by force.' When it is not possible to secure her, spies should enrage the parties; but when she is secured, quarrel will necessarily follow."

Love of women marks the leaders' character, or the lack of it and often brings them to their doom. Some are devoted to their wives but likely to suffer from jealousy. Others run after prostitutes and female entertainers (*kauśikīstrīyo nartakīgāyana*). Some chief forcibly abducts the ladylove perhaps into the forest or a secret pleasure chamber, where he may be killed by an assassin. At the behest of astrologers some may carry away betrothed maidens; others, perhaps even a poor absentee *Brāhmaṇa's* wife, sister, daughter or daughter-in-law. The complaint of the aggrieved *Brāhmaṇa* against the aggressor may or may not succeed. Occasionally, even the complainant himself may be killed. A rich widow instituting suits can have intrigues in the matters of heart with the chief, judging the case. "Widows or women, employed as spies with secret instructions may dispute among themselves about the claim for a deposit kept with the king and attract the chiefs of the corporation."

The great epic also speaks of tempting the *gaṇas* with beauty.[13] The *Mahāparinibbāṇa Sūtta* enjoins upon the Vajjian confederacy not to detain women or girls by force or abduction.[14]

The *Mahābhārata*, however, points out: "The *gaṇas* are torn asunder by the enemies, not by exertion, intellect or tempting them

---

[13] *Mbh.* Śānti. 107, 31-32.

[14] *SBE.* Vol. XI. 3-8.

with beauty, but by creating dissensions and offering bribes. So it is said that unity is the chief refuge of the *gaṇas*."[13]

Both Kauṭilya and the *Mahābhārata* indicate similar modes of creating disunion among the members of the corporation. While the *Mahābhārata* directs the major portion of its discussion towards a constructive line for the strength and solidarity of the corporations, Kauṭilya in the main devotes his chapter to the methods of disrupting them. Yet Kauṭilya ends his chapter with a moral teaching and indicates the correct line of conduct to be followed by the chief of a corporation. Such conduct includes justice (*nyāya*), welfare (*hita*) and self-control (*dānta*). "The chief of corporations," concludes Kauṭilya, "should endear himself to all the people by leading a virtuous life, by controlling his passions and by pursuing that course of action which is liked by all those who are his followers." The constructive outlook evinced by Kauṭilya in this passage compares favourably with the conditions set out in the *Mahāparinibbāṇa Sūtta* for the welfare of the Vajjian confederacy and the Buddhist Saṁgha.[14] Among the conditions are concord in meetings and undertakings, acting in accordance with ancient institutions and not detaining women or girls by force or abduction. Such moral weakness of the leaders Kauṭilya constantly harps on.

Chapter XIX

SANCTIONS OF MORALITY AND ITS ENFORCEMENT

Kauṭilya takes pains to prescribe a large number of rules of human conduct. It is interesting to enquire what, according to him, causes them to be observed. ". . . . . moral conduct is commonly associated with a sense of duty to do certain things and to abstain from certain others. The question then naturally arises concerning the authority of this sense of duty to command or to prohibit actions as the case may be. This is the problem of the sanction of morality. . . . . Generally speaking, most people who are moral lean on some outside authority as their moral sanction."[1] Kauṭilya too relies upon various sanctions to back the rules enunciated by him.

As an exponent of the school of politics Kauṭilya mainly depends upon *daṇḍa* or political sanction. According to him, *daṇḍanīti* or science of politics is the root of threefold human knowledge.[2] It governs the way of life (*tasyāmāyattā lokayātrā*).[3] The coercive power of the state keeps all people on the right path. Yet, Kauṭilya does not rely upon coercion *simpliciter*. It must be properly exercised.

"My teacher says: To keep people under control, there is no better instrument than the coercive power (*daṇḍa*). Not so, says Kauṭilya. Severe coercion indeed causes people to fret. Light coercion causes defect. One who exercises coercion as deserved is commended. Coercive power, when exercised with due consideration, directs the people towards spiritual, economic and sensual pursuits."[4] Thus in Kauṭilya's view the coercive power of the state, when properly exercised, furthers the threefold objective of life. Without coercion the reign of anarchy

---

[1] *Encyclopaedia Britannica*, 14th Edn. Vol. 8. p. 760 (Ethics).
[2] *AŚ.* I. 4.
[3] *Ibid.*
[4] *Ibid.*

ensues (*apraṇītohi mātsyanyāyamudbhāvayati*).[5] Dr. Bandopadhyaya observes: "The superior efficacy of coercion was recognised by all and almost everywhere in the globe. In India, too, the more ancient thinkers had recognised this. Kauṭilya following in their footsteps could not remain blind to it and brief as he is, he enters into a consider-tion of how this coercive authority be regulated and exercised."[6]

According to Kauṭilya, the king is the wielder of coercive power (*daṇḍadhara*). It is his paramount duty to prevent all people from swerving from personal duties (*svadharma*).[7]

The king preserves the duties of the four *Varṇas* and the four *Āśramas*. So he is the fountain of justice (*rājādharmapravartaka*).[8] In Kauṭilya's view the king's law (*rājaśāsana*) gets the foremost place among the sources of law.[9]

In view of the important status of the king in the social order, Kauṭilya, as we have seen, prescribes various duties for the ruler himself. His own conduct must be above board. He must avoid injury to another's wife and property. He should himself guarantee the security of family and private property. Himself exemplary of conduct, the king should compel others to perform right conduct. The complex machinery of the state, described by Kauṭilya with meticulous details, is employed for the preservation of the social order. Yet the king is not above the law. For in Kauṭilya's view, the king who punishes another unjustly shall pay thirty times the amount of the punishment.[10]

The state might inflict punishment in various ways, *viz*., death, mutilation of limbs, imprisonment, fine, forfeiture of property rights, banishment, branding, whipping, torture and so on. But Kauṭilya shows a tendency towards replacing harsh punishments by milder ones.[11]

In spite of his firm reliance upon political sanction, Kauṭilya is not oblivious of religious sanction. It certainly exerts great influence upon popular mind. Like the orthodox Dharmaśāstra-writers Kauṭilya believes in heaven and hell. "The performance of personal duties

---

[5] Bandopadhyaya, *Kauṭilya*, p. 43.
[6] *AŚ*. I. 3.
[7] *AŚ*. III. 1.
[8] *AŚ*. III. 1.
[9] *Ibid*.
[10] *AŚ*. IV. 13.
[11] Bandopadhyaya, *Kauṭilya*, pp. 234-38.

(*svadharma*) leads one to heaven and eternity."[12] He knows that the weakness of the political sanction lies in the personal factor of the king himself. If the ruler fails to discharge his duties, the religious sanction becomes more effective. By protecting the subject according to law and causing them to follow the rules regarding inter-caste marriage, the king, says Kauṭilya, goes to heaven.[13] In default he too falls into hell.

The concept of heaven and hell tends to induce common people as well to stick to the right path. So Kauṭilya asks the *Purohita*, the *Sūta* and the *Māgadha* (royal bards) to impress upon faltering people the importance of these concepts (*sūta māgadha... svargamasvargam... varṇayeyuḥ*).[14] The fear of hell protects the family relationship also. Thus a prince conspiring to kill his father is asked to desist, as otherwise, the patricide will descend to hell (*narakapāta*).[15]

Kauṭilya, moreover, has a high regard for the Vedas. He deduces the norm of *svadharma* from the Vedas. "As the three Vedas indicate the respective duties of the four *varṇas* and the four *āśramas*, they are useful (*aupakārika*)."[16] He also observes: "For, the whole world, when maintained in accordance with injunctions of the three Vedas, will surely progress, but never perish."[16] The Vedas show what is right and what is wrong (*dharmādharmau*).[17] The moral imperative of *svadharma* thus follows from the sanctity of the Vedas themselves.

Religious sanction exercises its effect on popular mind through the concepts of heaven and hell. It also presupposes the idea of sin (*pāpa*). It naturally suggests a distinction between legality and morality. Kauṭilya is conversant with this distinction. He does not mention the various gradations of sins and their corresponding religious penalties (*prāyaścitta*) so elaborately set out in many well-known Smṛiti works. Yet the idea of sin leaves a clear impression on Kauṭilya's mind. Even the king incurs sin for punishing an innocent man. When the king punishes an innocent man, he shall throw into water dedicating to god Varuṇa a fine equal to thirty times the unjust imposition; and

[12] *AŚ*. I. 3.
[13] *AŚ*. II. 1., also III. 7 (*Svargamāpnoti rājā narakamanyathā*).
[14] *AŚ*. X. 3.
[15] *AŚ*. I. 17.
[16] *AŚ*. I. 3.
[17] *AŚ*. I. 2.

this amount shall afterwards be distributed among the *Brāhmaṇas*. By this act, the king will be free from the sin of unjust imposition, for king Varuṇa is the ruler of sinner among men."[8] The Vedic faith in Varuṇa as the mentor of sinful persons persists in Kauṭilya's mind. He prescribes a mode of expiation for the sin of unjust punishment. If this religious sanction is available against the king, certainly it applies to the case of his subjects as well. For instance, if a wife goes out with a man other than her husband, she is in one case not only fined but also deprived of her right to participate in her husband's religious activities (*sarvadharmalopaśca*).[19] A suicide is denied the advantage of funeral ceremonies.[20]

When a *Brāhmaṇa* is found guilty of offences like violating an elder's wife, he cannot be punished by physical torture but is deprived of his civil rights (*vyavahārapatanāya*).[21] Sacrificial merit is supposed to diminish if the rites are performed in the presence of a man who violates a guru's bed.[22]

One well-known mode of inflicting religious punishment is the degradation from one's caste. For instance, a *śūdra* having sexual connection with a *caṇḍāla* woman is degraded to her caste.[23] The outcast, as we have seen, is a pathetic figure. Against him combine the religious, the political and the social sanctions. The law forfeits his right to inherit. The punishment visits his children (*patitājjāta*) who too are not entitled to inherit. His wife is asked to abandon him. None is allowed to associate with him in the matters of sacrifice, teaching and sex. The society shuns him and the state confirms his disabilities.

Kauṭilya, moreover, knows other social sanctions of morality. "The social sanction is that exercised by society or one's social environment, in a less formal and less explicit manner than is done by the state as a political organisation. There are social customs and traditions which carry much weight though not embodied in laws or regulations...."[24] Kauṭilya gives his approval to custom (*caritra*) as a source of law. In conflict of laws he places *caritra* (custom) above

---

[18] *AŚ*. IV. 13.
[19] *AŚ*. III. 4.
[20] *AŚ*. IV. 7.
[21] *AŚ*. IV. 8.
[22] *AŚ*. III. 14.
[24] *Encyclopaedia Britannica, ibid.*

dharma and *vyavahāra* but below the king's ordinance[25]. Public opinion receives due respect from him.[26] He advises the king to refrain from causing anger of the people. Public opinion goes against the ruler if he fails to rule properly. All sections of the people, the *gṛihastha*, the *vānaprastha* and the *parivrājaka*, get enraged if the coercive power is exercised badly.[27]

The civil judges (*dharmastha*) are told by Kauṭilya how to gain great popularity (*lokasampriyaḥ*) by proper enforcement of the laws.[28] Spies are employed to rouse the public opinion against a foreign ruler[29] and the chiefs of corporation.[30] A prince bent upon killing his father is advised to stop lest public opinion will go against him (*saṁkrośaḥ prajābhiḥ*) and the public will stone him to death (*ekaloṣṭra vadhaśca*).[31]

On a smaller scale the social sanction expresses itself through the permissible use of force by the members of a family. So Kauṭilya, as we have seen, allows the husband to chastise a wayward wife or even to inflict some amount of physical punishment on her. Likewise the wife may use similar methods for correcting a husband who finds joy with prostitutes (*bāhyavihāra*).[32] During the husband's absence, an adulterous wife may be restrained by the husband's relatives (*bāndhava*) and even by his slave. The husband might condone the offence of the wife. In that case she and her paramour are not liable to punishment.[33] In these stray references we find how the family takes part in dealing with the rules of correct conduct.

Of course, all these sanctions cannot be placed in water-tight compartments. Prof. Roscoe Pound says: "The major agencies of social control are morals, religion, and law. In the beginnings of law these

---

[25] *AŚ*. III. 1.

[26] "In Homeric times, the Greek culture was a shame culture, in which the fear of losing the good opinion of others was the chief sanction. Gradually this sanction became internalised and men came to fear the rebukes of their own conscience. In Homeric times, all the forces which we should regard as unconscious were projected outside the self and described as gods or demons: it was part of this process that gods appeared to reproach one for evil actions intended or committed." R. Taylor, *Sex in History*, p. 242.

[27] *AŚ*. I. 3.

[28] *AŚ*. III. 20.

[29] *AŚ*. I. 14.

[30] *AŚ*. XI.

[31] *AŚ*. I. 17.

[32] *AŚ*. III. 3.

[33] *AŚ*. IV. 12.

are not differentiated. Even in so advanced a civilisation as that of the Greek city-state the same word is used to mean religious rites, ethical custom, the traditional course of adjusting relations, the legislation of the city, and all of these looked on as a whole; as we should say, including all these agencies of social control under the one term which we now translate law."[34] In many cases, law, religion and custom will go hand in hand to enforce right conduct, as for example, in the case of *patita*, as we have already noted. Sometimes legal and religious punishments will go together, as, for instance, in the case of an eloping wife, she is fined and also deprived of some religious rights.

Goodhart writes: "There is no reason why religious laws should not be enforced by an earthly tribunal, even though the ultimate punishment be transcendental one. Similarly, the breach of moral law may entail the sanction of expulsion from the community even though there is no formal machinery by which this sanction can be enforced. The sanction which in fact makes certain state laws effective may not be the sanction which the law itself provides. Thus, during the recent war, the effectiveness of many of the rules prohibiting the purchase of food and of goods on the black market was due, not to the fines provided by the rules themselves but to the social stigma which was attached to the breach of these rules."[35]

The Kauṭilyan law takes advantage of public humiliation as an additional means of securing respect for morality. A wayward wife is in one case directed to be whipped by a *caṇḍāla* five times in the middle of the village before the public gaze.[36] The dead body of a suicide is dragged along the public street.[37] A *Brāhmaṇa*, who cannot be awarded physical torture, is branded by various marks of dogs, genital organs, etc., on his forehead and exposed to public ridicule (*sarvāparādheṣva-pīḍanīyo brāhmaṇaḥ/tasyābhiṣaṣṭāṅko lalāte syād ... brāhmaṇaṁ pāpa-karmāṇamudhṛiṣyāṅkṛitavraṇaṁ*).[38]

It is interesting to note that Professor Roscoe Pound refers to a condition of undifferentiated religion, morals and law and concludes

---

[34] *Social Control through Law*, p. 18 quoted in Goodhart, *English Law & Moral Law*, p. 44.

[35] A. L. Goodhart, *English Law & Moral Law* (Stevens, 1953).

[36] *AŚ*. III. 3.

[37] *AŚ*. IV. 7.

[38] *AŚ*. IV. 8.

that "law, as we now think of it, that is, social control through the force of politically organized society is the least in scope and the least in efficacy of the three." Kauṭilya, however, puts much reliance on *daṇḍa* or the political sanction.[39]

BIBLIOGRAPHY

The following list does not contain all the works consulted. It is a list of works from which specific facts have been drawn or understanding of a particular problem gained. The author expresses his deep sense of gratitude to the writers of these works.

I. Original sources: (Text and Translation).

INDIAN

Arthaśāstra of *Kauṭilya*—Edited by Dr. R. Shama Sastry, (Mysore 1924). Edited with commentaries by T. Ganapati Sastri, (Vols. I-III) (Trivandrum 1921-25). Edited by Dr. J. Jolly and Dr. R. Schmidt, (Lahore 1925). English translation by Dr. R. Shama Sastry, (Mysore 1923). English translation with a study by R. P. Kangle, (Bombay 1965). Bengali translation by Dr. R. G. Basak, Vols. I & II, (Calcutta 1950-51).

Aśoka's Inscriptions—*Corpus Inscriptionum Indicarum*, Vol. I, E. Hultzsch (London 1925).

Āpastambīya Dharma Sūtram—Edited by G. Bühler, (Bombay 1923).

Baudhāyana Dharma Sūtram—Kāshī Sanskrit Series, (Benares 1934).

Daśakumāra Carita of *Daṇḍin*—Edited by T. Bhattacharyya, Chowkhamba Sanskrit Series, (Benares 1965).

Divyāvadāna—Edited by E. B. Cowell and R. A. Neil, (Cambridge 1886).

Gautama Praṇīta Dharma Sūtram—Ānandāśrama Sanskrit Series.

Jatakas—Edited by V. Fausböll, 7 Vols. (London 1877-97). English translation edited by E. B. Cowell. 7 Vols. (Cambridge 1895-1913). Bengali translation by Isana Chandra Ghose, (Calcutta).

Kāmandakīya Nītisāra—With Hindi translation by Jawala Prasad Misra, (Bombay Saka 1926).

Kāmasūtra of *Vātsyāyana*—With commentary *Jayamaṅgala* of Yaśodhara, Edited by G. D. Sastri, (Benares 1929). English translation by K. Rangaswami Iyenger, (Lahore 1921).

Mahābhārata—With commentary of Nīlakaṇṭha. Edited by Panchanan Tarkaratna 2 Vols. (Calcutta Saka 1930). Bengali translation by Kali Prasanna Singha (Basumati Sahitya Mandir, Calcutta) 4 Vols.

Mahāvaṁsa—English translation by W. Geiger. (London 1908).

Mānava Dharmaśāstra—Edited by Dr. J. Jolly (London 1887).

Manu Saṁhitā—With commentaries of Medhātithi and Kullūka and Bengali translation by Bharat Chandra Siromani (Basumati Sahitya Mandir) 2 Vols. English translation with notes by G. Jha. 5 Vols. (Calcutta 1922 to 1929).

Nārada Smṛiti—English translation by J. Jolly, (London 1876). Also SBE. Vol. 33, (Oxford 1880).

Nāṭyaśāstra of *Bharata*—English translation by Dr. M. Ghose, (Calcutta).

Pariśiṣṭaparvan of *Hemachandra*—Edited by H. Jacobi, (Calcutta 1932).

Smṛitīnām Samuccaya—Ānandāśrama Sanskrit Series.
Therīgāthā—Edited with Bengali translation by Bijayachandra Majumdar, (Dacca).
Vāsiṣṭha Dharmaśāstram—Edited by A. Führer, (Poona 1930).
Yājñavalkya Smṛiti—With commentary *Mitākṣarā*, edited by W. L. S. Pansikar, (Bombay 1936).

FOREIGN

Ancient India: Its invasion by Alexander the Great—J. W. McCrindle, (Westminster 1896).
Ancient India as described by Megasthenes and Arrian—J. W. McCrindle, (Calcutta 1926).
Aristotle's *Ethics*—English translation, (Carlton House, New York).
Machiavelli's *The Prince*—Everyman's Library.

II. Modern works: (on Indian History and Culture).

BANDYOPADHYAYA, N. C.—*Kauṭilya*, (1927 Calcutta).
BANERJEE, GOORODAS—*Hindu Law of Marriage and Stridhana*, (Calcutta 1913).
BARNETT, L. D.—*Antiquities of India*, (London 1913).
BASHAM, A. L.—*The Wonder that was India*, (London 1954).
BHANDARKAR, D. R.—*Aśoka*. (Calcutta).
BHATTACHARYYA, S.—*Mahābhārater Samāj*, (Calcutta).
CHAKLADAR, H. C.—*Social Life in Ancient India:* Studies in Vātsyāyana's *Kāma-Sūtra* (Calcutta 1929).
FICK, R.—*Social Organisation in North-East India in Buddha's Time*, English translation by S. K. Maitra (Calcutta 1920).
GHOSE, B. K.—*Hindu Ideal of Life*, (Calcutta).
GHOSAL, U. N.—*Beginnings of Indian Histriography and other essays*, (Calcutta).
JAYASWAL, K. P.—*Hindu Polity*, (Bangalore, 1943). *Manu and Yājñavalkya*, (Calcutta 1930).
JHA, GANGANATH—*Hindu Law in its sources* (Allahabad 1930).
JOLLY, J.—*Hindu Law and Custom*, English translation by B. K. Ghose, (Calcutta 1928).
HOPKINS, W.—*Ethics of the Hindus.*
KANE, P. V.—*History of the Dharmaśāstras* 4 Vols. (Poona).
LAW, N. N.—*Studies in Ancient Hindu Polity.*
MAJUMDAR R. C.—*Corporate Life in Ancient India. History and Culture of the Indian People*, Vols. I & II, (General Editor), (Bhāratīya Vidyā Bhavan, Bombay).
MAYNE—*Hindu Law and Usage*, (Calcutta).
MEHTA, RATILAL—*Pre-Buddhist India*, (Bombay 1939).
MITRA, T.—*Law relating to the Hindu Widow*, (Calcutta 1881).
MOOKERJI, R. K.—*Candragupta Maurya and his times*, (Second Revised Edition, Delhi & Bombay 1952). *Local Government in Ancient India.*
MEYER, J. J.—*Sexual Life in Ancient India*, (Calcutta 1952).

NILAKANTA SASTRI, K. A.—*The Age of the Nandas and Mauryas*, (Bharatiya Itihas Parisad, Benares, 1952).
RADHAKRISHNAN, S.—*Indian Philosophy*, 2 Vols. (London, reprint, 1941).
RAPSON, J.—*The Cambridge History of India*, Vol. I, (Editor) (Cambridge 1922).
RAY, H. C.—*The position of Brāhmaṇa in Kauṭilya*, (Proceedings of the Second Oriental Conference). *Economic policy and function of Kauṭilyan State.*
RHYS DAVIS, T. W.—*Buddhist India*, new edition, (Calcutta).
SENGUPTA, N. C.—*Evolution of Ancient Indian Law*, (Calcutta and London 1953).
SIVASWAMY AIYAR, P. S.—*Evolution of Hindu Moral Ideals*, (Calcutta 1935).

III. Modern Works: General

CROCE, BENEDETTO—*Politics and Morals*, English translation by S. J. Castiglione, (London 1946).
DE COULANGES, FUSTEL—*The Ancient City*, English Translation by W. Small (Boston 1901).
DURANT, Will—*The Story of Civilization, Our Oriental Heritage*, (New York 1942).
ELLIS, HAVELOCK—*Psychology of Sex*, 2 Vols.
GOODHART, A. L.—*English Law and Moral Law*, (London 1953).
HOBHOUSE, L. T.—*Morals in Evolution*, (London 1915).
HOCKING AND OTHERS—*Preface to Philosophy*.
JAMES, E. O.—*Marriage and Society*, (London 1952).
KEIFER, OTTO—*Sexual Life in Ancient Rome*, (Calcutta 1951).
LECKY, W. E. H.—*History of European Morals*, 2 Vols. (London 1946).
LICHT, HANS—*Sexual Life in Ancient Greece*, (5th Edition, 1949).
POUND, ROSCOE—*Law and Morals*, (London 1926).
RATTRAY TAYLOR, G.—*Sex in history*. (London 1953).
RUSSELL, BERTRAND—*Marriage and Morals*, (New York).
SABINE, G. H.—*A History of Political Theory*, (London 1941).
WESTERMARCK, E.—*Ethical Relativity*.
The Future of Marriage in Western Civilization, (London 1936).
The History of Human Marriage, (London 1901).

IV. Encyclopaedia:

Encyclopaedia Britannica—14th Edition.
Encyclopaedia of Sexual Knowledge—Edited by Norman Haire, 5th Edition, (London 1938).
Encyclopaedia of Sex Practice—Do. 2nd Edition Reprint, (London 1952).

V. Statue:

Hindu Marriage Act 1955.

VI. Journals:

CALCUTTA REVIEW, APRIL, 1924—Winternitz, *Kauṭilya Arthaśāstra.*

DO. SEPTEMBER-DECEMBER, 1934—Law N. N. *Kauṭilya.*

INDIAN CULTURE, VOL. IV, 1937-8—Bose, Atindranath, *The date of the Arthaśāstra.*

JOURNAL OF THE AMERICAN ORIENTAL SOCIETY, VOL. 71—Sternbach. *Legal position of the Prostitutes according to Kauṭilya's Arthaśāstra.*

JOURNAL OF THE ROYAL ASIATIC SOCIETY, 1929—Johnston, E. H. *Two studies in the Arthaśāṣtra of Kauṭilya.*

NEW INDIAN ANTIQUARY, II, 1939-40—Narahari, H. C. *Society in Mauryan India.*

ABBREVIATIONS

Āpastamba. = Āpastambīyadharmasūtra.
AŚ. = Arthaśāstra of Kauṭilya.
Baudh. = Baudhāyana Dharma Sūtra.
EHMI. = Evolution of Hindu Moral Ideals by Sir Sivaswamy Aiyar.
ESK. = Encyclopaedia of Sexual Knowledge.
ESP. = Encyclopaedia of Sex Practice.
Gautama. = Gautama Dharmasūtra.
HCIP. = History and Culture of the Indian People (Bhāratīya Vidyā Bhavan).
HDS. = History of Dharmaśāstra by Mahāmahopādhyāya P. V. Kane.
HLC. = Hindu Law and Custom (English Translation)—Jolly.
IC. = Indian Culture.
J. = Jātaka.
JAOS. = Journal of the American Oriental Society.
JRAS. = Journal of the Royal Asiatic Society.
KS. = Kāmasūtra of Vātsyāyana.
Manu. = Manu Saṁhitā.
Mbh. = Mahābhārata (Śānti, Udyoga, etc. refer to the parvans).
MC.I. = McCrindle's Ancient India: its Invasion by Alexander the Great.
Meg. = McCrindle's Ancient India as described by Megasthenes and Arrian.
Mm. = Mahāmahopādhyāya.
Nārada. = Nārada Smṛiti.
NŚ. = Bharata's Nāṭyaśāstra.
PBI. = Pre-Buddhist India by Ratilal Mehta.
PE. = Pillar Edict of Aśoka.
Rām. = Rāmāyaṇa.
RE. = Rock Edict of Aśoka.

SBE.	=	Sacred Books of the East.
SLAI.	=	Sexual Life in Ancient India by J. J. Meyer.
SLAG.	=	Sexual Life in Ancient Greece by Hans Licht.
SLAR.	=	Sexual Life in Ancient Rome by Otto Kiefer.
SRE.	=	Separate Rock Edict of Aśoka.
Vaśiṣṭha.	=	Vāśiṣṭhadharmasūtra.
Yāj.	=	Yājñavalkya Smṛiti.

INDEX

* * * *